# rio de janeiro

# NATIONAL GEOGRAPHIC
# TRAVELER

# rio de janeiro

by Michael Sommers
photography by Peter M. Wilson

National Geographic
Washington, D.C.

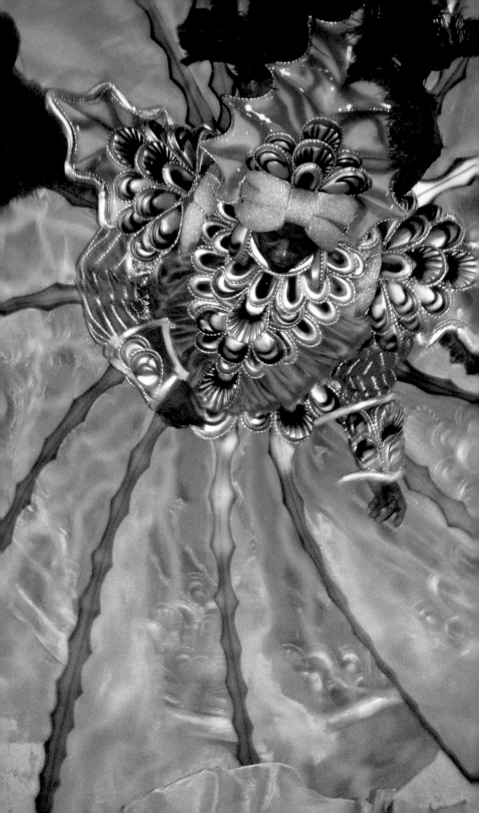

# CONTENTS

TRAVELING WITH EYES OPEN  6

CHARTING YOUR TRIP  8

Pages 2–3: View of the Biblioteca Nacional from the rooftop of the Theatro Municipal
Left: Spectacle and fantasy combine in the samba school parades during Carnaval.

# TRAVELING WITH EYES OPEN

Alert travelers go with a purpose and leave with a benefit. If you travel responsibly, you can help support wildlife conservation, historic preservation, and cultural enrichment in the places you visit. You can enrich your own travel experience as well.

To be a geo-savvy traveler:

- Recognize that your presence has an impact on the places you visit.

- Spend your time and money in ways that sustain local character. (Besides, it's more interesting that way.)

- Value the destination's natural and cultural heritage.

- Respect the local customs and traditions.

- Express appreciation to local people about things you find interesting and unique to the place: its nature and scenery, music and food, historic villages and buildings.

- Vote with your wallet: Support the people who support the place, patronizing businesses that make an effort to celebrate and protect what's special there. Seek out shops, local restaurants, inns, and tour operators who love their home—who love taking care of it and showing it off. Avoid businesses that detract from the character of the place.

- Enrich yourself, taking home memories and stories to tell, knowing that you have contributed to the preservation and enhancement of the destination.

That is the type of travel now called geotourism, defined as "tourism that sustains or enhances the geographical character of a place—its environment, culture, aesthetics, heritage, and the well-being of its residents." To learn more, visit National Geographic's Center for Sustainable Destinations at *www .nationalgeographic.com/travel/sustainable.*

# rio de janeiro

## ABOUT THE AUTHOR & THE PHOTOGRAPHER

**Michael Sommers** has lived and worked in Brazil as a journalist for nearly 15 years, in the country's original capital of Salvador, Bahia. As a writer and photographer, he has contributed travel articles to the *New York Times,* the *Globe and Mail,* and the *International Herald Tribune.* He is the author of the guidebooks *Moon Brazil* and *Moon Rio.*

**Peter M. Wilson** hails from North Yorkshire, England. After earning a B.A. degree in photography and film, he moved to Lisbon, Portugal, where he photographed a project examining the interweaving of social and religious rituals. This culminated with a major exhibition of his work, "Ritual in Portugal," at London's Barbican Centre. After returning to London, he began shooting assignments in the fields of travel, editorial, and photojournalism. His work has appeared in leading U.K. publications such as the *Sunday Times, Guardian, Independent,* and *Daily Telegraph,* as well as in international magazines such as *Condé Nast Traveler* and *Vogue.* He has also shot many titles in the Dorling Kindersley Eyewitness Travel Guide series. His work has taken him around the world.

# Charting Your Trip

Despite being a large, sometimes chaotic metropolis, Rio is also a laid-back city where punctuality is an elastic concept and chilling out is a highly valued pastime. The best way to tap into its pulse is by ignoring the clock, dispensing with schedules, and succumbing to its relaxing rhythms.

### Getting Around

Due to geography, much of Rio is laid out in a very long and narrow band. Depending on where you're going, this can translate into long distances and terrible traffic jams. Try to organize your daily outings around specific regions that you can cover by foot (or quick cab rides) so that you spend time enjoying the city instead of navigating it.

Rio has two principal modes of public transport: the Metrô (subway) and buses. The Metrô (*www.metrorio.com.br*) is clean, efficient, and (blessedly) air-conditioned. It has two lines: Linha 2 connects Centro to the vast suburbs of the Zona Norte; Linha 1 links Centro to the Zona Sul as far as Ipanema. A new line, Linha 4, will link Ipanema to Barra da Tijuca when completed in 2015. The Metrô/bus system allows users who buy an *intergração* ticket to transfer from hub stations to express buses (known as the Metrô Na Superfície) that service areas in the Zona Sul and Zona Oeste. The Metrô allows you to avoid Rio's increasingly pervasive gridlock. During rush hour, it gets crowded.

Municipal buses, operated by private companies under the auspices of Rio Ônibus (*www.rioonibus.com*), go everywhere, at all times—and if not hampered by traffic, they go roller-coaster fast. The final destination (and route number) is on the front of the bus, while main points along the route are listed along the side. While buses are generally safe during the day and into the evening, at night it's safer to take a taxi. Easily hailable taxis are also ideal if you're in hurry or want to get to and from an off-the-beaten path destination.

**Cristo Redentor, atop Corcovado**

### If You Only Have a Few Days

A major part of Rio's allure is its emphasis on living it up and relaxing to the hilt. The urban ethos is more about improvisation than efficiency. Go with the Carioca—the term for a citizen of Rio—flow by not planning too much, and know that lolling on a mountain-fringed beach with an *água de coco* (coconut water) and sitting in a neighborhood bar, listening to samba and watching the world go by, count as Rio experiences, too. Nonetheless, if you have only a few days to indulge, the following itinerary includes attractions that shouldn't be missed.

Most flights from North America and Europe are overnight hauls that get you to Rio in the morning. After arriving at your hotel, start **Day 1** by heading to Ipanema Beach, where you can shift into relaxation mode. Shelter from the hot sun at a juice bar or restaurant in Ipanema, then wander the leafy streets, checking out boutiques. In the midafternoon, take a bus or cab around the sparkling waters of the Lagoa Rodrigo de Freitas to the cool, green refuge of the Jardim Botânico and then walk to the nearby Parque Lage, which sits in the shade of Corcovado. Both jungly gardens have wonderful cafés for chilling. After dusk, the surrounding neighborhoods of Jardim Botânico and adjacent Leblon are home to some of the city's most reputed restaurants. If you don't want a big meal, head to Palaphita Kitch, an Amazonian-themed bar overlooking the *lagoa,* where you can lounge in the company of sublime views, exotic snacks, and *cupuaçu* caipirinha cocktails.

Kick off **Day 2** with a long, leisurely walk along the 2.5-mile (4 km) length of Copacabana Beach, from the Forte de Copacabana to the Pedra do Leme, making strategic stops along the way. One of these can be poolside breakfast or drinks at the legendary Copacabana Palace hotel, while another can be ogling the art deco buildings surrounding the Praça do Lido. At Leme, those with energy to spare can make the short ascent to the Forte Duque de Caxias; the views from the fort are bewitching. Otherwise, head straight to Bar do David, in the Chapéu Mangueira favela, for delicious homemade cooking. From Leme, it's only a quick cab or bus ride to Urca. Arrive midafternoon to walk around the great hump of Pão de Açúcar (Sugarloaf) on the Claudio Coutinho trail before taking the cable car to the summit in time to watch the sun set over the city. Consider dinner in nearby Botafogo or Copa, both of which also have interesting bar/club scenes.

**Day 3** is a good day to head to Centro, where you can spend a few hours immersing yourself in Rio's history. The Museu Histórico Nacional provides an excellent overview of Brazilian

**NOT TO BE MISSED:**

Years of Brazilian history at the Museu Histórico Nacional   **62–63**

Listening—and dancing—to live music in Lapa's streets, bars, and clubs   **104–109**

A stroll along Santa Teresa's cobblestoned streets   **114–115**

Experiencing, up close, the embrace of Cristo Redentor   **135–138**

Watching the sun set over the city from the top of Pão de Açúcar   **143–145**

A stroll along the glorious length of Copacabana Beach   **158–159**

**Visitor Information**

To stay up to date with what's new and happening in Rio, pick up a free, compact, and bilingual guide published monthly by the city's tourist bureau, **RioTur** *(www.rioguia oficial.com.br),* also available (in a more expanded version) online. In addition to fairly extensive listings of things to do see, eat, and drink as well as places to stay, it provides practical information and timely articles. You'll find copies at RioTur kiosks and many hotels. In a pinch, you can dial 1746 for the bilingual 24/7 tourist hotline, also reachable through apps.

## When to Visit

Rio's tropical climate makes it inviting year-round. Summer is the high season, which means fun and *festas* galore (from Réveillon to Carnaval), but also inflated prices and temperatures (not to mention heavy humidity and short but torrential rains). Winter can be lovely, but cold fronts from the south can bring cool temperatures and rain that can last for days. Spring and fall coincide with the off season; aside from lower prices, you'll be treated to moderate temperatures and lots of clear days, ensuring that from Corcovado's summit you can see forever.

history in less than two hours and is close to one of Rio's oldest colonial buildings, the Paço Imperial, as well as the baroque churches of Igreja de Nossa Senhora do Carmo da Antiga Sé and Igreja da Ordem Terceira de Nossa Senhora do Monte Carmo. From Praça XV, explore the winding cobblestoned streets of the *centro histórico*, which are lined with palaces housing myriad cultural centers, among them the formidable Centro Cultural Banco do Brasil. Satiate your Brazilian baroque fix by visiting the splendid Mosteiro de São Bento, a monastery built by the Benedictines, and then head toward Largo do Carioca to be dazzled by the Igreja da Ordem Terceira de São Francisco da Penitência, making sure to stop for a coffee at the sumptuous belle epoque Confeitaria Colombo café. From Largo da Carioca, hop a minibus to the lovely hilltop neighborhood of Santa Teresa. After visiting the Museu da Chácara do Céu, spend the late afternoon wandering the cobblestoned streets of "Santa" before having drinks and/or dinner at a charming local bar or restaurant. Cap off the night by soaking up some live samba, either in the bohemian *bairro* of Lapa or the up-and-coming port neighborhoods of Saúde and Gamboa, both of which are quick cab rides away.

**Mountaintop Attractions:** Begin **Day 4** by catching the first train up to Corcovado and the statue of Cristo Redentor with the dual aim of beating the crowds and catching the sun spreading its golden rays over the city below. Afterward, check out the vivid collection of artworks at the nearby Museu Internacional de Arte Naïf. In the early afternoon, continue exploring Rio's summits by treating yourself to a (prearranged) tour of one of two (literally) top Carioca

## Body Lingo

When it comes to communication, Rio's citizens are notoriously expressive—not in terms of just verbal language, but body language as well. Although some Brazilian gestures look identical to those used in North America, be aware that the meanings may be very different. Here are some common bodily expressions:

- Tapping your fingers under your chin = "You don't know what you're talking about."

- Rubbing your thumb against your index finger = "That's expensive!" or "I don't have enough money."

- Encircled thumb and forefinger (the North American hand signal for "OK") = "Screw you!"

- Shaking your hand back and forth while wagging your raised index finger = "No way."

- Thumbs up = "OK!" or "Cool!"

A *clássico* between two homegrown Rio *futebol* favorites: Flamengo and Botafogo

attractions: Those with an interest in urban matters should embark on a hilltop favela (slum or shantytown) tour, while nature lovers can explore the jungle-clad peaks of the Parque Nacional da Tijuca, on foot or by jeep. A lovely place to applaud the sunset is from atop the Pedra do Arpoador, the rocky promontory that separates Ipanema from Copacabana. Once the spectacle is over, while away your final evening dining and soaking up the ambience in the adjacent neighborhoods of Copacabana, Ipanema, or Leblon.

## If You Have More Time

If you're staying longer in Rio, the culturally inclined should visit the city's premier modern art museum, the **Museu de Arte Moderna,** and the adjacent **Parque do Flamengo.** Aside from temporary exhibits, the landmark house and beautiful gardens of the **Instituto Moreira Salles** are worth the side trip to Gávea. A half day can be spent visiting the **Sítio Roberto Burle Marx,** encompassing the home, atelier, and gardens of the acclaimed artist/landscaper, and the **Casa do Pontal,** which houses Brazil's largest collection of folk art. Both are located an hour from the Zona Sul, past the Zona Oeste beach of Recreio. In the same vicinity are Rio's most primitively alluring beaches, **Prainha** and **Grumari** (best accessed by car or taxi).

With a full day at your disposal, hop across beautiful Guanabara Bay to **Niterói** and alternate visits to colonial fortresses with gazing at Oscar Niemeyer–designed modernist monuments along the Caminho Niemeyer. Also day-trip worthy is a trip to the imperial mountain city of **Petrópolis,** home to Pedro II's summer palace, only an hour's drive north from Rio. Meanwhile, you'll kick yourself if you don't spend at least two nights exploring and decompressing in the charming beach-strewn peninsula of **Búzios,** on the unspoiled island of **Ilha Grande,** or in and around the jewel-like colonial town of **Paraty,** all several hours from Rio along the coast. ∎

# History & Culture

The Museu Nacional de Belas Artes possesses the nation's most important collection of 19th-century Brazilian art.

# Rio de Janeiro Today

**Rife with contrasts and contradictions, Rio de Janeiro is mesmerizing and musical, complex and sometimes chaotic, but never, ever boring. It possesses enough historical, cultural, and natural attractions to keep a visitor occupied for months—but don't forget that in Rio, relaxation is a serious art form.**

Rio de Janeiro is one of those magical metropolises whose combination of beauty and ethereal, otherworldly *je ne sais quoi* transcends mundane, factual description and can only be duly, and lyrically, summed up in song. Not surprisingly, like for a select handful of the world's truly great cities, songs have been written about Rio—scads of them.

Throughout Brazil, and around the world, Rio is most frequently and famously referred to as the Cidade Maravilhosa, or Marvelous City. What most people don't

**The bewitching view from Pão de Açúcar (Sugarloaf) of the sun setting behind Corcovado**

know is that this eternally apt designation is actually the title of a Carnaval march. Written in 1934 by André Filho (1906–1974), it sung Rio's praises with such flair that in 1960 it was adopted as the official municipal anthem.

Squeezed between dramatic mountains, carpeted in lush jungle, and the impossibly blue southern Atlantic ocean, Rio impresses even before one actually touches down at Antônio Carlos Jobim International Airport. Indeed, it's fitting that Rio's airport would be named after Tom Jobim (1927–1994). One of the greatest Brazilian composers of all time and a pioneering force involved in the creation of the quintessentially cool and carefree Carioca musical style known as the bossa nova, Jobim was passionate about his hometown. The city inspired many of his lyrics, including the poignant paean "Samba do Avião," in which he describes the sensation of gazing down upon Rio from an airplane

**Rio is not only Brazil's top tourist destination, it also receives more visitors than any other metropolis in the Southern Hemisphere.**

after a trip abroad: "*My soul sings. / I see Rio de Janeiro. / I'm dying of longing. / Rio, your sea, your endless beaches. / Rio, you were made for me.*"

## An Exceptional Natural Setting

Jobim's excitement is likely to infect those who arrive in Brazil's second largest city, of 6 million (12 million in terms of metropolitan area), for the first time—and then return again on subsequent occasions due to the fact that Rio is one of those highly intoxicating places for which there is no cure. Rio is not only Brazil's top tourist destination, it also receives more visitors than any other metropolis in the Southern Hemisphere. In 2012, UNESCO declared Rio to be a World Heritage site due to the magnificence of its natural landscapes, which encompass its towering granite peaks, the lush Tijuca rain forest, and glorious Guanabara Bay.

Indeed, Rio's setting is truly exceptional. Stretching 111 miles (179 km) along a slender strip of alluvial plains, the city is tightly hemmed in between the South Atlantic and the foothills of the Serra do Mar, an ancient gneiss-granite mountain chain covered in the native Mata Atlântica (Atlantic Forest). The city's downtown core—Centro—grew up around the 16th-century colonial settlement that was built upon an inlet of the natural harbor formed by Guanabara Bay.

To the north of Centro lie the sprawling industrial, working-class and poor neighborhoods—including many of Rio's favelas (slums)—of the Zona Norte (North Zone). To the south, the oldest upscale and middle-class Zona Sul (South Zone) neighborhoods of Glória, Catete, Flamengo, Bota-fogo, Urca, and Laranjeiras are separated by mountains from the famous beach *bairros* of Copacabana, Ipanema, and Leblon, which stretch out languorously along the open Atlantic. Like Gávea, Lagoa, and Jardim Botânico, lush residential neighborhoods that ring the saltwater lagoon of Lagoa Rodrigo de Freitas, these neighborhoods are among Rio's wealthiest and most eternally fashionable.

More mountains—largely covered by the Parque Nacional da Tijuca and favelas such as Rocinha and Vidigal—separate the Zona Sul from the much newer, constantly swelling, and more suburban neighborhoods of the Zona Oeste (West Zone). Home to more than 50 percent of Rio's population, the Zona Oeste is growing at breakneck speed, due in large part to the confines of the city's geography, which preclude expansion in older, more central areas. While the Miami-like bairros along the beaches of Barra and Recreio are well-to-do neighborhoods full of high-rises, those inland, going north, are dominated by poorer and working-class areas.

## An Ethos of *Alegria*

From its glistening beaches lapped by the sea to the outstretched arms of the statue of Cristo Redentor (Christ the Redeemer), Rio is geographically, and culturally, an open city that warmly embraces new influences, ideas, and people—and has done so throughout its five centuries of history. Although the original settlement founded by the Portuguese in 1503 began life as a muddy, mosquito-infested swampland, over time São Sebastião do Rio de Janeiro blossomed into a major port city from which Brazil's consecutive riches—sugarcane, gold, and coffee—set sail around the world. Along the way, the city enjoyed increasing prominence as Brazil's colonial capital (1763), capital of the United Kingdom of Portugal, Brazil, and the Algarves (1815), capital of the independent Empire of Brazil (1822), and capital of Brazil's first democratic republic (1889), becoming increasingly sophisticated, cosmopolitan, modern, and trendsetting as the centuries wore on.

**[T]he thing about Rio is that, aside from being drop-dead gorgeous, it's suffused with a spirit of *alegria* (joy) that makes it quite simply, and effortlessly, fun.**

When the federal capital moved to Brasília in 1960, Rio lost some of its political clout (although it became capital of the newly created state of Rio de Janeiro in 1975). And during the latter part of the 20th century, it saw much of its economic, financial, and cultural dominance eclipsed by that of São Paulo. However, Rio never lost its zest for life and its place in the world's collective imagination. Indeed, one can rest assured that while political bigwigs and financial magnates spend the week toiling away in Brasília and São Paulo, they are dreaming of spending a romantic and relaxing weekend in Rio de Janeiro, sprawled on a white-sand beach with a caipirinha drink in hand, chatting up a small storm in a neighborhood bar, or samba-ing the night away in a Lapa dance hall. Because the thing about Rio is that, aside from being drop-dead gorgeous, it's suffused with a spirit of *alegria* (joy) that makes it quite simply, and effort-lessly, fun.

This was the case even in the 1990s and early mid-2000s, when Rio's reputation was badly tarnished by national and global headlines detailing the violent civil war between

## The Lush Mata Atlântica

When the Portuguese first arrived in Rio, the landscape was richly carpeted in green. Known as Mata Atlântica, or Atlantic Forest, this ancient tropical rain forest (comparatively, the Amazon is a mere adolescent) once covered Brazil's entire coastline from north to south and stretched far—often as much as 125 miles (200 km) into the interior. Five centuries of brazilwood extraction, sugar and coffee cultivation, farming, logging, industrialization, and urbanization have wreaked havoc on this unique ecosystem. Today, a mere 7 percent of virgin rain forest survives in small, protected patches along the coast of Rio de Janeiro state as well as those of São Paulo, Paraná, and Bahia states.

Due to its age and its isolation, the Mata Atlântica possesses an incredibly rich biodiversity—60 percent of its fauna and 40 percent of its flora exist nowhere else on Earth—which makes the endangered status of much of its inhabitants all the more critical (and has led to its designation as a World Biosphere Reserve).

Among the rain forest's most striking, and endangered, species are the black-faced lion tamarin, the woolly spider monkey, the maned sloth, and the blonde capuchin, whose platinum hair is quite dazzling. The muriqui holds the title of largest primate in the Americas, while the Brazilian golden frog can lay claim to being the tiniest frog in the Southern Hemisphere. Endemic flora includes rare species of orchids, ferns, and bromeliads, as well as some resistant specimens of *pau brasil*, the tree that bequeathed its name to Brazil.

drug traffickers and police that brought the city to its knees and made life akin to living in an urban combat zone. Although the worst of the violence took place in the city's drug-lord-controlled hilltop favelas—numbering close to a thousand, they are home to approximately 20 percent of Rio's population—not even citizens in the wealthiest neighborhoods were immune to stray bullets.

However, while Rio may have been down, it was never out. In the last few years, the city has experienced a miraculous turnaround and is now once again riding high as one of the world's "It" cities. The economy—the city has the second largest GDP in Brazil after São Paulo—is flourishing, driven in part by the enormous offshore oil finds off the northern coast of Rio de Janeiro state, as well as booming service, telecommunications, media, cultural, and tourist sectors and a mushrooming IT segment. It's also created a massive building boom as well as nightmarish traffic jams, an overheated real estate market—these days, wealthy Cariocas prefer to buy their penthouses in Miami or New York instead of Ipanema or Leblon—and an escalating cost of living that sometimes shocks foreigners. While Rio is considerably safer than it's been in the past, it's also much more costly. In 2012, it was rated as the world's 13th most expensive city in terms of overall cost of living.

Having scored hosting duties for both the 2014 FIFA World Cup (soccer) and the 2016 Summer Olympics has given the city an impetus to go on a major development spree, revitalizing areas such as the historic port district, revamping its woefully insufficient public transportation system, and opening up new museums and cultural centers, not to mention restaurants and hotels. It's also served as a catalyst for Rio's traditionally look-the-other-way government to finally tackle the enormous twin problems of the drug trade and urban violence.

Since 2008, many of the drug lords who ruled over some of Rio's most prominent and centrally located favelas have been arrested or sent packing. In their place, specially trained Police Pacification Units (UPPs) have moved in, with the aim of maintaining security and also allowing these once marginalized communities to be integrated into the rest of the city. In conjunction with other public programs aimed at bridging the traditional gap between Rio's haves and have-nots, these initial yet watershed efforts have met, so far, with a degree of success that has infused the city with a palpable optimism.

## Life Is a Beach

Not that residents of Rio—known as Cariocas—are lacking in this regard. While all Brazilians are justifiably famed for their warmth, hospitality, relaxed charm, and effortless flair for seizing the day (not to mention the night and the morning after), Cariocas take it one step beyond. In Brazil, a popular saying points out that while residents of São Paulo play to work, Cariocas work to play. The truth is you'll be hard-pressed to find a major city where so much of daily life revolves around enjoying life to the hilt. Of course, the prevalence of such an ethos is unsurprising in view of the fact that virtually every inch of this metropolis is within strolling distance of a beautiful beach.

Rio possesses a mind-bogglingly sophisticated beach culture that embraces everything from fashion to health. Ever since it titillated the world with its provocative use of the *fio dental* (dental floss) bikinis in the 1970s, Rio has been globally celebrated for its cutting-edge beachwear. Meanwhile, one of the reasons the sporty city boasts such a

Throngs of *foliões* (revelers) take to the streets of Ipanema during Carnaval.

high number of soccer fields and volleyball courts, running and cycling paths, gyms and juice bars, is so Cariocas can proudly display their bronzed and buffed bodies on the beach (in Rio, vanity is considered a positive attribute).

Rio's beaches are microcosmic mirrors of the city at large. From afar, they constitute democratic spaces where tanned and flip-flopped citizens from all walks of life mix and mingle regardless of race, class, background, and education; yet up close, they are also stratified, with specific patches of sand acting as territories for particular urban *tribos* (tribes). The famed Zona Sul beaches of Copacabana, Ipanema, and Leblon, for instance, possess casually demarcated sections that are divided up among surfers, favela kids, hipsters, gays and lesbians, aging '60s leftists, soccer junkies, and young wealthy families with babies (and nannies). Indeed, in Rio, one is always experiencing the intense paradox in which shocking disparities and inequalities—the juxtaposition of precarious favela shacks literally suspended on top of luxury condominiums—coexist with a natural proclivity to blend together and mix it all up.

## A Culture of Mestiçagem

This melting-pot tendency is most apparent in Rio's culture, a heady mélange of high and low, traditional and avant-garde, which is constantly reinventing itself on multiple levels and in unexpected ways. Such eclecticism is unsurprising given the city's unique history of *mestiçagem* (mixing of races and ethnicities). For centuries, of course, Rio drew many waves of Portuguese immigrants. And to this day, most Cariocas can lay claim to some Portuguese ancestry as well as a seemingly genetic predilection for culinary delights of Portuguese origin ranging from crunchy *bolinhos de bacalhau* (codfish balls) to custardy *quindins*.

**EXPERIENCE:**
## Live & Learn

There's nothing more frustrating than not being able to communicate with the locals—especially in Rio, where the locals conversing always appear to be having such fun. In Ipanema, the nonprofit language school **Casa do Caminho** *(Rua Farme de Amoedo 135, tel 21/2267-6552, www.casadocaminho-languagecentre.org)* offers group (three hours a day for three or five days a week) and individual (on an hourly basis) Portuguese lessons, at all levels. In addition to classroom work, the school organizes activities such as samba lessons, beach volleyball games, and weekend hikes. If you're serious about immersing yourself in the language and culture, Casa do Caminho also organizes homestays with local families. As a bonus, all student fees are used to fund an orphanage, cultural center, and environmental training center in the town of Xerem (where students can also volunteer).

However, until the 19th century, the vast majority of the city's population was of African ancestry. During the 1800s, Rio received more African slaves (mainly from regions today occupied by Nigeria, Angola, and Mozambique) than any other New World metropolis. Subsequently, today close to 50 percent of Cariocas classify themselves as either black or mixed race.

This Afro-Brazilian heritage bleeds into many aspects of Carioca culture. It's particularly pronounced in the city's astoundingly diverse music, which embraces rap, hip-hop, and funk as well as samba in all of its derivations (from roots-inflected samba-pagode to samba-rock, samba-rap, and samba-reggae). It's also apparent in the number of Cariocas of all colors and backgrounds who adhere—seriously as well as sporadically—to

**Young men play table football in the Tavares Bastos favela, near Catete.**

Afro-Brazilian religions such as Candomblé and Umbanda. It's very common, for instance, to walk along the shores of Copacabana and encounter a washed-up rose, a favorite offering to Iemanjá, an *orixá* (deity) whose title is Queen of the Seas.

That said, Cariocas are a very eclectic bunch when it comes to spiritual matters. While Brazil boasts the largest population of Roman Catholics on the planet—and Rio boasts a splendid ensemble of baroque churches, convents, and monasteries—only 50 percent of Cariocas are practicing Catholics, while a whopping 14 percent are atheists. Followers of Protestantism—in the form of constantly multiplying evangelical and Pente-costal churches—and Spiritism (see sidebar opposite) are growing in number. The city is also home to a small but pronounced Jewish population.

From day one, Rio had always attracted a small number of adventurous Europeans—ranging from explorers and traders to the artists and architects of the French Artistic Mission, who were hired by King João VI to modernize the city. However, the late 1800s and early 1900s witnessed a veritable immigration explosion. Lured first by Rio's coffee boom, and subsequently by its burgeoning commercial and industrial opportunities, waves of Spaniards, Italians, Germans, Lebanese, Syrians, and Japanese set up shop in the thriving capital, each leaving a small but indelible imprint upon the city.

Beginning in the mid-20th century, Rio also began receiving truckloads of poor migrants from the Brazilian Northeast who arrived searching for work. With little money

or education, many ended up living in favelas and doing menial labor. Traditionally, there was a certain stigma attached to these newcomers. Over time, however, *nordestino* (Northeast) elements have crept into the city's cultural life; their influence is particularly pronounced in the realms of music and cooking.

In the last few years, as North American and Western European economies have floundered and life has sped up and become more stressful, a new breed of immigrant—highly educated, chronically unemployed, and burned-out First Worlders—have been moving to Rio in record numbers. While for some the motivation is necessity or opportunity, for many others it's the unrivaled beauty, unparalleled warmth, and unlimited possibilities of the city itself.

In 1969, during the darkest days of Brazil's military dictatorship and cultural censorship, composer/singer Gilberto Gil was arrested and spent two months in a military prison in Rio. Released on Ash Wednesday, he was so overjoyed to emerge into the vibrant street life of Rio de Janeiro that he started composing a song in which he paid homage to the young favela girls, Portela samba school musicians, and Flamengo team soccer fans that he encountered as Carnaval wound down.

Gil recorded the samba-inflected "Aquele Abraço" ("That Embrace") prior to going into exile in London. He later explained that the title referred not only to the outstretched arms of the statue of Cristo Redentor, clearly visible from all over Rio, but also to the warm embrace of the city itself and his eternal desire to return to it. It's a sentiment that's common among all who are fortunate enough to feel the embrace of Rio and its people. Once they've experienced it, they long to come back. ∎

## Spiritual Matters

In 19th-century France, after attending a séance, French educator Allan Kardec (1804–1869) began studying the phenomenon of spirits in earnest. He subsequently authored a series of books on Spiritism that became hugely influential—particularly in Brazil.

Today, Brazil boasts the largest number of believers in Espiritismo, a philosophy and/or religion that centers on the reincarnation and eternal presence of human spirits. In fact, over the last ten years, the number of adherents has doubled. Rio possesses the country's largest number of Espiritistas (6 percent of the population), many of whom are white, middle class, and well educated. A considerable number work for the Globo television network, whose nightly *novelas* (soap operas) are watched by tens of millions. This results in soap protagonists who are killed off, but whose spirits remain among the cast—a phenomenon as popular as it is common.

# Rio de Janeiro's History

Rio has packed a fantastic amount of colorful history into its 500 years. From a fortified outpost perched on Guanabara Bay, the city rose from a swampy colonial backwater into the seat of the Portuguese Empire and capital of the first Brazilian republic before blossoming into one of the world's most captivating modern metropolises, rife with perpetual contrasts and incomparable verve.

## Prehistory

The earliest traces of human civilization in Rio de Janeiro are fragments of pottery that date back to 1000 B.C. By the time the first Europeans arrived on the scene in A.D. 1500, an estimated 400 indigenous ethnic groups inhabited Brazil, each with distinctive variations with respect to language and customs. Most lived in villages where their livelihoods depended upon hunting, fishing, and harvesting nature's bounty, which grew in profusion in the lush Atlantic rain forest that covered the entire coast of Brazil.

"Landing of Pedro Álvares Cabral in Porto Seguro, in 1500," by Oscar Pereira da Silva, 1902

## The Man Who Gave Rio Away

In 1531, Martim Afonso de Sousa (1500–1571), a Portuguese explorer and childhood friend of King João III (1502–1557), was sent to Rio. His joint mission was to establish a colony and discover El Dorado, tales of which had been passed on to early explorers by Brazil's native peoples. Afonso spent two years scouring the Brazilian interior for riches. During this time, the Spanish tumbled upon their own El Dorado in the form of the gold-drenched Inca Empire, while the hapless Portuguese were decimated by native attacks and tropical diseases. By 1533, Afonso was disgusted with Brazil and journeyed to India, where spoils were guaranteed. Wanting nothing to do with the territory gifted to him by the king—which encompassed Rio—he happily gave the land away for free to other colonists, saying that whoever took it off his hands would be doing him "the greatest mercy and greatest honor in the world."

The "Indians" who inhabited the coast of Rio de Janeiro belonged to groups that spoke Tupi. The two principal Tupi ethnic groups were the Temiminó and the Tamoio. Early Portuguese explorers were astonished by their casual nakedness, their ceremonial dances, and their impeccable hygiene (Tupi females insisted that European sailors adopt the habit of regular bathing). While the hospitable Temiminó forged an alliance with the Portuguese and easily succumbed to catechism, the fierce Tamoio became their mortal enemies.

### Colonization

Brazil was discovered by Europeans in April 1500 when Portuguese navigator Pedro Álvares Cabral (1467–1520) landed on the southern coast of Bahia. Planting a cross on the shores of what today is the town of Porto Seguro, Cabral claimed the territory in the name of Portugal's king, Manuel I (1469–1521).

Portugal's maritime explorations were motivated by the heavily indebted monarchy's desperate search for "undiscovered" virgin territories whose spoils they could plunder to fill up their chronically empty coffers. Cabral returned to Portugal with samples of a native tree known as pau brasil; while pau means "wood," brasil is thought to be a derivative of brasa (hot coal). This exotic reddish timber, brazilwood, was found to yield a rich crimson dye that became extremely coveted by European aristocrats. Before long, weaving factories were clamoring for this precious brasil, whose name came to designate the uncharted land where this cash crop grew in profusion.

On January 1, 1502, another Portuguese expedition, led by navigator Gaspar de Lemos, sailed into the breathtaking bay that the Tamoio referred to as Guanabara ("breast of the sea"). Believing the half-mile (1 km) entrance to the bay was in fact the mouth of a river, Lemos mistakenly baptized it Rio de Janeiro (River of January)—and the name stuck. When it was discovered that the lush Mata Atlântica surrounding the bay was rife with brazilwood,

Sugarcane, brought to Brazil by Portuguese colonists, is now one of Brazil's most important crops.

the Portuguese wasted no time in plying the native Tupi with trinkets in return for chopping down and harvesting the valuable timber. During this period, the Portuguese built a trading post on Praia do Flamengo, near the point where a river flowed into the sea. Surprised by the strange architectural style of the structure, the Tupi referred to it as *carioca* ("house of the white man"). Over time, "Carioca" became the name given to the river that supplied fresh water to the city, and its inhabitants became known as Cariocas.

Meanwhile, the French were also lured by the potential riches of the vast new Brazilian territory. While the Portuguese focused their attentions on the northeast, where decimated forests had already given way to the colony's next cash crop—sugarcane—the French set their sights on creating a French Antarctica. After forging a strategic alliance with the Tamoio, in 1555, Nicolas Durand de Villegaignon (1510–1571) built a fort on Serijipe Island (today known as Ilha Villegaignon) and began an occupation of Rio.

Years of battles ensued until, in 1560, Portuguese troops succeeded in driving the French out of Guanabara Bay. On January 20, 1563, the foundations of the settlement of São Sebastião do Rio de Janeiro were laid when Capt. Estácio de Sá (1520–1567) presided over the completion of a military fort, erected in the shadow of Sugarloaf.

## Founding of Rio de Janeiro

It would be another two years before the Portuguese succeeded in taking total possession of Rio and the surrounding region. Those of Rio's original inhabitants that weren't killed in battle or sent to live on Jesuit reservations succumbed to diseases brought by the Europeans. To safeguard against further attacks—both native and foreign—in 1567, the village of São Sebastião do Rio de Janeiro was transferred to the more secure higher ground of a fortified hilltop known as Morro do Castelo, near present-day Cinelândia. By the early 1600s, Rio was already Brazil's third largest settlement after the colony's capital of Salvador, in Bahia, and the adjacent towns of Olinda and Recife, in Pernambuco. Inspired by the riches from the Northeast's thriving sugarcane economy, Portuguese settlers in Rio began investing in sugarcane plantations as well as in the African slaves that were essential for their operation. As a result, over the following decades, Rio de Janeiro became one of the primary slave ports in all of the Americas, receiving a significant number of the estimated total of four million Africans who arrived in Brazil.

By 1700, the vast majority of Rio's 10,000 inhabitants were either African slaves or free mixed-race citizens boasting some African heritage; white Europeans were a small minority. Despite brutal attempts to prohibit Africans from speaking their ancestral languages and worshipping their deities, many cultural and religious practices survived and were absorbed into the fabric of daily life, where they remain present to this day.

It wasn't sugarcane, however, but gold that catapulted Rio to prominence. After centuries of searching high and low for a mythical El Dorado reputed to be located deep in the Brazilian interior, in the early 1700s vast amounts of gold and gemstones were finally discovered deep in the mountains and riverbeds of neighboring Minas Gerais. As the primary port from which all of Minas's riches were shipped off to Lisbon, Rio grew in importance as it became the primary transportation and taxation hub of Portugal's American colony. By 1763, Rio de Janeiro's strategic significance had eclipsed that of Salvador and the city became the new capital of Brazil. By this time, it had expanded in size and its population now numbered some 50,000 inhabitants.

**By 1763, Rio de Janeiro's strategic significance had eclipsed that of Salvador and the city became the new capital of Brazil.**

## Seat of Empire

Its newfound political and economic clout aside, throughout the 18th century, Rio continued to be a dirty, mosquito-ridden backwater plagued by chaos and disease. With the dawn of the 19th century, however, the city's destiny changed suddenly—and dramatically.

In 1808, Napoleon Bonaparte invaded Portugal, sending the Portuguese royal family into exile. Along with his family and a retinue of 15,000 ministers, aristocrats, courtesans, and other attendants, King João VI (1767–1826) fled across the Atlantic and sought refuge in Rio. The tropical colony proved so irresistible to the king that following Napoleon's 1815 defeat at Waterloo, João VI decided not only to remain in the Americas but to legitimize his preference by declaring Rio de Janeiro to be the capital of the newly invented United Kingdom of Portugal, Brazil, and the Algarves.

Rio flourished as the new seat of the Portuguese Empire. The port was opened up for international trade with Portugal's European allies. Foreign merchants, many of them English, set up businesses in the city center, which quickly grew into a thriving commercial hub. Meanwhile, under royal patronage, the arts and sciences flourished. A strong French influence in the development of academies and institutions led to the creation of a sophisticated, educated elite and the development of a cultural scene that was extremely cosmopolitan.

In 1821, uprisings in Portugal left João VI with no choice but to return to Lisbon, but he left his only son, Pedro I (1798–1834), to govern over Brazil. Months later, when he demanded that Pedro return as well, he was shocked when his rebellious son not only refused but promptly declared Brazil's independence from Portugal on the historic date of September 7, 1822. Shortly afterward, Pedro I proceeded to have himself crowned Brazil's first emperor.

To live up to its new role as capital of the only empire in the Americas, Rio de Janeiro was treated to a major, and much needed, overhaul. Elegant palaces sprang up along the paved and illuminated grand *avenidas* (avenues) that cut through Centro. In the 1860s, newly installed *bondes* (streetcars) provided the city's first public transportation system. Initially powered by mules, they were promptly modernized when electricity came to Rio in the 1880s. By the mid-19th century, the great fortunes once generated from sugar and gold had all but dried up, leaving in their wake a sizable class of poor, unemployed slaves who migrated to the city's expanding slums. Meanwhile, new wealth was being made from Brazil's newest cash crop: coffee, plantations of which carpeted the surrounding mountains and valleys.

In 1831, Pedro I was obliged to return to Lisbon to occupy the vacant throne left by his father, who had died in 1826. In his place, he left as prince regent his son Pedro II

## The Education of Pedro II

Pedro II had a lonely upbringing in Rio. When he was two, his mother died, and when he was five, his father returned to Portugal. The little emperor spent the next ten years being groomed for his future role. Amid a barrage of lessons in everything from philosophy and astronomy to fencing and ballroom dancing, he had only two hours a day of leisure time. He couldn't even protest the grueling schedule: He was instructed never to lose his temper or express emotions in public.

As emperor, Pedro II was a fervent believer in education. He founded many schools, universities, and academic institutes and was a patron of the arts and sciences. Multilingual, he traveled the world and eagerly met, and subsequently

corresponded with, leading intellectuals, including Friedrich Nietzche, Victor Hugo, Lewis Carroll, and Louis Pasteur. In Philadelphia, he encountered Alexander Graham Bell, who demonstrated a new invention: the telephone. After picking up the receiver of the ringing phone, Pedro was so stunned to hear the phrase "To be or not to be . . ." that he yelled, "My God! This thing talks!" He installed the nation's first telephone line in his Petrópolis palace.

Pedro never stopped his continuing education. Exiled from Brazil, he spent the last months of his life in Paris visiting museums and attending university seminars. It was while returning home from a lecture that he caught a cold that worsened into the pneumonia that killed him.

Pedro Américo's "Independence or Death" (1888) depicts Pedro I's famous "cry" of independence.

(1825–1891)—who at the time was only five years old. Groomed from early childhood to assume his imperial duties, Pedro II (see sidebar opposite) was crowned at the tender age of 15 in 1840. The crowds who watched the coronation at the Paço Imperial were overjoyed to have a homegrown leader after centuries of colonial rule.

## Imperial Capital

Educated, progressive, and tolerant, Pedro II was considered an illuminated monarch for much of his 58-year reign. However, as the 19th century wore on, there was mounting social pressure for radical change. Increasingly, Rio became a hotbed for two escalating national movements: abolition and republicanism. Fanned by European liberalism, both issues were fiercely debated in the city's increasingly influential newspapers and among its rising intellectual class. Already in 1850, as a result of pressure from England—Portugal's major European ally and trading partner—Brazil had been pressured into abolishing the slave trade (although a thriving black market trade persevered). However, so as not to antagonize the powerful landowning elites, Pedro II espoused only a gradual abolition stance (despite having liberated all his own slaves in 1840). It was thus over a period of decades that laws such as 1871's Lei do Ventro Livre, which freed all children born to slaves, and 1885's Lei dos Sexagenários, which liberated all slaves over the age of 65, were passed. And it wasn't until May 13, 1888, that Pedro II's daughter Princesa Isabel (1846–1921) would sign the Lei Áurea (Golden Law). In one fell pen stroke, Brazil's 700,000 remaining slaves (out of a total national population of 15 million) were liberated—and Brazil earned the dubious honor of becoming the last independent nation in the Americas to abolish slavery.

   With the signing of the Lei Áurea, Brazil's plantation economy went into a tailspin. The state of Rio de Janeiro's slave-intensive coffee economy was profoundly affected and, like other rural elites throughout the country, the coffee barons expressed their displeasure with the monarchy by allying themselves with the growing republican forces. Meanwhile, the newly strengthened army was also harboring discontent in the aftermath of Brazil's involvement in the Paraguayan War (1864–1870), which pitted Brazil, Argentina, and Uruguay against their neighbor Paraguay and left Brazil with considerable casualties and a large public debt.

On November 15, 1889, in Campo de Santana, Marshal Manuel Deodoro da Fonseca (1827–1892) headed a military coup that deposed Pedro II and declared Brazil to be a republic. Days later, the imperial family set sail for Europe, never to return. In 1891, following the passage of a new constitution, Deodoro became the first president of the United States of Brazil.

## Rio's African Prince

**Pedro II wasn't Rio's sole regal presence. The grandson of a Yoruba king whose son was sold into slavery, Dom Oba II (born Cândido da Fonseca Galvão in 1845) grew up in a Bahian diamond-mining town, where his father taught him to read and write. As a young man, he volunteered to fight in the Paraguayan War, where, due to his courage, he was made an honorary army lieutenant. Moving to Rio, this tall African prince in a frock coat, gold pince-nez, and gloves cut an exceptional figure, inviting ridicule and reverence. A fervent abolitionist who was worshipped by the city's Afro-Brazilian population, he was also a monarchist and great friend of Pedro II, whom he frequently visited at the palace. When the empire fell, so did Dom Oba; he was stripped of his military honors and died in 1890.**

## First Republic

The First Republic (1889–1930) came to be known as the era of *café com leite*. This is because, despite the fact that Rio was the new republic's capital, most of the government's power originated in the states of São Paulo, ruled over by rich coffee barons, and Minas Gerais, where wealthy milk-producing landowners called all the shots. As a result of the privileges enjoyed by these oligarchs and the crony corruption that ensued, it wasn't long before popular revolts began to break out in Rio and around the country.

Between 1891 and 1894, navy officers in Rio staged a revolt known as the Revoltas das Armadas in which rebels questioned the legitimacy of President Deodoro and his successor, Floriano Peixoto (1839–1895). In 1893, they went so far as to launch an attack upon Rio's army-controlled fortresses. Although it lasted less than a year, Cariocas were terrified by the constant thunder of cannon fire.

In 1896, a second revolt—this one of rural workers and freed slaves in Canudos, in the interior of Bahia—also had major repercussions on Rio. Following the army's squelching of the revolt, demobilized Northeastern soldiers who had fought for the government were promised land on an unoccupied hilltop *(morro)* in Rio's Centro. When the government reneged on its offer, the frustrated migrants occupied the area, which soon became known as Morro da Favela *(favela* is a plant native to the arid Northeastern interior). Henceforth, all hilltop communities invaded by poor migrants came to be called favelas.

Despite these upheavals, as capital of the republic, Rio continued to expand and prosper as the 20th century dawned. The end of slavery coupled with the city's economic potential attracted an increasing number of European immigrants, who started businesses and were also instrumental in establishing some of the city's first industrial factories. Inspired by Baron Haussmann's elegant overhaul of Paris, between 1902 and

1906 Rio's Centro was treated to a belle epoque revamping complete with tree-lined grand avenues and monumental squares flanked with elegant palaces and theaters. Entire blocks of centuries-old buildings were obliterated to make way for the multilaned thoroughfare of Avenida Central (today Avenida Rio Branco).

Much of this modernization process was motivated by the insalubrious conditions in which Rio's poor lived—and very often died due to frequent epidemics of yellow fever, measles, and bubonic plague. In 1904, a municipal law was passed making inoculation against measles obligatory. This early attempt at public health care led to an enormous popular uprising known as the Revolta da Vacina (Vaccine Revolt). Meanwhile, one of the side effects of this developmental fervor was the expulsion of Centro's poor (mostly black) residents to the burgeoning favelas.

Centro wasn't the only part of Rio that was under transformation. In 1892, a tunnel blasted through the mountains opened up access to what would quickly emerge as the most fashionable beach neighborhood in the city, if not the planet: Copacabana. During the 1930s and '40s, the Cidade Maravilhosa captured the world's imagination as a tropical Paris, an image reinforced by a wave of South American–themed Hollywood movies such as *Flying Down to Rio, That Night in Rio, Road to Rio,* and even *Charlie Chan in Rio*. With its glamorous nightclubs, swanky casinos, and luxurious Copacabana Palace Hotel, Copacabana rapidly became the hub of a progressive and hedonistic Rio that sparkled, impervious to the fact that Brazil was living under a dictatorship.

**In 1891, following the passage of a new constitution, Deodoro became the first president of the United States of Brazil.**

## Vargas & the Estado Novo

The increasing dissatisfaction with café com leite politics came to a head in 1930 when the Great Depression knocked the bottom out of Brazil's coffee market. To rescue the coffee barons from ruin, the government spent a fortune purchasing coffee at a fixed rate, only to burn the harvest when no foreign buyers materialized. Workers and the rising urban middle class as well as political opposition leaders were furious. Popular revolts broke out in Rio as well as in the Brazilian northeast and south, home to a charismatic politician from Rio Grande do Sul by the name of Getúlio Vargas (1882–1954). Vargas had run for president in 1930, but lost due to purported fraud. When a bloodless military coup that year ousted President Washington Luís (1869–1957), Vargas was installed in his place—for the next 15 years.

A staunch nationalist, wily politician, and unabashed populist, Vargas ushered in a new era. He gave a major boost to Brazil's nascent industry by nationalizing key sectors, including oil, mining, and electricity, all of which flourished. At the same time, he won over the poor and working classes by launching public health and social welfare systems, legalizing unions, and creating labor laws and a minimum wage. He also extended to women the right to vote.

Vargas carried out such sweeping reforms by declaring himself dictator under a regime known as the Estado Novo (New State). Following its implementation in 1937, opposition parties were banned, the press censored, and dissidents imprisoned. Meanwhile, at the expense of democracy, Vargas's centralized government succeeded in finally splintering the power of the old landowning oligarchies.

Rio became the Estado Novo's symbolic showcase. It was during this time that Avenida Presidente Vargas was constructed. Lined with imposing, vaguely fascist high-rises, this daunting, multilaned thoroughfare cut a wide swath through Centro, creating an essential artery that connected the mushrooming neighborhoods of the Zona Sul and the Zona Norte areas. Amid great military pomp, the avenue was inaugurated by Vargas himself on September 7, 1944.

With the breakout of World War II, Brazil initially remained neutral. Behind the scenes, however, Vargas was flirting with both the Allies and the Axis. He finally joined the Allied cause, after being seduced by offers of American financial aid in return for permission to install U.S. military bases along Brazil's strategic northeast coast. As a result, in 1942, Brazilian troops joined the Allied Forces in the invasion of Italy. Ultimately, however, the paradox between fighting for freedom abroad while operating a fascist dictatorship at home proved difficult to sustain. In 1945, amid military pressure to step down, Vargas resigned.

In 1930, Getúlio Vargas is sworn in as provisional Brazilian president at the Palácio do Catete.

Vargas's mass popularity never waned, and in 1950 the masses returned him to power once again—as a democratically elected president. Without his absolute powers to deflect criticism, though, his term was tarnished by accusations of corruption. The most strident attacks came from Carlos Lacerda (1914–1977), a Carioca journalist and politician with presidential aspirations of his own. When an assassination attempt on Lacerda was linked to one of the president's security staff, the resulting scandal led to calls for Vargas's resignation. Instead, on the evening of August 4, 1954, the president went into his bedroom at Rio's Palácio do Catete and shot himself in the heart after leaving a dramatic suicide note addressed to the Brazilian people. The subsequent outpouring of grief was such that Lacerda fled the country.

In 1956, Juscelino Kubitschek (1902–1976) was elected president on the basis of a catchy campaign slogan vowing that he'd accomplish in 5 years what other politicians did in 50. The ambitious former governor of Minas Gerais immediately set about making good on his promise by hiring a forward-thinking group of urban planners and architects—under the talented auspices of Lucio Costa and Oscar Niemeyer—to build a brand-new capital from scratch in the geographic center of Brazil (that is, in the middle of nowhere).

Kubitschek's utopian mission in creating Brasília was to settle and develop Brazil's vast, yet deserted, interior. Countless critics called him crazy, among them ministers and other politicos who shuddered at the thought of abandoning the glamorous haunts and balmy beaches of Rio for the flat, dry, and dusty isolation of Brazil's center-west. Yet, Kubitschek persevered. On April 21, 1960, he presided over the unveiling of the new (but not fully completed) capital. The crazy part, however, was the astronomical cost of building Brasília, which Kubitschek resolved by printing excessive amounts of money. This shortsighted strategy resulted in a massive long-term debt and rampant inflation.

By the time the capital moved to Brasília, Rio had begun to resemble the modern city that can be seen today. With the exception of a few stray baroque churches and some grand palaces, many of which formerly sheltered government ministries, Centro succumbed to the beginnings of verticalization with the breakneck construction of commercial high-rises. The 1950s and '60s also witnessed the creation of the vast waterfront Parque do Flamengo, the opening up of more tunnels through the mountains, and the building of multilane freeways to ease steadily growing traffic. Rio's new look was mirrored by the new ideas that were percolating among the city's new generation of intellectuals and artists. Although no longer the seat of government, the city continued to be a magnet for the Brazilian vanguard, whose members held casual court on the sands and in the bars of the cool new beach neighborhoods of Ipanema and Leblon.

## Military Regime

Brazil's escalating economic problems dovetailed with growing social unrest that saw conflicts escalate between urban workers and factory owners and tensions rise between wealthy landowners and the rural poor. Kubitschek's replacement, Jânio

### Land of the Future

During the 1930s and '40s, many Jewish refugees sought sanctuary in Brazil. Yet none of them caused as much commotion as Stefan Zweig (1881–1942). Accompanied by his young wife, Lotte, the Austrian writer arrived in Rio de Janeiro in 1941 and rented a chalet in the imperial town of Petrópolis. That same year, he published Brazil, Land of the Future, in which the utopian Zweig waxed so enthusiastic about his adopted homeland that Brazilian critics accused him of being paid off by the Vargas dictatorship. It turns out that, while the best-selling author didn't lack for funds, he apparently had agreed to produce a book in return for quick residency visas. His love for Brazil notwithstanding, after only five months in Brazil, Zweig convinced Lotte to enter into a suicide pact. Despite his untimely death, his catchphrase title lives on in the collective consciousness as Brazilians constantly wonder if the future has arrived.

Quadros (1917–1992) lasted only months in power before being succeeded by João Goulart (1918–1976), a left-leaning politician who actively supported trade unions and rural peasant organizations and whose first act was to increase the minimum salary by 100 percent. This enraged Brazil's conservative elites, not to mention the military, which—contaminated by Cold War paranoia—accused "Jango" of harboring communist sympathies. On March 31, 1964, with the implicit backing of the U.S. government, a small group of right-wing generals, led by Marshal Humberto de Alencar Castelo Branco (1897–1967), deposed Goulart in a swift and bloodless coup, plunging Brazil into a military dictatorship that would last 21 years.

Castelo Branco became the first in a long series of generals to rule the country with an iron fist. The first order of business included dissolving Congress, outlawing political parties and unions, and censoring the media. However, the darkest days of the dictatorship arrived in 1969 when Gen. Emílio Garrastazú Medici (1905–1985) came to power. The five years of his reign—known as the *anos de chumbo* (lead years)—were the bleakest and most brutal of the military regime. Thousands of Brazilians were arrested, imprisoned, tortured, and killed for holding political beliefs considered subversive or for expressing ideas deemed unacceptable by the regime. Many of Brazil's leading artists, academics, politicians, and intellectuals—among them composer-musicians such as Caetano Veloso, Gilberto Gil, and Chico Buarque and future president Fernando Henrique Cardoso—spent years in exile. Although Brazil's dictatorship was less brutal than those in neighboring Argentina and Chile, where hundreds of thousands "disappeared," there was widespread loathing for the generals who were as corrupt as they were cruel.

**The dictatorship's harshest years coincided with years that saw economic growth surpassing 10 percent a year.**

Even during the most repressive years of the regime, Rio's liberal and subversive voices weren't silenced. In 1968, the Passeata dos Cem Mil (March of the Hundred Thousand) occurred when thousands of citizens took to the streets to protest a military policeman's public shooting of an innocent student. The following year, in retaliation for American support of the military coup, a handful of young guerrillas kidnapped the U.S. ambassador, demanding that 15 political prisoners be released (an episode that is dramatized in the 1998 film *O Que É Isso, Companheiro? (Four Days in September)*.

**Economic Miracle:** The dictatorship's harshest years coincided with years that saw economic growth surpassing 10 percent a year. Dubbed Brazil's "Economic Miracle," the period was marked by a massive industrial boom, which attracted vast numbers of poor migrants from the Northeast to Rio and, especially, São Paulo in search of manufacturing jobs. While many found employment in factories and performing other low-wage tasks, an overwhelming number remained miserable. In Rio, many of these newcomers settled in the favelas crowning the city's hilltops, which began to expand exponentially in size and number.

Although a small minority of Brazilians grew very rich, the Economic Miracle quickly became an economic disaster with the onset of the 1973 oil crisis. By the early 1980s, inflation had skyrocketed to absurd levels (in 1983, annual inflation hit 200 percent)

In 1968, thousands of people parade through Rio in opposition to Brazil's military regime.

as the country struggled to pay off foreign creditors that had financed pharaonic and incredibly costly public projects such as Itaipu, the world's largest hydroelectric dam, at Iguaçu Falls, and the (never fully paved) Trans-Amazonian Highway, which cut a 2,485-mile (4,000 km) swath through the previously impassable rain forest all the way to Peru.

Increasingly unhappy with censorship, corruption, and the disastrous economic situation, members of Brazil's working and middle classes together with students, artists, labor leaders, and intellectuals took to the streets of Rio and other major cities to protest their opposition to the military regime. In São Paulo, workers initiated a series of crippling strikes led by Luiz Inácio da Silva (1945–), a leader of one of the illegal unions. Known by the nickname "Lula," da Silva was a fiery young factory worker from the northeastern state of Pernambuco who had lost a finger in a factory accident. When the government sent in troops to quell the strike, Lula and his colleagues refused to surrender. The government was obliged not only to back down but to legalize unions as well.

As popular revolts continued to spread, President João Figueiredo (1918–1999) began to enact reforms, part of a gradual *abertura* (opening) that was meant to mark a transition to Brazil's return to democracy. Measures included the relaxation of censorship codes and amnesty that permitted dissidents to return to Brazil from foreign exile. In 1982, the first democratic state and municipal elections took place, while federal elections were held in 1985.

## The New Republic

When Tancredo Neves (1910–1985), a popular politician from Minas Gerais, was swept into power in 1985, Brazilians took to the streets to celebrate the end of the dark years of dictatorship. However, the rosy dawn of the New Republic was extremely short-lived; the night prior to his inauguration, Neves suddenly died from a stomach tumor. His vice president and successor, José Sarney (1930– ), was an uninspiring conservative from the northeast state of Maranhão who proved unable to rein in Brazil's skyrocketing inflation, which had reached almost 2,000 percent in 1989.

Sarney's successor in 1990, a playboy millionaire named Fernando Collor de Mello (1949– ), was dashing but disastrous. While infuriating the middle class by freezing their bank accounts, he and his cronies funneled billions of dollars in public money into private accounts.

When Collor was forced to step down in 1992, his elected successor was Fernando Henrique Cardoso (1931– ), a respected sociologist who, during the military regime, had spent years in exile studying in the United States. In 1994, "FHC" rescued Brazil's flailing economy by creating a new currency, the *real,* and pinning its value to the U.S. dollar. In doing so, he brought soaring inflation to a halt for the first time in decades.

During Cardoso's two terms (1994–2002), Brazil's economy enjoyed steady growth, fueled by the opening of its borders to foreign capital, the privatization of corrupt and often inefficient public companies, and a reduction of import barriers. Economic reforms were accompanied by the beginnings of urgently needed political and social reforms.

### Fuel for Thought

In late 2007, when international oil prices suddenly skyrocketed, Brazil became the envy of many panicked countries when the nation's oil giant, Petrobras, tapped into an immense deepwater reserve off Rio de Janeiro state's northern coast. It's estimated that the Tupi reserve contains as much as eight billion barrels of oil—although it's not as if Brazil is prey to a nasty oil habit. In the aftermath of the 1973 oil crisis, the government's inspired solution was to convert sugarcane into ethanol as an inexpensive, nonpolluting fuel for all vehicles. As a result, today Brazil is the world's top producer of sugarcane alcohol, and all Brazilian vehicles are flex-fuel models that run on gas, alcohol, or a blend of both.

## Lula, Dilma, & the Worker's Party

After running—and being narrowly defeated—in every presidential election since 1990, in 2001, Lula da Silva, the former São Paulo union leader and head of the Partido dos Trabalhadores (PT; Workers' Party), finally scored a historic victory on his fourth attempt. The election of Lula as president was a watershed moment. Throughout its five centuries of history, Brazil had always been ruled by scions of the upper-class elite. That a poor boy from the parched interior of Pernambuco, without a university degree, could rise to the highest post in the land was nothing short of miraculous.

While Lula was adored by the masses and by many of Brazil's traditionally left-leaning artists and intellectuals, the corporate class was fearful of the former Marxist who flaunted his friendships with Cuba's Fidel Castro and Venezuela's Hugo Chavez. As president, however, the man the press dubbed "Lula Light" hewed to a centrist path, continuing to promote Brazil as an increasingly important economic player in the global marketplace and presiding over unprecedented rates of economic growth. At the same time, his government made significant strides in tackling some of the most flagrant social inequalities that have plagued Brazil, and Rio, since early days. Notably, the PT government spearheaded a host of wide-ranging programs that allowed Brazil's traditionally neglected poorer and working classes unprecedented access to education, affordable housing, and loans to start small businesses.

**Of Romanian descent, Dilma Rousseff is Brazil's first female president, elected in November 2010.**

These efforts, coupled with a flourishing economy, rising salaries, and record low unemployment, resulted in the ascension of an unprecedented number of poor Brazilians into the ranks of the middle class. Unsurprisingly, when Lula completed his second term in 2010, he had a historic approval rating of 83 percent. Indeed, it was largely as a result of his great popularity that Dilma Rousseff (1947–), his chief of staff and groomed successor, was elected Brazil's first female president in November 2010.

For the most part, Dilma—a former member of an underground military group who was jailed and tortured during the military regime—has followed in Lula's footsteps, attempting to lead Brazil toward increased economic prosperity while not forsaking the fight for social justice and equality. To date, Brazil has made great strides in becoming a mature and stable democracy with a robust economy. It's emerged as a regional leader in Latin America and a source of inspiration to other nations.

In recent years, Rio de Janeiro's progress has mirrored that of Brazil. In fact, increasingly, the city has once again been at the forefront of progress. Its economy buoyed by substantial offshore oil discoveries, its pride (and urban development) invigorated by its dual hosting gig of the 2014 FIFA World Cup (soccer) and the 2016 Summer Olympics, and its deep and chronic rift between the poor of the morros and the wealthy of the *asfalto* (asphalt, i.e. the city proper) at long last receiving the healing attentions it deserves, Rio of the 21st century is emerging stronger, more vibrant, and more *maravilhosa* than ever before. ■

# Food & Drink

While Rio has no signature regional cuisine of its own, the city is a food and drink lover's delight. From haute cuisine to street (and beach) food, you'll find an intoxicating mixture of homegrown and international, gluttonously fattening and übernutritious.

Traditionally, *feijão* and *arroz* (beans and rice) have comprised the twin pillars of the Brazilian diet.

While other regions of Brazil—such as Bahia, Minas Gerais, and the Amazon—are endowed with a rich and distinctive culinary heritage, Rio de Janeiro—hewing true to the *mestiçagem* that defines so many other aspects of Carioca life—is all about the inspired and often improvised mélange of the myriad influences that wash up on its shores.

## Portuguese Influences

A legacy of its past as Portugal's colonial and imperial capital means that Portuguese dishes and delicacies maintain a strong hold on the city's collective stomach. *Bacalhau* (salted cod) is popular, particularly in the form of crunchy fried *bolinhos,* which are a mainstay of the city's bars. Other legacies include *cozido* (a hearty stew made with slow-cooked meat and a cornucopia of vegetables) and myriad rich, eggy desserts, many of whose centuries-old recipes originated in Portuguese

convents. Among the most delectable is lustrous yellow *quindim,* a sweet cupcake-shaped custard to which African slaves added the inspired touch of shredded coconut.

Portugal's greatest culinary gift to Brazil is the heady, dense stew of beans (*feijão*) and meat that's become the national dish par excellence: *feijoada.* Actually, "dish" is a misnomer, since feijoada is a full-out meal. It consists not only of the beans (which in Rio are invariably black), simmered for hours with various pork parts and sausages such as *linguiça* and *paio,* but all the attendant trimmings as well. These vary throughout Brazil, but in Rio you can count on a *feijoada completa* being served with rice, sautéed collard greens, orange slices, and *farofa* (manioc flour toasted to crunchiness in butter). Sometimes, just to underscore the pork element, crisp *torresmos* (fried pork rinds) make a cameo appearance. The presence of Brazil's classic cocktail, the caipirinha, as a loyal sidekick

## EXPERIENCE: Saturday Is *Feijoada* Day

Owing to the effort involved in both eating and digesting *feijoada*, you should indulge in this dish on Saturday afternoons, when it is traditionally served. In Santa Teresa, **Bar do Mineiro** *(Rua Paschoal Carlos Magno 99, tel 24/2221-9227)* does a righteous version that invites lines out the door. Also succulent is the Feijoada da Tia Surica, which can be savored on the last Saturday of the month at Centro's legendary **Teatro**

**Rival** *(Rua Álvaro Alvim 33–37, tel 21/ 2240-4469)*. Since "Aunt" Surica is a venerated member of the Portela samba school, it's no surprise that her version comes with a side of live samba. For a weekday hit, try the **Casa da Feijoada** *(Rua Prudente de Moraes 10, tel 21/2247-2476)* or its sister establishment, **Brasileirinho** *(Rua Jangadeiros 10A, tel 21/2513-5184)*, both in Ipanema.

is inspired—the zest of the crushed lime and the alcoholic edge of the cachaça cutting through all that salty richness.

### Brazilian Flair

A consequence of Rio's cosmopolitanism is the ease with which you can encounter food from all over Brazil—Bahian seafood *moquecas* (stews), heady Amazonian *pato* (duck) *no tucupi,* and succulent *churrasco* (barbecue) from down Rio Grande do Sul way—as well as all over the globe at its many restaurants. Moreover, in recent years, a new generation of chefs has moved away from Eurocentric menus and has successfully been applying Old World techniques to Brazil's New World abundance of exotic and often unexploited fish, meats, vegetables, grains, and fruits in an attempt to create a contemporary Brazilian cuisine.

Speaking of fruit, you'll find an avalanche of tantalizing shapes, scents, and tastes on offer from Brazil's tropics. Aside from the fact that run-of-the-mill bananas and mangos come in numerous varieties and taste ambrosial, there is also the exotica you've never heard of from the Amazon *(cupuaçu, bacuri),* Northeast *(umbu, siriguela),* and Central-West's Cerrado region *(mangaba, cagaita).* While these won't show up at the breakfast table, you'll easily encounter them at Rio's many *bares de suco* (juice bars), where health-conscious Cariocas don't just quench their thirst but grab nutritious snacks.

Indeed, Rio's warm climate, coupled with the extroverted, sporty, and casual tendencies of its residents, means that food is often enjoyed communally and outside—at a sidewalk bar, on the beach, or in a lively square. It's common for friends to share several portions of *petiscos* (bar appetizers)—not to mention rounds of icy *cerveja* (beer), Cariocas' beverage of predilection—in lieu of dinner, or to substitute lunch with a couple of deep-fried meat *pastéis* washed down with *água de coco* (coconut water) from a freshly macheted green coconut.

*Água* (water) from green coconuts can be purchased *gelada* (cold) and *natural* (unchilled).

# The Arts

Rio's wondrously hybrid cultural legacy is as dazzling as its beaches. Once the city slipped free of the yoke of colonialism, the wildly innovative mixtures—of foreign and local, high and low, traditional and cutting-edge, formal and improvised, Euro, Afro, and *índio*—led to the creation of a unique literary, artistic, cinematic, and musical landscape that continues to evolve and fascinate.

## Fine Arts & Architecture

The first recorded examples of "Brazilian" art date back to colonial times when European artists—many of whom accompanied early exploring expeditions—began registering the lush, untamed landscapes, and their exotic indigenous inhabitants, on canvas. Back in Europe, their works helped fuel and perpetuate the myth of tropical Brazil as an earthly albeit primitive paradise.

It wasn't until the 18th century that Rio began to develop an artistic scene. One of the earliest painters of note was Leandro Joaquim (1738–1798), a young mulatto who was known for his vivid landscapes and seascapes, rendered in rich colors. Joaquim was part of the Escola Fluminense de Pintura, a school of painters that blossomed in the early 1700s around Ricardo Pilar (1630–1702). Considered one of colonial Rio's most talented figures, Pilar was also a friar who was most famously responsible for the 14 exquisite decorative panels in the 17th-century Mosteiro de São Bento.

> **Most of the earliest artworks created in Rio during colonial times were executed by anonymous monks, underscoring the degree to which religion, art, and architecture were intertwined.**

Most of the earliest artworks created in Rio during colonial times were executed by anonymous monks, underscoring the degree to which religion, art, and architecture were intertwined. It's significant that, excluding the Paço Imperial, Rio's sole surviving colonial buildings are all churches built by various Portuguese religious orders. Apart from the magnificent Mosteiro de São Bento, the Benedictine monastery that constitutes a high point of Carioca baroque, other notable examples of ecclesiastical architecture include the Igreja de Nossa Senhora do Carmo, the Igreja de Ordem Terceira de São Francisco de Penitência, and the Santuário e Convento do Santo Antônio, all of which are located in Centro.

**Barroco Mineiro:** Many early Brazilian artists slavishly copied styles fashionable in Europe. However, over time, a few renegades began to subtly, and sometimes subversively, tropicalize them by weaving distinctly Brazilian elements into their works. The most remarkable instance of this tendency resulted in the emergence of *barroco mineiro*, a version of Portuguese baroque that emerged in the neighboring state of Minas Gerais during the 18th century. As a result of its historic gold rush, Minas's suddenly wealthy mining towns were adorned with splendid churches that set themselves apart from the baroque norm with their use of vivid colors and

**The Theatro Municipal's sumptuous main staircase is wrought from two types of onyx.**

exaggerated decorative flourishes, not to mention the integration of local elements ranging from the black facial features of sculpted cherubs to the presence of tropical flora and fauna in painted panels and gold-drenched altars.

The leading figure of barroco mineiro was a mulatto builder and sculptor named Antônio Francisco Lisboa (1738–1814), who was more commonly known as Aleijadinho (Little Cripple) as a result of the leprosy that plagued him in his later years. Considered one of the greatest baroque artists ever, Aleijadinho's influence was enormous.

Rio de Janeiro's answer to Aleijadinho was Valentim da Fonseca e Silva (1745–1813). A prolific and talented mulatto sculptor and architect, Mestre Valentim was the originator of a unique style that fused elements of baroque and rococo with neoclassicism. In addition to the many carvings and sculptures he produced for churches such as the Igreja de Nossa Senhora do Carmo da Lapa do Desterro, he designed Lapa's Passeio Público, Rio's (and Brazil's) first public park. He is also the author of two monumental stone fountains: the Chafariz do Mestre Valentim in Centro's Praça XV and the Chafariz das Saracuras, which anchors Praça General Osório in Ipanema.

## Portraitist of Imperial Brazil

The Parisian portraitist Jean-Baptiste Debret was left flailing after his patron, Napoleon, was exiled from France in 1815. Fortunately, Debret and other patroned artists were still in favor overseas. Debret's 1816 arrival in Rio coincided with the death of João VI's mother, Maria, whose funeral Debret was hastily hired to paint. Other royal commissions followed. Yet Debret's most important work was the detailed portraits produced during the 15 years he spent living in Rio and traveling through Brazil. Published in the 1830s under the title *Voyage Pittoresque et Historique au Brésil*, Debret's lithographs of indigenous chiefs, African slaves, rural and urban workers, and celebrants of folk and religious festivals were accompanied by descriptive texts whose historical value is as important as their artistic merits. Today it is considered one of the most important registers of 19th-century Brazilian life.

**French Influences:** Napoleon's invasion of Portugal in 1808 and the subsequent flight of João VI and his royal retinue to Rio had a profound effect upon Brazil's artistic milieu. As seat of the Portuguese empire and capital of independent Brazil, Rio quickly adapted to its role as the nation's artistic and cultural center. In 1816, João VI summoned a group of renowned French artists, known as the Missão Artística Francesa (French Artistic Mission), to beautify and modernize the city. It was also their duty to disseminate the philosophies and methods of romanticism and neoclassicism, both of which were in vogue at the time in France, to a generation of young Brazilian artists who came to study at newly created art academies, such as the Escola Nacional de Belas Artes (National School of Fine Arts), established in 1826.

Among the French Artistic Mission's most prominent members were architect Auguste Grandjean de Montigny (1776–1850) and two painters, Nicolas-Antoine Taunay (1755–1830) and Jean-Baptiste Debret (1768–1848; see sidebar this page). With anthropological vigor, Debret captured vignettes of daily street life, with a particular emphasis on human forms and expressivity. Taunay, meanwhile, was seduced by Rio's natural attributes.

**"Transportation of Coffee,"** one of 153 lithographs included in Jean-Baptiste Debret's *Voyage Pittoresque et Historique au Brésil,* **which depicts life in 19th-century Brazil**

His awe-filled yet botanically detailed renderings of its tropical landscapes were suffused with elements of the sublime. Taken together, both artists' works constitute an important iconographic legacy of Rio in the 19th century. Their romanticism infused the imaginations—and the canvases—of Carioca painters such as Pedro Américo (1843–1905), Vítor Meireles (1832–1903), and Rodolfo Amoedo (1857–1941), who depicted historic events and national heroes in a sweeping, dramatic style.

Meanwhile, Grandjean de Montigny was single-handedly responsible for introducing neoclassicism to Rio when he constructed the Casa França Brasil in 1919. He then went on to help design many of the sober, symmetrical, multicolumned neoclassical palaces that became lasting symbols of Rio's 19th-century elegance, among them the Biblioteca Nacional and the Escola Nacional de Belas Artes (later transformed into the Museu Nacional de Belas Artes), where Grandjean de Montigny was a professor in the mid-1800s. In the late 19th and early 20th centuries, neoclassicism merged with other architectural styles—among them Gothic and Italian Renaissance—to become the eccentric but popular architectural mishmash known as eclecticism, the most stunning example of which is Rio's sumptuous Theatro Municipal.

French influence continued to hold sway over Rio's early 20th-century architecture, as a brief flirtation with art nouveau in the 1920s developed into a full-blown love affair with art deco in the 1930s and '40s. The most prominent example of art deco is, of course, the statue of Cristo Redentor hovering above Corcovado (although, technically, it's a made-in-France import).

**Brazilian Modernism:** The 1920s were seminal for Brazilian art. For the first time, Brazilian artists broke away from dominant European tendencies and sought to create works that were distinctly Brazilian in terms of form, themes, and subject matter. In 1922, the intellectuals and artists who gathered in São Paulo for the Semana de Arte Moderna (Week of Modern Art) produced an artistic manifesto that proposed a concept of Brazilian art and culture. Tarsila do Amaral (1886–1973), Anita Malfatti (1889–1964), and Emiliano Di Cavalcanti (1897–1976) were among the first generation of Brazilian modernists concerned with creating a uniquely Brazilian art in the 1920s, '30s, and '40s. They were followed by a second generation that included important painters such as Alberto de Veiga Guignard (1896–1962), Cândido Portinari (1903–1962), and Flávio de Carvalho (1899–1973) and sculptors such as Bruno Giorgi (1905–1993), Alfredo Ceschiatti (1918–1989), and Maria Martins (1894–1973).

Apart from creating their own works, some of these modernists lent their talents to the decoration of a new spate of public buildings that were being built. Both Portinari and Di Cavalcanti contributed beautiful murals, to the Palácio Gustavo Capanema and the Teatro João Caetano, respectively. Then there were the modernists who actually created the buildings themselves. Two of the most legendary are Lúcio Costa (1902–1998) and Oscar Niemeyer (1907–2012). Disciples of the pioneering and purist Swiss modernist

**Oscar Niemeyer's futuristic Museu de Arte Contemporânea (MAC) overlooks Guanabara Bay.**

Le Corbusier (1887–1965), both cut their architectural teeth in their hometown—working on the Palácio Capanema (formerly the Ministry of Health and Education building) under Le Corbusier—before going on to everlasting fame as the creators of Brazil's cutting-edge capital of Brasília in the late 1950s.

While classic modernism espoused pared-down minimalism, linearity, and functionality, Niemeyer's genius was to "Brazilianify" the style's boxlike rigidity by adding soft and sensual curves inspired by Rio's undulating landscape of mountains, ocean waves, and voluptuous women. By the time Niemeyer passed away in 2012, at the age of 104, he had sealed his reputation as one of the world's most recognizable and influential architects of the 20th century. He had also left a lasting legacy of more than 600 works, many of which—including his personal residence, the Casa das Canoas, considered by some to be his masterpiece—are situated in his beloved Rio as well as neighboring Niterói, where a number of his later projects, including the UFO-like Museu de Arte Contemporânea, are located.

Another important modernist who left an indelible mark on Rio was Roberto Burle Marx (1909–1994), a prolific and multitalented artist and landscape architect. Although his most iconic work is the black-and-white "wave" mosaic sidewalk that lines Copacabana Beach, Burle Marx revolutionized parks and gardens in his hometown by doing away with imported shrubbery and anachronistic Greco-Roman statues, replacing them with unsung tropical flora rescued from all four corners of Brazil.

## Artistic Cannibalism

During the Semana de Arte de São Paulo, Oswald de Andrade (1890–1954) unleashed a guiding principle for Brazilian modern art: antropofagia—that is, cannibalism. Andrade was inspired by some Brazilian indigenous groups' ritual eating of their enemies, which wasn't about hunger appeasement, but based on a belief that doing so would allow them to ingest the best qualities of their fiercest foes. Indeed, prior to being cooked, enemies were pampered like VIPs, receiving special food and lodging and the ministrations of local maidens.

Andrade proposed that Brazilian artists take a similar cannibalistic approach, devouring elements of the European vanguard and feasting on native indigenous and Afro-Brazilian arts, all with the aim of creating a new Brazilian art.

**Beyond Modernism:** The 1950s saw the emergence of abstract and concrete art whose major Carioca proponents included Ivan Serpa (1923–1973), Franz Weissman (1911–2005), Ferreira Gullar (1930–), and Lygia Clark (1920–1988). In the 1960s, Clark and Hélio Oiticica (1937–1980) produced challenging art installations that riffed on the relationships between objects and the space surrounding them. Among the provocative Oiticica's most iconic works was a parangolé, a capelike work of "wearable art" donned by singer-composer Caetano Veloso at the height of his late '60s fame.

In recent decades, the most interesting Carioca art and architecture have attempted to adhere to the tenets of antropofagia (see sidebar this page) by creatively mixing global media, trends, and technology with local materials, contexts, and styles. Some of the best known Carioca-based contemporary artists include Adriana Varejão (1964–), Tunga (1952–), Beatriz Milhazes (1960–), Nelson Leirner (1932–), Daniel Senise (1955–), Sergio Camargo (1930–1990), and Waltercio Caldas (1946–).

## Literature

Rio's beauty, complexity, and vibrant cultural scene have always inspired writers. Over the centuries, Carioca scribes—not to mention the city itself as both backdrop and supporting or main character—have played a seminal role in the development of Brazilian literature. From the very beginning, Rio acted as a fertile muse for those who set their eyes upon its paradisiacal setting. Brazil's first colonial governor-general, Tomé de Souza (1503–1579), was the first to go on record touting Rio's bewitching natural attributes, in a letter penned to the king of Portugal in 1552. Although countless other foreigners and visitors raved about Rio in letters, journals, and chronicles, it wasn't until the Portuguese crown moved to Rio in 1808 that the city's own literary life took off, spurred on by the emergence of the city's first printed press, which enabled European literary trends to circulate widely.

**Romanticism & Realism:** The first major European trend to cross the Atlantic and take hold of Rio's writers was Romanticism. Brazil's first generation of Romantics sought to nationalize European tendencies by focusing on the specifics of its unspoiled exotic nature and short but dramatic history. The pure and primitive "noble savage" embodied by the native Tupi was an oft-used figure that appeared in such novels as *O Guarani* (1847). Set in the mountains around Rio, this influential novel was written by the father of Brazilian Romantics, José de Alencar (1829–1877). The city itself also proved custom-made for sweeping social romances such as Alencar's *Senhora* (1875) and Joaquim Manuel de Macedo's (1820–1882) *A Moreninha* (1844), both torrid love tales set amid the complex and often hypocritical mores of 19th-century bourgeois Carioca society.

> From the very beginning, Rio acted as a fertile muse for those who set their eyes upon its paradisiacal setting.

The 19th century also saw the emergence of one of the greatest Carioca literary figures: Joaquim Maria Machado de Assis (1839–1908). Born poor and mulatto in the Rio neighborhood of Saúde, Machado rose above his humble circumstances to become a literary deity in Brazil, where he became the first president of the National Academy of Letters. More recently discovered by international critics and literati, Brazil's pioneering realist is routinely championed as one of the finest writers of modern fiction. In addition to creating an album of rich, idiosyncratic characters (particularly females), Machado applied a surprisingly modernist sensibility and style, suffused with sharply honed irony, to his descriptions of the lives and times of the wealthy and corrupt in late 19th-century Rio. Among his most famous novels are *Posthumous Memoirs of Brás Cubas* (1881), *Quincas Borba* (1891), and *Dom Casmurro* (1899), but he is also known for short stories and plays.

**Modernism & More:** As realism segued into modernism, a new generation of Carioca writers came to the fore. Among the best known was Afonso Henriques de Lima Barreto (1881–1922), who, like Machado, was skilled at satirizing Rio's high society in such novels as *Triste Fim de Policarpo Quaresma* (1911). Both Machado and Lima Barreto were major influences on future generations of Carioca writers working in all media who used irony and irreverence to slyly skewer Rio's ruling elites.

# Art Deco Rio

**Although Rio is known for its baroque and modernist architectural gems, few people are aware that the city is said to possess more art deco architecture than any other city in the Southern Hemisphere. At last count, there were some 400 aerodynamic edifices ranging in appearance from pristinely preserved to completely dilapidated.**

Art deco became all the rage in Rio during the 1930s and '40s during a period marked by industrialization, rampant modernization, and the explosion of ritzy nightclubs, luxury hotels, and casinos—all of which were reflected in the style's dominant aesthetic characteristics: bold geometric forms, rich colors, and lavish ornamental details. It dovetailed perfectly with the development of Rio's newest, most modern, and glamorous neighborhood: Copacabana.

Copa possesses more deco buildings than any other *bairro* in Rio. One area in particular is especially dense with deco gems: the **Praça do Lido** neighborhood. Here, numerous sleekly stylized residential buildings line the streets, particularly Rua Ministro Viveiros de Castro, Rua Ronaldo de Carvalho, Rua Fernando Mendes, and Rua República de Peru. Copa is also home to Rio's sole surviving art deco movie theater, the **Roxy** (*Av. Nossa Senhora de Copacabana 945*). Inaugurated in 1938, this plush palace with its grand swirling staircase still screens films.

In its decorative flourishes, art deco drew upon the simple geometrical motifs of ancient and exotic civilizations such as the Egyptians and Aztec. In Rio, deco architecture embraced the indigenous influence of the sophisticated Amazonian Marajoara culture, drawing inspiration from ceramic urns and vessels painted with intricate geometric forms. Architects created what was known as Marajoara art deco. The most captivating example by far of this deco is the **Edifício Itahy** (*Av. Nossa Senhora de Copacabana 252*), whose rich, impossibly glossy, malachite green entrance is guarded by an indigenous mermaid caryatid surrounded by stylized tropical marine life.

Estação Central do Brasil, completed in 1943

After Copacabana, Flamengo—which was still very fashionable in the early 20th century—boasts a considerable number of impressive deco buildings. The most attention-grabbing is the **Edifício Biarritz** (*Praia do Flamengo 268*), with its splendid balconies tricked out in intricate wrought-iron railings and its front doors tailor-made for a giant.

Centro has also managed to preserve some striking examples of art deco. Among the most notable are Rio's main train station, the **Estação Central do Brasil** (*Praça Cristiano Otóni*) with its prominent clock tower, and the "modern" branch of the 19th-century café **Casa Cavé** (*Rua Sete de Setembro 133*).

But despite Rio's wealth of deco buildings, it's worth noting that the city's most famous deco monument is the 1931 **statue of Cristo Redentor** on Corcovado, the work of French sculptor Paul Landowski.

**Paulo Lins, acclaimed author of the semiautobiographical novel *Cidade de Deus (City of God)***

One of Brazil's most intelligent and ferociously witty 20th-century writers was Clarice Lispector (1920–1977). Of Ukrainian Jewish origin, her family moved to Recife when she was a baby, but from the age of 12 onward she lived in Rio. Lispector revolutionized Brazilian fiction by writing in a Portuguese that was dense and often fragmented, but also poignantly intimate. Although widely celebrated for her intricately crafted short stories, she also wrote novels: Her *A Hora da Estrela* (*The Hour of the Star,* 1977) is a succinct yet powerful tale of a poor, homely Northeastern migrant girl's daily struggles in Rio.

Among important contemporary Carioca writers is Rubem Fonseca (1925–), who mines the city's gritty underbelly as a backdrop for raw but gripping novels, short stories, and film screenplays in which crime, sex, and violence dominate. His most acclaimed novel, *Agosto* (1990), mixes fiction and fact in the creation of intrigue that culminates in the suicidal death of Getúlio Vargas. Indeed, in recent times, many of the city's most pressing social questions have been put under the fictional microscope, most notably in the engrossing *Cidade de Deus* (*City of God,* 1997), whose author, Paulo Lins (1958–), grew up in the eponymous favela amid the violence of gangs and drug dealers that permeate this novel (later made into Fernando Meirelles's acclaimed film of the same name).

## Music

Perhaps more than all other art forms, music is the one most synonymous with Rio, capturing the soul of the place and its people. While Rio's contributions to the world musical scene are incalculable, in the city itself music seeps into every aspect of daily life: from the singsong chants of beach vendors and the improvised sambas that adolescents beat out on the side of municipal buses to the multitude of street celebrations, both sacred and profane, whose most extravagant example is Carnaval. Music in Rio is also inseparable from dance. Regardless of the melody, it's nearly impossible for any Carioca to sit still for more than a few intro beats before he or she is moved to break into a dance.

The sheer originality and variety of Carioca music is directly linked to the miscegenation of Brazil's indigenous, African, and European populations. In early colonial times, Jesuit missionaries felt they'd have a better chance in converting the natives to Christianity if they added indigenous rhythms and Tupi lyrics to traditional Portuguese hymns. Later, African slaves crossed the Atlantic with drums, rattles, and other percussion instruments that provided musical accompaniment to secular and religious rituals. Disapproving Portuguese aristocrats tried to prohibit these rhythms, claiming they aroused libidinal behavior. Yet, ironically, it was the European masters who ended up slaves to the rhythms that contaminated plantation houses and urban mansions and began infecting 19th-century musical styles. The polka was an early victim; its contact with Afro-Brazilian *lundu* spawned the popular Rio musical style known as *maxixe*. In 1914, when the wife of President Hermes da Fonseca hosted a party at the Palácio do Catete, all anyone could talk about was a performance of "Corta-jaca," a saucy maxixe penned by Carioca composer Chiquinha Gonzaga (1847–1935), a mulatta. Although the song created an uproar, the scandal lasted only as long as it took Rio's crème de la crème to appropriate the new style—all the rage in poor black neighborhoods—as their own preferred sound track.

> **Perhaps more than all other art forms, music is the one most synonymous with Rio, capturing the soul of the place and its people.**

**Samba:** Maxixe paved the way for the birth of Rio's most indelible rhythm: samba. Samba first emerged at the turn of the 20th century, in the old port neighborhoods of Saúde and Gamboa, where freed slaves from Bahia often held impromptu communal jams set to the accompaniment of drums and guitars. It wasn't until 1917, however, that the first recorded samba—"Pelo Telefone," written by a young musician-composer who went by the name of Donga

---

## EXPERIENCE: Bring On the Funk

On any given weekend, you can dance through the night at one of the more than 100 *bailes do funk* that are held in Rio. Most bailes take place in favelas, but few carry the edgy sense of danger of yesteryear when singers performed for drug gangs. These days, most bailes are led by DJs, and among the sweat-soaked dancers are young gringos hungry for a raw slice of Carioca favela life. **Be a Local** (tel 24/9643-0366, http://bealocal.com) offers tours that include a baile. Funk has also made its way out of the favelas and pitched camp on the beaches and streets of Rio. Join in the action at the **Eu Amo Funk** bailes—popular with the Zona Sul crowd—held at venues such as Lapa's **Circo Voador** (Rua dos Arcos, tel 21/2533-0354), where formerly underground performers get a chance to go mainstream.

(1890–1974)—made its debut during Carnaval. From then on, there was no turning back. When Rio's first samba school took to the streets in 1929, it sealed forever the marriage between samba and Carnaval. Meanwhile, in the early 1930s, the dawn of Brazil's Rio-based phonographic and radio industries resulted in the most popular sambas being broadcast around the country.

Samba's golden age—the 1930s and '40s—yielded compositions by Ary Barroso (1903–1964), Noel Rosa (1910–1937), Cartola (1908–1980), Lamartine Babo (1904–1963), and Ismael Silva (1905–1978) that became hits when sung by such musical stars as Francisco Alves (1898–1952), Araci de Almeida (1914–1988), and the immensely popular Carmen Miranda (1909–1955; see sidebar p. 130) in her pre-tutti-frutti-hatted days. Known as *samba-canções,* these slow-tempo "samba-songs" were performed by interpreters accompanied by small bands. They were quite different from the more frantically paced Carnaval *sambas de enredo,* featuring one or two singers backed by an army-size samba school of percussionists and backup singers. Among the many other styles of samba is *samba pagode,* a more traditional roots-inflected form popularized in Rio's bars and dance halls during the 1990s. One of the best loved Carioca performers of pagode is Zeca Pagodinho (1959–). Other stars who have left a mark upon the samba firmament over the last few decades include Elza Soares (1937–), Clara Nunes (1943–1983), Beth Carvalho (1946–), Paulinho da Viola (1942–), and Martinho da Vila (1938–), whose daughter Mart'nália (1965–) has deftly followed in his footsteps.

## "Chega de Saudade"

**Saudade is one of Portuguese's most maddeningly untranslatable words. Although its Latin root—*solitatem*—means "solitude," *saudade* also contains elements of yearning, nostalgia, wistfulness, and missing (someone or something). English writer A. F. G. Bell made a valiant attempt in 1912 when he referred to it as "a vague and constant desire for something that does not and probably cannot exist."**

**Brazilians make liberal use of the term in day-to-day conversation, and Brazilian music is filled with references to this complex state of mind (and soul). It's fitting that the first bossa nova song ever written was "Chega de Saudade." It's also telling that the melody composed by Tom Jobim captures the word's meaning far better than the song title's English translation: "No More Blues."**

*Choro:* Hardly known outside Brazil, *choro* is a Carioca style that emerged in the 19th century. Intimate, with a tinge of wistfulness about it (*chorar* means "to cry" in Portuguese), this sophisticated instrumental style counts among its disparate influences traces of Argentine tango as well as European mazurka and waltz. Choro catapulted to popularity in the 1930s due to the prolific output of local composer Pixinguinha (1897–1973). Traditionally, choro is played in a relaxed, jazz-inspired style by a trio consisting of a flute, guitar, and *cavaquinho* (a four-string instrument resembling a ukulele), with the percussive accompaniment of a tambourine-like *pandeiro.* The early 20th-century composer Heitor Villa-Lobos (1887–1959)—who revolutionized Brazilian erudite music by infusing it with elements borrowed from popular and regional styles—wrote many choros, including some for orchestras. In recent times, choro has been revitalized in Rio and can often be heard in many of the city's bars and parks.

**Bossa Nova:** In the 1950s, it was common for Rio's artists, intellectuals, and bohemians to host all-night get-togethers in apartments and bars in the hip new beach *bairros* of Copacabana and Ipanema. Late-night musical jams were de rigueur, and from an inspired mélange of imported American jazz and local samba, a new, decidedly cool and sophisticated urban style of music was born: bossa nova.

Bossa nova's pioneering force was João Gilberto (1931–), a composer and musician from Bahia whose 1959 album *Chega de Saudade* is considered to be the first bossa nova record. The album's title was also the name of the first bossa nova song ever

Heitor Villa-Lobos seated at his piano, on which he composed many of his *choro* tunes

written (see sidebar opposite)—by a pair of Cariocas named Antônio Carlos Jobim (1927–1994) and Vinícius de Moraes (1913–1980). "Tom" Jobim was a classically trained pianist, while Moraes was a diplomat and poet, in addition to being a lyricist. Together, the two great friends, talented musicians, and legendary bon vivants created a succession of bossa nova classics, among them "A Garota de Ipanema" ("The Girl From Ipanema"), which became an international hit when sensually crooned (in English) by Astrud Gilberto (1940–), who was married to João at the time. Bossa nova's languorous vibe and syncopated rhythms favored the cool Carioca style's easy migration into jazz territory. Covered by artists ranging from Stan Getz (1927–1991) and Frank Sinatra (1915–1998) to Ella Fitzgerald (1917–1996) and Miles Davis (1926–1991), many bossa nova songs became jazz standards that catapulted Brazilian music onto the world stage for the first, but not the last, time.

(continued on p. 53)

# Carnaval

Rio may not play host to the only Carnaval (Carnival) on the planet, but it's hard to dispute that the city's eye-popping, ear-exploding, mind-blowing extravaganza is the most spectacular—and fun—of all. It's impossible for many (if indeed any) foreigners to conjure up Rio without Carnaval; the city and the four-day *festa* are joyously and inextricably linked.

## Sambódromo Action

In truth, most people associate Carnaval with the extravagant *desfiles* (parades) in which the city's top 12 *escolas de samba* (samba schools) strut their magnificent stuff down the main *avenida* of the Sambódromo. Designed by modernist Oscar Niemeyer and inaugurated in 1984, this purpose-built, giant concrete stadium now (after renovations in 2012) holds up to 78,000 people.

The desfiles take place on the Sunday and Monday nights of Carnaval. Starting at 9 p.m. and lasting until dawn, each of the 12 escolas is allotted 90 minutes to parade down the 765-yard (700 m) stretch of Rua Marquês de Sapucaí. Aside from bleachers full of shimmying spectators, there is a table of judges who award points for the strength of various performance elements, including floats, costumes, choreography, drumming, and the *samba de enredo* (theme song). Each year, fired by the dream of being crowned champion, the escolas invest vast quantities of time, talent, and hard work, not to mention money. The

## Birth of Carnaval: Subversive Fun

The origins of Rio's Carnaval stem from the Portuguese Festas de Entrudo (Shrovetide Festivals), variations of which were first celebrated in Rio in the 18th century. Subversion ruled as the poorer classes tossed flour, *limões de cheiro* (literally "scented lemons," but actually wax balls filled with perfume), and foul-smelling fluids in the streets and at the homes of the city's elites. Rio's elites were scandalized—but seemingly envious of the fun, they started throwing costume balls inspired by the masquerade balls of Venice and parading up and down the streets in allegorical carriages.

Rio's largely black masses were permitted to watch these processions, but banned from joining in. Without missing a beat, they organized their own *blocos* (groups) and *bandas* (musical bands) that were precursors of today's *escolas de samba* (samba schools). Consisting of drummers, string and woodwind musicians, and costumed dancers, these groups would parade through the streets and then dance from dusk till dawn. Over time, the conflicts between the upper and lower classes's festas dissipated amid their overlapping hedonistic frenzy. The masses adopted the lavish costumes and floats of the upper crust, while the latter surrendered to the intoxicating Afro-Brazilian rhythms of samba. The resulting celebration was an original hybrid, quintessentially Carioca in nature.

In the early 20th century, some of Rio's most talented musicians began to pen music expressly for Carnaval. Broadcast throughout the country, some became enormous hits. Samba schools began courting top composers to produce lyrics that would then inspire the choreography and allegorical themes of their processions. In 1932, the first Carnaval competition between samba schools took place, launching a tradition that lives on today.

Some samba schools may spend up to US$150,000 on a lavishly ornate *carro alégorico* (Carnaval float).

glittery, gaudy-hued fruits of their astonishing labors is spectacle on the grandest, most delirious scale imaginable.

**Tickets & More:** Most revelers purchase their desfile tickets far in advance. Indeed, many travel agents and scalpers snatch up the best seats when they first go on sale (usually in January). Two good sources are **Rio Services Carnival** *(www.rio-carnival.net),*

which sells online tickets via PayPal, and **Rio-tur** *(www.rioguiaoficial.com.br),* the city's tourist secretariat, which can snag you expensive (and comfortable) seats in private boxes. Otherwise, steel your buns for the concrete bleachers (although chances are you'll be samba-ing more than sitting). Sections 5, 7, and 9 offer the best views of the action.

The best way to get to the Sambódromo is to take a taxi or the Metrô (it operates

Banda de Ipanema, one of Rio's most traditional *blocos* (groups), takes to the streets during Carnaval.

round-the-clock during Carnaval) to Praça Onze (for even-number seating sectors) or Central (for odd-numbered sectors).

## Carnaval *da Rua*

The Sambódromo desfiles are the best known and most lavish of Rio's Carnaval events. However, for good old bacchanalian fun, many Cariocas prefer the traditional street Carnaval. In recent years, Carnaval *da rua* has enjoyed a major resurgence as *foliões* (Carnaval revelers) have flocked to the many neighborhood and resident association *blocos* (groups) and *bandas* (musical bands). Among the most traditional Carnavalesque groups are those in Centro (Bafo de Onça, Cacique de Ramos, Cordão do Bola Preta), Santa Teresa (Carmelitas de Santa Teresa), Botafogo (Barbas, Bloco de Segunda, Dois Pra Lá, Dois Pra Cá), Copacabana (Bip Bip), and Ipanema (Símpatia é Quase Amor, Banda de Ipanema, Banda Carmen Miranda). To join in, just show up at the blocos' headquarters on the days and times of their parades (Riotur has online schedules). Costumes aren't obligatory—although some are hilariously inventive, and there are a lot of men in drag—but you might want to dress in the bloco's traditional colors or purchase a T-shirt on the spot. Complementing the street celebrations are the free shows and festivities organized by the city of Rio. Among the most popular are the festas held outside the Sambódromo at the Terreirão do Samba, the Baile da Cinelândia in Centro, and the alternative Rio Folia, which unspools beneath the Arcos da Lapa.

## Glittering Balls

Meanwhile, the city's clubs and hotels host private *bailes* (balls) featuring live samba bands and guests whose extravagant costumes (usually obligatory) mask their loosened inhibitions. The most lavish, and expensive, of them all is the **Magic Ball** at the Copacabana Palace. Among the still fabulous (and more affordable) runners-up are the **Baile Vermelho e Preto,** where revelers honor the Flamengo soccer team by dressing in the team colors of crimson and black, and the gay-friendly, bacchanalian **bashes held at the Scala Club**'s Cinelândia digs.

**MPB:** *Música popular brasileira,* or MPB, is a somewhat vague but all-embracing term that covers all forms of popular urban Brazilian music. The expression emerged in the early 1960s as Brazil sought to reinvent its national identity against the increasingly censorious climate imposed by the military regime. Brazilian television, which was in its nascent stages, began to broadcast *festivais de música popular,* wildly popular live competitions in which young singers performed original songs by young composers. Victors not only landed recording contracts but often became very famous. The champion that emerged from the first of these televised festivals, held in 1965, was a diminutive 20-year-old from Rio Grande do Sul with an outsize, emotionally charged voice named Elis Regina (1945–1982), whose feisty demeanor earned her the nickname "Pimentinha" (Little Hot Pepper) from Vinícius de Moraes. After moving to Rio, Elis set the standard for MPB, covering songs by a bright new generation of composers. Among the most prolific was a famously shy Carioca named Chico Buarque (1944–), who would emerge as one of Brazil's most acclaimed and lyrical composers.

> During the late 1960s and '70s, amid great controversy, MPB went electric, and artists began integrating new influences and styles . . . into their music.

During the late 1960s and '70s, amid great controversy, MPB went electric, and artists began integrating new influences and styles—both regional and international

**Improvised samba jam on Praia do Leme**

(primarily American)—into their music. Jorge Ben (1942– ) and Tim Maia (1942–1998), both Carioca and Afro-Brazilian, were among the most original figures who innovatively fused homegrown samba with Afro-American funk and soul. In the 1980s, Rio was the base of an exploding rock scene that saw the emergence of such seminal bands as Barão Vermelho and Os Titãs, along with such composer-rockers as Cazuza (1958–1990), Lulu Santos (1953– ), Fernanda Abreu (1961– ), and Marina Lima (1955– ). While today's rock—whose main audience skews white and middle class—packs a lesser wallop, the city continues to possess a potent indie band scene.

In the 1980s, the urban favelas were the cradles of Brazilian rap and funk. Like their U.S. counterparts, Rio's young black rappers, among them MV Bill (1974– ) and Marcelo D2 (1967– ), riffed on relevant social themes such as violence and economic and racial inequality. Meanwhile, funk is a distinctly Carioca phenomenon that mingles a variety of influences including Miami bass, European techno, and traditional Afro-Brazilian beats. Hugely popular in favelas where funk *bailes* (enormous open-air street parties; see sidebar p. 47) regularly take place, funk usually ruffled a lot of feathers due to the sexual explicitness and misogynistic references included in some of the lyrics.

## Cinema

Given how much the camera loves Rio, it's not surprising that Rio has historically dominated Brazil's cinemascape. Rio was where the country's first movie theater opened in 1897, on Centro's fashionable Rua do Ouvidor, and where, in 1907, the first Brazilian film made with actors, *Os Estranguladores,* was made, bringing to celluloid life a heavily sensationalized strangling murder.

By the late 1920s, Praça Floriano was more commonly known as Cinelândia due to the quartet of glamorous art deco movie palaces that attracted Hollywood-loving hordes. Shortly after that, in the 1930s, Rio became the cradle of Brazil's own film industry with the establishment of studios such as pioneering Cinédia and Brasil Vita Filmes, whose provocative *A Favela dos Meus Amores* (1935) depicted life in a local favela. Before 20th Century Fox signed her, Carmen Miranda, then Brazil's most popular recording star, appeared in homegrown musicals produced by Sonofilmes.

**A 2009 stamp pays homage to Carmen Miranda in all her glory.**

In the 1940s and '50s, Atlantida and Vera Cruz were major studios that produced popular melodramas as well as *chanchadas,* burlesque musical comedies that often lampooned Hollywood blockbusters of the day. Hollywood's studio system also inspired Vera Cruz to construct a giant soundstage for the making of big-budget Westerns and murder mysteries.

Meanwhile, in the 1950s, a new generation of cineastes came on the scene. Repelled by the commercialization and Americanization of the Brazilian cinema industry, these

# EXPERIENCE: Carnaval out of Season

Although Carnaval in Rio is a unique and unforgettable experience, there are several downsides, such as the weather (invariably hot and humid), the crowds (enormous, loud, and invariably inebriated), and the prices (inflated airfare and accommodation costs are as ritualized as Carnaval itself). Happily, you can avoid the latter inconveniences by traveling to Rio at other times and still manage to get a small but meaningful taste of the splendid full banquet.

## Pre-Carnaval

Long before the main extravaganza erupts, the samba schools begin rehearsing. As early as September of the preceding year, they start holding weekly *ensaios* (rehearsals), many of which are open to the public at large. While you won't get to see the dazzling floats or costumes, you will be treated to a privileged behind-the-scenes look at the making of a successful *desfile* (parade), in addition to drinking a lot of beer and hearing (and dancing to) a lot of great samba. Among the most popular and easy to get to are ensaios held by Salgueiro, Mangueira, Portela, and Unidos da Tijuca.

The convenient proximity of **Salgueiro** *(Rua Silva Teles 104, Andarai, tel 21/2238-0389, www .salgueiro.com.br)* to Centro has made it a favorite with foreign visitors (which also accounts for the higher entrance fee). Rehearsals are held in a vast hall where an elevated platform ensures you can see the drummers in all their percussive glory.

Founded in 1928 on the historically significant hill of the same name, immensely popular **Mangueira** *(Rua Visconde de Niterói 1072,*

*Mangueira, tel 21/2567-4637)* has won 17 championship titles, including the first ever to be awarded in the Sambódromo, in 1984.

One of Rio's oldest and most traditional schools, **Portela** *(Rua Clara Nunes 81, Madureira, tel 21/2489-6440)* has been in existence since 1923. Although it hasn't won a championship in decades, its history has assured it a loyal following.

> In January, as the countdown to Carnaval begins in earnest, the top 12 samba schools hold free dress rehearsals ... in the Sambódromo itself.

Almost as old, in recent times **Unidos da Tijuca** *(Av. Francisco Bicalho 47, São Cristóvão, tel 21/2263-9679, http://unidosdatijuca.com.br)* has gotten a new lease on life (which resulted in championship victories in 2010 and 2012). Rio's only openly gay- and lesbian-friendly samba school, the rehearsals draw a mixed crowd who stick around for the DJ-spun

tunes after the samba winds down.

In January, as the countdown to Carnaval begins in earnest, the top 12 samba schools hold free dress rehearsals (although the sequins and feathers are kept under wraps) in the Sambódromo itself. Usually occurring on Sunday evenings, they are open to the public. January is also when many of the neighborhood groups hold rehearsals. These often take place on weekends, in and around local bars—the groups' unofficial headquarters—which ensures the presence of plenty of food and drink.

## Post-Carnaval

Another thing to consider is showing up on the weekend after Carnaval, when all the streets have been cleansed of beer and trash and the city is still calmly nursing its collective hangover. On the Saturday following the desfiles of the samba schools, the newly crowned champion and a handful of other top schools perform in the Parade of the Champions, held at the Sambódromo. In addition to getting to view a choice compilation of the main event (for a much more affordable price), you don't have to lose a night of sleep.

young lions looked to Italian neorealism as a source of inspiration for shoestring-budget, shot-on-location films that emphasized the harsh realities of Brazilian life. One of the most influential works of this Cinema Novo (New Cinema) was Nelson Pereira dos Santos's (1928– ) heat-and-concrete-saturated portrait of five favela kids, *Rio 40 Graus* (1955). Cinema Novo didn't survive the censorious dictates of Brazil's military regime. However, in 1969, the generals created Embrafilme, a state-run production and distribution company that provided capital to Brazilian filmmakers. Despite the bureaucracy and limitations placed on free expression, seminal (albeit apolitical) films of a national character were made during the 1970s and '80s by acclaimed directors such as Bruno Barreto (1955– ), Cacá Diegues (1940– ), and Hector Babenco (1946– ).

**A Cinema Renaissance:** Following the demise of both the military regime and Embrafilme, the early 1990s witnessed a slow but steady resurrection of Brazilian cinema. A film that jump-started this revival was Carioca actor-director Carla Camurati's (1960– ) 1993 *Carlota Joaquina,* an irreverent historical comedy chronicling the adventures of Portugal's royal family in early 19th-century Rio. Avid to see their lives projected on a giant screen, Brazilians flocked in record numbers to movie theaters. Filmmakers responded by ramping up the quantity—and quality—of their movies, which began to earn them international accolades. Bruno Barreto's (1955– ) 1997 *O Que É Isso, Companheiro? (Four Days in September)* and Walter Salles Jr.'s (1956– ) 1998 *Central do Brasil (Central Station)*—both of which were set in Rio—received Oscar nominations for best foreign-language film.

## Rio on Celluloid

Over the decades, the eternally photogenic *Cidade Maravilhosa* has enjoyed many onscreen moments. Not just a pretty backdrop, it has often played a key supporting role in foreign films.

*Flying Down to Rio* (1933): A genius first-time pairing between Fred Astaire and Ginger Rogers, who cut a rug together on the terrace of the just-built Copacabana Palace. The duo's dancing of "The Carioca" made it a staple of dance academies across the United States.

*Notorious* (1946): It doesn't get much better than this: Alfred Hitchcock as director, Cary Grant as a suave FBI agent, Ingrid Bergman as the daughter of a Nazi spy, and Rio in lush, expressionistic, film noir mode.

*Black Orpheus* (1959): Shot on location at Morro da Bablilônia, Marcel Camus's setting of the Orpheus myth in a Rio favela

during Carnaval is lyrical, particularly due to the bossa nova sound track by composers Tom Jobim and Luiz Bonfá.

*Moonraker* (1978): Not one of James Bond's best, but Roger Moore's breathtaking tousle with the steel-dentured villain Jaws while ascending Pão de Açúcar (Sugarloaf) in a cable car is iconic.

*Blame It on Rio* (1984): The intoxicating city and its sensual citizens get all the blame when Michael Caine loses his inhibitions on a family vacation (Caine's daughter is played by a young, hang-gliding Demi Moore).

*Rio* (2011): *Ice Age*–director (and Carioca native) Carlos Saldanha brings his hometown to vivid life in this 3-D computer-animated musical comedy featuring two adorable and endangered blue macaws trying to escape the clutches of poachers during Carnaval.

Although gripping and poignant, these films didn't shy away from Rio's glaring problems and paradoxes. Instead, they unleashed a new generation of filmmakers who have found in Rio's urban jungle an ideal backdrop for the exploration of poverty, violence, and other pressing issues. In 2002, the film *Cidade de Deus (City of God)* made a major impact, both domestically and around the world. To tell this story of survival amid the drug-fueled wars of the Cidade de Deus favela, Fernando Meirelles (1955–) hired favela

**Director José Padilha at a U.S. screening of his 2010 film** *Tropa de Elite 2 (Elite Squad: The Enemy Within)*

residents to play the protagonists and made creative use of fragmented jump cuts and breakneck editing to create a new aesthetic, echoes of which appeared in subsequent films. Among them are the controversial *Tropa de Elite* (*Elite Squad*, 2007) and *Tropa de Elite 2* (*Elite Squad: The Enemy Within*, 2010), films by José Padilha (1967–) that provided a harrowing glimpse of the armed warfare between drug lords and a special military police unit created to protect favela residents. Based on true events, the first film was so anticipated that an estimated 12 million Brazilians snatched up pirated copies in the street before it was even released, making it the most watched national film of all time until the (carefully guarded) sequel broke all box-office records. ■

Rio's historic heart, where Brazil's colonial, imperial, and republican pasts rub shoulders with the 21st century

# Centro

Rio's Theatro Municipal is one of the most prestigious theaters in South America.

# Centro

Rio's downtown is a busy and beguiling mishmash of cobblestoned alleyways and traffic-clogged avenues, where baroque churches and neoclassical palaces vie for space with 20th-century skyscrapers. A commercial and cultural nexus, Centro is Rio's historic heart, whose pulse, spurred on by new projects, is more vibrant than ever.

Centro was where Rio first began, in 1567, with the São Sebastião do Rio de Janeiro settlement atop a hilltop known as Morro do Castelo; however, aside from a handful of opulent churches, few colonial vestiges remain. During the 19th century, Rio strove to transform itself from a stagnant backwater into a cosmopolitan metropolis of tree-lined boulevards, elegant parks, and grandiose public buildings. But Centro declined in the 1960s, when the federal government moved to Brasília and São Paulo became the nation's financial center. In recent times, however, the area has been in the throes of a major revitalization. Former government palaces are now home to cutting-edge cultural centers. Historic streets shelter funky galleries and bistros as well as decades-old restaurants and bars. And as Rio prepares to host the 2014 FIFA World Cup and 2016 Olympic Games, the

## NOT TO BE MISSED:

**Years of Brazilian history at the Museu Histórico Nacional 62–63**

**Having a *cafezinho* amid the belle epoque splendor of the Confeitaria Colombo 73**

**Getting an art fix at the Centro Cultural Banco do Brasil 80**

**The gold-doused baroque interior of the hilltop Igreja e Mosteiro de São Bento 81**

**Samba-ing the night away amid the crowds at Pedra do Sal 92–93**

**Tasting the testosterone at a *futebol* game played at the famous Maracanã soccer stadium 98**

historic port area is getting a major makeover, promising to turn it into the city's next hot spot.

## Castelo & Cinelândia

In the 1920s, the Morro do Castelo was razed to make way for wide avenues and office buildings; only a few colonial landmarks—such as the Fortaleza de Santiago, part of which houses the Museu Histórico Nacional—in Castelo survived. Neighboring Cinelândia—so called because of the 1920s construction of a quartet of movie palaces around Praça Floriano—sprang to life during a similar urban transformation: when the city's first grand boulevard, Avenida Central (today Avenida Rio Branco), was becoming Centro's new nerve center. Cinelândia is home to the splendid Theatro Municipal.

## Praça XV & Praça Tiradentes

One of the city's oldest and most famous squares, Praça XV constitutes Rio's symbolic and historic epicenter. Bordered by Guanabara Bay and anchored by the Paço Imperial

(Imperial Palace), it is the gateway to the heart of colonial Rio, a maze of centuries-old dwellings and narrow streets lined with bars and cultural centers. Farther inland, Praça Tiradentes is a large square surrounded by a mess of cluttered streets and bustling avenues. By day, this area hums with commercial activity. By night, patrons flock to theaters, restaurants, and *gafieiras* (dance halls).

## Port Zone & São Cristóvão

Formerly home to Rio's largest slave market, the Port Zone's adjacent *bairros* of Saúde and Gamboa increasingly pay homage to Afro-Brazilian culture with open-air samba jams and clubs. A quick bus or Metrô ride away, the vibrant working-class bairro of São Cristóvão is home to Quinta da Boa Vista, a vast park housing the former royal palace. Nearby is Brazil's most famous soccer stadium, Maracanã. ■

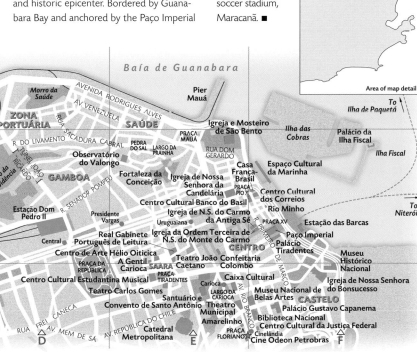

# Castelo & Cinelândia

Stretching back from the shores of Guanabara Bay, the teeming avenues and innocuous high-rises surrounding Castelo and Cinelândia are interspersed with a wealth of baroque churches, museums, and monumental edifices such as the Theatro Municipal and the Biblioteca Nacional.

A 19th-century funeral carriage on display in the Museu Histórico Nacional's Carriage Hall

**Museu Histórico Nacional**

- 🅰 61 F1
- ✉ Praça Marechal Âncora
- ☎ 21/2550-9220
- 🕐 Closed Mon.
- 💲 $
- 🚇 Metrô: Cinelândia

## Castelo

When you set foot in the area known as Castelo, it's difficult to conjure up the 16th-century settlement whose dwellings clung precariously to the hill known as Morro do Castelo. Originally surrounded by beaches and swampland, the *morro* was strategic in that it guarded the entrance to Guanabara Bay. In the 1920s, the hilltop was leveled and the earth was used to shore up the coastline of neighboring Glória. Today, the area is as flat as a pancake and bisected by major thoroughfares that run through Centro. It holds a few interesting sights.

### Museu Histórico Nacional:

A visit to the National History Museum is a fitting beginning to any tour of Centro and provides a great introduction to Brazil in all its fascinating complexity. The museum is installed in a gleaming white architectural complex that embraces a trio of historical buildings, the oldest of which, a fortress known as the Fortaleza de Santiago, dates from 1603.

Reserve a couple of hours to tour the permanent collection, which earns high marks for providing descriptions that are both compelling and flawlessly translated into English. The exhibit begins with copies of prehistoric cave paintings found in the northeastern state of Piauí, which date back more than 60,000 years. It continues chronologically through room after room stuffed with artifacts that conjure up key moments and themes in Brazilian history. Of particular interest are the displays devoted to indigenous cultures (shark-tooth arrowheads and brilliant feather headdresses, not to mention a fascinating description of cannibalism rituals), Brazil's African legacy (the iron gags used to prevent slaves from swallowing precious gold and gemstones are harrowing), and Brazilian baroque (a banquet of gold-doused cherubs and angels galore).

Among the more unusual highlights is a 19th-century homeopathic pharmacy. Rescued in its entirety from a street in Centro, its burnished walnut shelves are stacked with crystal and opaline vials filled with potions. Also fun to ogle at are the many knickknacks that once belonged to members of Brazil's imperial family; Pedro I's toy boat carved from ivory and Pedro II's dragon-topped golden throne are particularly fine objects.

**Igreja de Nossa Senhora do Bonsucesso:** Behind the museum, on Largo da Misericórdia, the Igreja de Nossa Senhora do Bonsucesso is one of Rio's oldest churches. Since 1594, the original adobe chapel has undergone numerous reforms. The simple yet elegant facade that has survived is a classic example of 18th-century Jesuit baroque architecture. Inside, the restrained white-and-gold interior is typical of churches devoted to the Virgin Mary.

**INSIDER TIP:**

**Famous for its Carnaval costumes, Centro's Casa Turuna *(Rua Senhor dos Passos 122)* also has a marvelous selection of colorful *chita* or *chitão* fabrics perfect for making anything.**

—PRISCILLA GOSLIN
*Author of* How to Be a Carioca

**Palácio Gustavo Capanema:** From Nossa Senhora do Bonsucesso, crossing Avenida Presidente Antônio Carlos and walking toward Cinelândia brings you to a more recent architectural landmark. The Palácio Gustavo Capanema was constructed between 1937 and 1943 under the supervision of Franco-Swiss architect Le Corbusier by a team that included young upstarts such as Oscar Niemeyer and Lúcio Costa, the dynamic Brazilian duo who eventually went on to design Brasília, the capital of Brazil.

**Igreja de Nossa Senhora do Bonsucesso**
- 61 F1
- Largo da Misericórdia
- 21/2220-3001
- Closed Sat.–Sun.
- Metrô: Cinelândia

**Palácio Gustavo Capanema**
- 61 F1
- Rua da Imprensa 16
- Metrô: Cinelândia

## EXPERIENCE:
## Last Cinema Standing

You can experience the grandeur that inspired Cinelândia's name at the area's sole surviving movie palace, the **Cine Odeon Petrobras** *(Praça Floriano 7, tel 21/2240-1093)*, formerly the Odeon. Inaugurated in 1932, this restored art deco theater takes the seventh art seriously. Aside from showing first-run films on its giant screen, it hosts events ranging from star-studded opening nights to the annual Rio Film Festival. It's also a hot spot for young cinephiles, who flock to regularly scheduled events such as Cineclube LGBT, in which gay- and lesbian-themed shorts segue into a DJ-led dance-a-thon. If you're a hard-core film buff, consider one of the *maratonas,* all-night movie marathons with dancing intermissions in the lobby and breakfast served at "The End."

The former Ministry of Education and Health building is considered a masterpiece of modernism and served as a model of inspiration for architects throughout Brazil and the world. Among its signature features are the slender 33-foot-high (10 m) columns that support the structure, facilitating circulation—of light, air, and foot traffic—and allowing one to admire the intricate blue-and-white mosaic panels created by renowned artist Cândido Portinari. Other modernist highlights include the curvaceous sculptures by Bruno Giorgi and the tropical gardens landscaped by Roberto Burle Marx.

### Cinelândia
Until the turn of the 20th century, the region known as Cinelândia was filled with a hodgepodge of crumbling colonial dwellings and flophouses. Everything was swept away when Centro's main boulevard, Avenida Central (today's Avenida Rio Branco), was inaugurated in 1904, part of a major effort to modernize a Centro that was insalubrious, overpopulated, and prone to outbreaks of diseases such as yellow fever.

Stretching from the (then new) port at Praça Mauá to the city's outer limits, which in those days was Glória, Avenida Central quickly became the city's new hub. Along this wide boulevard, a series of grand edifices sprung up, including the Supremo Tribunal da Justiça, the Biblioteca Nacional, and the Theatro Municipal.

In the early 1920s, a Spanish entrepreneur named Francisco Serrador proposed a new development project whose intent was to transform the area around **Praça Floriano**—a vast square named for Brazil's second president, Floriano Peixoto (1839–1895)—into a Brazilian version of Broadway, awash in theaters and nightclubs. However, it was the four swanky movie palaces—the Império, the Odeon, the Glória, and the Capitólia—that inspired the area's popular nickname and lent it glamorous associations.

Much of the glamour was gone by the 1970s, when Cinelândia was significantly transformed by the building of Rio's Metrô. By then, like much of Centro, the area had taken a turn for the seedier. However, the size and central location of Praça Floriano, not to mention the presence of Rio's

Câmara dos Vereadores (Chamber of Councilmen) on its northwestern edge, made it a focal point for political protests, particularly during the darkest days of Brazil's military dictatorship.

Today, during the week, Cinelândia is a lively place where workers habitually gather for lunch and after-hours beer at open-air bars. The most famous of them all, **Amarelinho** *(Praça Floriano 55, tel 21/2262-3311 or 21/2240-8434)* has been around since the 1920s—and it's still an agreeable place to while away an hour or two. And while much of Avenida Rio Branco has been disfigured by concrete skyscrapers, Praça Floriano remains surrounded by several magnificent early 20th-century buildings.

### Theatro Municipal: The

most immediately eye-catching of these buildings is the Theatro Municipal, a beguiling fusion of understated neoclassicism and opulent baroque that is a shining example of the eclectic style that was in vogue in Brazil at the beginning of the 20th century. Don't be surprised if, upon first glance, it looks familiar. Designed by French architects Albert Guilbert and René Barba,

**Theatro Municipal**
- 🅰 61 E1
- ✉ Praça Floriano
- ☎ 21/2332-9134
- 💲 $$ (guided tour)
- 🚇 Metrô: Cinelândia

**NOTE:** Theatro guided tours offered Tues.–Fri. (12 p.m., 2 p.m., 3 p.m., & 4 p.m.) & Sat. (12 p.m. & 1 p.m.). Purchase tickets at the box office on Av. 13 de Maio 30 minutes ahead of tour or reserve by calling 21/2332-9220.

The sumptuous interior of the Theatro Municipal seats 2,244 people.

## A Kiss Is Just a Kiss

**Brazilians are famed for their friendliness. If you're greeting a woman—regardless if she's a stranger or an old friend—it's customary in Rio to exchange two *beijos* (kisses), one on each cheek. While women also kiss men, men stick to more conventional handshakes when greeting other males. However, among friends, family members, and even work colleagues, backslapping, *abraços* (hugs), and other amicable forms of physical contact are frequent between men. When it comes time to say goodbye, the same kissing, hugging, and handshaking rituals apply. Indeed, as a result of shared intimacies (and alcohol), they are often even warmer.**

along with Francisco Oliveria Passos, son of Rio's mayor Francisco de Pereira Passos (accusations of nepotism were rife at the time), the theater was modeled after Paris's Palais Garnier. Intended to be a showpiece of Pereira's brand-new Haussmann-inspired Centro, it was strategically located so that theatergoers could catch glimpses of Guanabara Bay while ascending the grand central marble staircase with its onyx banisters (sadly, development now obscures this view).

No expense was spared. Great Brazilian artists of the day such as sculptor Henrique Bernardelli and painters Eliseu Visconti and Rodolfo Amoedo were called upon to embellish both the facade and the interior using luxurious materials, including bronze, Carrara marble, and gold. The main foyer is particularly sumptuous with its profusion of gilded

mirrors, crystal chandeliers, and German stained-glass windows whose colorful allegories represent dance, theater, and music. No less extravagant, but far more surreal, is Assírio, the basement bar. The Pompeii-inspired mosaic floors, pillars topped with bulls' heads, and wall frescoes stamped with exotic Babylonian, Egyptian, and Persian motifs give the impression of having wandered into the abandoned set of a Cecil B. DeMille film.

**INSIDER TIP:**

**When choosing a place to eat dinner in Cinelândia or elsewhere, look for small restaurants that hold considerable wine collections—a must if you want to have a great meal.**

—ARTURO SANCHEZ-
AZOFEIFA
*National Geographic grantee*

Since opening its doors in 1909, Brazil's premier theater has hosted some of the world's most renowned orchestras and theater, dance, and opera companies, as well as such icons as Isadora Duncan, Sarah Bernhardt, Vaslav Nijinsky, Igor Stravinsky, and Maria Callas. It is still home to reputable symphony and dance companies. Unless you buy tickets to a performance, the only way to inspect the interior is to take a guided tour.

**Museu Nacional de Belas Artes:** Across Avenida Rio Branco from the Theatro Municipal, the design of the more somber, neoclassical Museu Nacional de Belas Artes was inspired by the Louvre. When completed in 1908, this building housed the national school of fine arts; in 1937, it was converted into a

Pedro Américo (1843–1905) and Victor Meirelles (1832–1903), both of whom excelled at depicting seminal events in Brazilian history with dramatic flair. More interesting for foreign eyes, however, is the early 20th-century collection, in which Brazilian artists such as Cândido Portinari, Anita Malfatti, Alfredo Volpi, and

**Museu Nacional de Belas Artes**

🏛 61 F1
✉ Av. Rio Branco 199
☎ 21/2219-8474
🕐 Closed Mon.
💲 $
Ⓜ Metrô: Cinelândia

The Biblioteca Nacional sits kitty-corner to the Theatro Municipal, it too facing Praça Floriano.

fine arts museum. Although there is a sprinkling of works by European masters, the real interest here is the national collection, which offers novices a useful historical overview of Brazilian painting. The 19th century is particularly well represented, with works by key figures such as

Emiliano Di Cavalcanti—his triptych *Návio Negreiro* (1961) is a highlight of the collection—broke free from dominant European influences and began experimenting with new and distinctly Brazilian subjects and styles. In addition to the permanent collection, temporary exhibitions also occur.

**Biblioteca Nacional**

🏛 61 F1

✉ Av. Rio Branco 219

☎ 21/2220-9484

🚇 Metrô: Cinelândia

**Two More Neoclassical Gems:** Next door to the Museu Nacional de Belas Artes, the **Biblioteca Nacional** is the largest library in Latin America. A mixture of neoclassical and art nouveau elements, the building is another example of the eclectic style that reigned at the time it was built (1906). The stacks hold every book ever published in Brazil, along with such rarities as first editions of Portuguese poet Luís de Camões's classic epic *Os Lusíadas*

Crossing Rua Pedro Lessa brings you to yet another palace, in which neoclassical and art nouveau characteristics are prominent. Between its inauguration in 1909 and 1960, the building was home to the Supremo Tribunal da Justiça (Supreme Court of Justice). Today it houses a cultural center, the **Centro Cultural da Justiça Federal,** with a small theater, a café, and galleries where free temporary exhibits are held. It's worth ascending the grand marble staircase, with its twirling art nouveau wrought-iron banisters, to the sumptuous Sala das Sessões (chambers) to admire the jewel-hued stained-glass windows, inlaid floors of precious Brazilian woods, and ceiling panels by renowned artist Rodolfo Amoedo.

---

## Traffic in Paradise

As Brazil's economy has boomed, Rio's traffic has stalled. Between 2001 and 2011, car ownership shot up by 63 percent, while the number of motorcycles soared by 338 percent. The city's geography makes building new roads difficult, and the slowly expanding Metrô has barely made a dent in the traffic. *Engarrafamentos* (bottlenecks) can happen at any time, but peak hours (7–10 a.m. and 4:30–7:30 p.m.) are notoriously bad. To avoid getting stuck in traffic, organize activities around specific neighborhoods. When possible, take the Metrô. Avoid leaving town on Fridays and returning on Sundays. And always give yourself plenty of lead time to catch buses or flights.

---

**Centro Cultural da Justiça Federal**

🏛 61 F1

✉ Av. Rio Branco 241

☎ 21/3261-2550

🕐 Closed Mon.

🚇 Metrô: Cinelândia

(1572), two Gutenberg Bibles from 1462, and correspondence exchanged between members of the Brazilian imperial family (although viewing of rare tomes is usually possible only during temporary exhibits). Even if you are not a bibliophile, you might want to take the guided tour *(free, offered hourly 10 a.m.–5 p.m.)* of the ornate interior.

**Largo da Carioca:** Following Avenida Rio Branco north past the Theatro Municipal brings you to Avenida Almirante Barroso. The modern high-rise on

Altar detail, Igreja da Ordem Terceira de São Francisco da Penitência

**Caixa Cultural**
- 63 1E
- Av. Almirante Barroso 22
- 21/3980-3815
- Closed Mon.
- Metrô: Carioca

the northwest corner houses the headquarters of the Caixa Econômica Federal national bank, the first two spacious floors of which function as a top-notch cultural center, the **Caixa Cultural.** Aside from two cinemas, a theater, and a concert arena, several small galleries host free exhibitions featuring up-and-coming contemporary artists that are often worth checking out.

The building looks out onto the Largo da Carioca, a sprawling square that is usually cluttered with hurrying pedestrians weaving in and out of informal street vendors known as *ambulantes*. The *largo* was originally covered by a lagoon. Its waters were drained in the early 1600s and replaced by this square in the middle of which a fountain with 17 taps provided water from the Rio Carioca to residents who

## Santuário e Convento de Santo Antônio

🏛 61 F1
✉ Largo da Carioca
☎ 21/2262-0129
🕐 Closed Sat. p.m. & Sun.
Ⓜ Metrô: Carioca

**www.convento santoantonio.org.br**

lined up daily with jugs. The water arrived from the hilltop neighborhood of Santa Teresa via the Arcos da Lapa aqueduct. The square eventually became known as Largo da Carioca—and residents of Rio became known as Cariocas.

**Morro de Santo Antônio:**
Contrasting with the surrounding office buildings and modern hustle and bustle are the placid

On the left, the **Santuário e Convento de Santo Antônio** dates back to the early 1600s, when the church and adjoining convent were constructed by Franciscan monks. Over subsequent centuries, both buildings have undergone numerous renovations, although they still retain their modest, unadorned facades. Many original paintings and sculptures have been

Among Centro's most interesting buildings is the futuristic Catedral Metropolitana (foreground).

facades of two colonial churches perched on Morro de Santo Antônio, the hill above Largo da Carioca. Together, they comprise the oldest and most important colonial architectural ensembles in the city.

conserved along with the delicate sacristy frescoes rendered in blue-and-white azulejos (ceramic tiles), which feature scenes from the life of St. Anthony. Adjacent to the front doors, a granite niche shelters a famous statue of the saint. When the French attacked Rio in 1710, the governor prayed to St. Anthony for victory. When his wish was granted, the governor not only made the statue a captain of the infantry but also awarded it a military salary, which was paid regularly to the convent until 1911.

For a more impressive example of baroque religious architecture, head next door to the **Igreja da Ordem Terceira de São Francisco da Penitência.** Stepping inside is like walking into a resplendent jewel box. The last 30 years of the church's construction—which began in 1657 and lasted 115 years—were spent dousing the finely sculpted cedar altars and nave in 880 pounds (400 kg) of pure gold. One of the earliest examples of Brazilian baroque, the Igreja São Francisco was a prototype for many other churches across the country, although few ever matched it in terms of magnificence. Also pioneering were the ceiling frescos by 17th-century painter and gilder Caetano da Costa Coelho. Depicting the glorification of St. Francis, they represent the first examples of perspective painting in Brazil. Stare long enough and it appears as if the angels are actually descending from the heavens.

### Catedral Metropolitana:

Breaking completely with baroque is the space-age concrete cone that houses the Catedral Metropolitana. Visible from Largo da Carioca—its pinnacle reaches a height of 328 feet (100 m)—the cathedral can be reached by walking up Avenida República do Chile. Built between 1964 and 1976, it took over the role of Rio's cathedral from the 18th-century Nossa Senhora do Carmo da Antiga Sé in 1979. Devoted to the

city's patron saint, St. Sebastian, it serves as the headquarters of Rio's archdiocese. The raw concrete exterior may strike some as *Blade Runner*-esque. However, passing through the gigantic 60-foot-high (18 m) front doors and into the interior—vast enough to hold 20,000 souls—one can't help but be awed by the profusion of light and the sense of airiness. Depending on the time of day, the gemstone patches of blue, red, yellow, and green refracted through the gigantic stained-glass windows are quite sublime. In the basement, a small

## Safety Tips

**Rio feels, and is, a lot safer than it used to be—a result of the pacification of many favelas and a beefed-up police presence in tourist areas such as the Zona Sul. Nonetheless, it pays to be cautious.**

**Invest in a money belt. Dress simply and avoid flashy jewelry. Don't carry around a lot of cash, a smartphone, a laptop, and so on. If you do, tuck them away in inconspicuous bags and remove them only in secure places. Be careful where you use your big-lensed professional camera (pocket-size cameras are more discreet). Don't advertise your tourist status by opening maps and guides in the street. Never take valuables to the beach or to crowded events such as shows or Carnaval.**

**Igreja da Ordem Terceira de São Francisco da Penitência**
- 🖂 Largo da Carioca
- ☎ 21/2269-0197
- 🕒 Closed Sat.–Sun.
- 💲 $
- 🚇 Metrô: Carioca

**Catedral Metropolitana**
- 🅰 61 E1
- 🖂 Av. República do Chile
- ☎ 21/2240-2669
- 🚇 Metrô: Carioca

Confeitaria Colombo's handsome belle epoque interior

sacred art museum *(open Wed. 9 a.m.–12 p.m. & 1 p.m.–6 p.m. & Sat. 9 a m –12 p.m. or by reservation, $)* displays relics such as the baptismal fonts used to christen children of the imperial family, a throne belonging to Pedro II, and the golden roses that Princess Isabel received from Pope Leo XII after abolishing slavery.

**Rua da Carioca:** On the far side of the Largo da Carioca, Rua da Carioca is one of Rio's most traditional thoroughfares. The street concentrates several music stores, such as **Casa Oliveira** *(Rua da Carioca 70,*

*tel 21/2508-8539, closed Sun.),* which sell typical Brazilian instruments, including the ukulele-like *cavaquinho* and the drums, tambourines, rattles, and other percussion instruments that are a *sambista*'s tools of trade.

Other decades-old institutions include **Bar Luiz** *(Rua da Carioca 39, tel 21/2262-6900, closed Sun.),* a German bar first opened in 1887 (in World War II, anti-Nazi protestors caused it to undergo a name change from Bar Adolph). Aside from schnitzels, sausages, and a famed potato salad, the bar is renowned for having one of the best *chopps* (drafts) in town.

Dating to 1909, **Cine Íris** *(Rua da Carioca 49, tel 21/2262-1729)* is an art nouveau movie palace that alternates porn-film screenings and striptease shows with the occasional weekend rave.

**Confeitaria Colombo:** Running north from Rua da Carioca, narrow Rua Gonçalves Dias hides an unexpected treasure and a Carioca institution. Open since 1894, the belle epoque Confeitaria Colombo café offers a glimpse into how swank life must have been for Rio's turn-of-the-20th-century elites. The cavernous salon dazzles with its Old World mix of Portuguese tiles, Italian marble, French stained glass, and Belgian mirrors, all accentuated by homegrown jacaranda woodwork. Join workers chasing traditional *pastéis de nata* (custard tarts) with *cafezinhos* at the front bar

**INSIDER TIP:**

The Confeitaria Colombo is one of my favorite places to get a glimpse of Rio's former imperial grandeur. It's a wonderful place to have a *salgadinho* (snack) and coffee or tea.

—KELLY E. HAYES
*Scholar of Brazilian religion, Indiana University*

or gaping tourists splurging for *chá da tarde* (afternoon tea). A special treat are the *gaufrettes,* which are ideal ice cream companions. Upstairs, a somewhat overpriced restaurant serves a buffet lunch during the week and *feijoada* on Saturdays to the strains of live piano. ∎

**Confeitaria Colombo**

🅐 61 E2
✉ Rua Gonçalves Dias 32
☎ 21/2505-1500
🕐 Closed Sun.
🚇 Metrô: Carioca
www.confeitaria colombo.com.br

---

## From Cidade da Morte to Cidade Maravilhosa

In the later 19th century, Rio's notorious nickname was Cidade da Morte (City of Death). As the city expanded and its population exploded, Centro became a breeding ground for disease. If foreign sailors feared docking at Rio like the plague, it was because many actually caught the plague (along with diphtheria, measles, tuberculosis, and yellow fever—which, in 1895, killed 234 out of a crew of 340 Italians who set anchor in the "port of filth").

Then along came an engineer named Francisco Pereira Passos (1836–1913). Elected mayor in 1902, Pereira Passos made it his mission to remodel and clean up Centro. Taking his inspiration from

Baron Haussmann's modernization of Paris in the 1850s and '60s, he razed buildings (more than 600 of them) and expelled Rio's poor to the surrounding hills. He was joined in his endeavors by Oswaldo Cruz (1872–1917), a bacteriologist who, as Rio's health minister, launched a citywide vaccination campaign. These obligatory injections were met with extreme protests that boiled over into the Vaccine Revolt of 1904 and led to the suspension of the campaign. Cruz was vindicated, however, when a 1908 smallpox epidemic sent Cariocas pleading for inoculations. In the aftermath, the newly sanitized and tropically belle epoque Rio became known as the Cidade Maravilhosa—Marvelous City.

# Praça XV & Around

From Praça XV, one of Rio's most historically significant squares, cobblestoned alleys wind toward the heart of colonial Rio. Here, a labyrinth of centuries-old houses shelters lively after-hours bars, and grand palaces lodge cutting-edge cultural centers.

The Estação das Barcas ferry terminal overlooks Praça XV de Novembro.

**Praça XV de Novembro**

61 F2

Metrô: Carioca or Uruguaiana

## Praça XV de Novembro

Stretching from Rua Primeiro de Março to Avenida Alfred Agache and the waterfront, Praça XV de Novembro is flanked by some of Rio's most important landmarks, including the former royal palace, the Paço Imperial. From the edge of Guanabara Bay, ferries depart from the Estação de Barcas (formerly the main city passenger docks) to Niterói and Ilha de Paquetá. Take note of the pyramid-shaped fountain, wrought out of granite and limestone. It was created in 1789 by Mestre Valentim (1745–1813), the son of a Portuguese diamond merchant and an African slave, who is considered one of colonial Brazil's finest sculptors.

The *praça*'s name refers to November 15, 1899, the date when Brazil's first president, Manuel Deodoro da Fonseca, declared Brazil a republic.

Since then, Praça XV—as it's referred to by Cariocas—has been the scene of countless events, ranging from early Carnaval parades to rodeos and bullfights. On Saturdays, it hosts one of Rio's oldest antiques fairs.

**Paço Imperial:** Dominating Praça XV is the whitewashed colonial complex known as the Paço Imperial (Imperial Palace). Completed in 1743, it initially served as the residence for Portugal's viceroys and governors before hosting the Portuguese royal family when João VI fled Napoleon's troops in 1808. When the royal family later moved to more luxurious digs at the Palácio da Quinta da Boa Vista (see p. 95) in São Cristóvão, the Paço Imperial was used to host receptions and events, including the traditional hand-kissing ceremony, which took place in the second floor's throne room. Among the historic events that occurred here were the coronations of João VI as king and Pedro II as emperor, and the signing of the Lei Áurea, which ended slavery, by Princesa Isabel, on May 13, 1888.

Today, the Paço's cavernous rooms welcome some of the city's premier art exhibitions. Overlooking the inner courtyard, the **Bistrô do Paço** (tel 21/2262-3613) is a popular spot for a light lunch. **Arlequim** (tel 21/2524-7242) is a bookstore that also boasts an excellent and varied collection of jazz, classical, and both erudite and popular Brazilian musical CDs and DVDs. The café is a cozy place

to cool your heels. Around happy hour, there are often CD launches and live musical performances.

**Palácio Tiradentes:** Exiting from Arlequim onto Avenida Primeiro de Março brings you face-to-face with an imposing neoclassical building crowned by a great dome. Built in the 1920s on the site of the old city jail, Palácio Tiradentes is named in honor of Brazilian independence hero Tiradentes (1746–1792), who was held captive here prior to his execution (a fiercely bearded statue of him guards the entrance). The palace housed the National Assembly until the capital moved to Brasília. Since then, the building has been occupied by Rio's State Assembly. Those with a penchant for political history can

---

### Beer Etiquette

Nothing beats Rio's 104°F-plus (40°C plus) heat like a *cerveja estupidamente gelada* (stupidly cold beer). Cariocas prefer theirs in large 600-milliliter (20.3 oz.) bottles, clad in a *véu de noiva* (bridal veil), a lyrical allusion to the thin coating of frost that announces a well-chilled beer. In upscale bars, smaller 350-milliliter (11.8 oz.) versions (known as "long necks") are the norm, while on beaches and at street parties, *latões* (big cans) and *latinhas* (little cans) reign.

In traditional neighborhood *botecos* (bars), Cariocas' beer of choice is *chopp* (draft) served in three types of glasses. While slender *tulipas* (tulips) and squat *garotinhos* (little boys) are popular, mug-size *canecas* are rare due to the firmly held belief that the larger the glass, the warmer—and less drinkable—the beer.

---

**Paço Imperial**

61 F2
Praça XV de Novembro 48
21/2215-2622
Closed Mon.
Metrô: Carioca or Uruguaiana

**Palácio Tiradentes**

61 F2
Rua Primeiro do Março
21/2588-1251
Metrô: Carioca or Uruguaiana

**Igreja de Nossa Senhora do Carmo da Antiga Sé**

- 61 F2
- Rua Sete de Setembro 12
- 21/2242-7766
- Metrô: Carioca or Uruguaiana

take a free guided tour (offered in English as well as Portuguese), although the interesting collection of period photos requires no translation. During the week, from the second floor, one can observe Carioca legislators in action (or looking bored). An overhead skylight features a stained-glass reproduction of the city sky exactly as it was on November 15, 1889, at 9:15 p.m.—the precise moment at which the Brazilian republic was proclaimed.

**Twin Churches:** Back along Avenida Primeiro de Março, directly across from Praça XV, sit a pair of baroque churches. Perched on the corner of Rua Sete de Setembro, the **Igreja**

**INSIDER TIP:**

For some rare peace and quiet, take the ferry from Praça XV to the island of Paquetá, one of the few places in Brazil from which automobiles have been banned.

—SHAWN W. MILLER
*Scholar of Rio urban land use, Brigham Young University*

**de Nossa Senhora do Carmo da Antiga Sé** served as Rio's royal chapel as well as its cathedral *(antiga sé)* until 1976, when its role was taken over by the Catedral Metropolitana.

Rua do Ouvidor, near Praça XV, is one of Rio's oldest—and most animated—streets.

## A Trip to Ilha de Paquetá

A 70-minute ferry ride away from Praça XV, bucolic Ilha de Paquetá makes for a pleasant day trip if you have extra time on your hands and feel like getting away from Rio's urban fray. To preserve the small island's calm, no cars are allowed; you can explore the isle on foot, by (cheap) rental bike, or by horse-drawn carriage.

Originally inhabited by Tamoio Indians, Paquetá was home during colonial times to wealthy landowners and their slaves, who cultivated timber, fruits, and vegetables. In the 19th century, João VI was a frequent visitor. He was responsible for the construction of the São Roque Chapel, where the five-day Festival de São Roque takes place in August. Since then, the island's charming (if dilapidated) houses and pretty (if polluted) beaches have

been a favorite Carioca getaway. For this reason, avoid crowded weekends; visit during the week, when you'll have the small coves to yourself. Rumor has it, the cleanest beaches are Moreninha, Imbuca, and José Bonifácio. Although much of the original native Atlantic Forest has been decimated, lots of greenery remains, including some two dozen baobab trees. Look on Tamoios beach for the biggest and oldest baobab, known as Maria Gorda (Fat Maria); according to local legend, if you make a wish and kiss Maria's trunk, your wish will come true.

Boats to Paquetá leave at two- to three-hour intervals from the Praça XV Estação das Barcas ferry terminal (tel 0800-7211-0126, fare). The voyage across Guanabara Bay is a scenic one.

Following its completion in 1761, many of the city's most important religious commemorations were held here, including Emperor Pedro I's coronation and the baptism and marriage of Emperor Pedro II. While the facade has undergone significant modifications, the interior is a rococo banquet, featuring altars dripping in silver and gold. Vestiges of the original 16th-century chapel that preceded the church can be viewed at the small **Museu e Sítio Arqueologico** (closed Sun.). The archaeological museum is free, but there is a fee for guided tours, which need to be pre-booked (tel 21/2242-7766, $).

Next door, the **Igreja da Ordem Terceira de Nossa Senhora do Monte do Carmo** dates back to 1750. Its sober granite

facade, completely unadorned, is rare and clashes with the gold-doused rococo interior, whose six altars represent the stations of the Via Crucis (Way of the Cross). In the main altar, sits a wooden statue of Christ's seldom depicted great grandmother, St. Emerenciana, in the company of her daughter St. Anne and her granddaughter, the Virgin Mary, who is holding baby Jesus in her arms.

**Arco do Teles:** Directly across Praça XV from the Paço Imperial, an imposing stone arch beckons. Built in 1743 by the wealthy Teles de Menezes family, it originally served as a covered passageway that connected two wings of the family's posh residence. Although the house burned down in 1790, the archway, known as Arco do

### Igreja da Ordem Terceira de Nossa Senhora do Monte do Carmo

- ⓐ 61 F2
- ✉ Rua Primeiro do Março 14
- ☎ 21/2242-4828
- 🕐 Closed Sun.
- Ⓜ Metrô: Carioca or Uruguaiana

Rio de Janeiro's palatial former customhouse, built in the 1880s, engulfs tiny Ilha Fiscal.

## Espaço Cultural da Marinha

🅰 61 F2
✉ Av. Alfred Agache
☎ 21/2104-6025
🕐 Closed Mon.
🚇 Metrô: Carioca or Uruguaiana

Teles, survived. Passing beneath this gateway is like stepping back in time. Wander down the **Travessa do Comércio** (also known as Beco de Teles) and the equally narrow pedestrian streets of **Rua Visconde de Itaboraí** and **Rua do Ouvidor** to get a feel for what 18th- and 19th-century Rio was like. Originally home to wealthy merchants and subsequently to beggars and whores, today this atmospheric maze of cobblestoned streets shelters dozens of traditional bars and restaurants, where Centro's workers gather for lunch and happy hour drinks. Friday nights are particularly lively.

Open since 1884, **Rio Minho** *(Rua do Ouvidor 10, tel 21/2509-2338, closed Sat.–Sun.)* is Rio's oldest restaurant still in operation. The unassuming Portuguese tavern, specializing in seafood, is the birthplace of *sopa Leão Veloso*, a tropical version of French bouillabaisse that has become a Carioca culinary classic. Also of historical interest is **No. 13 Travessa do Comércio,** which was the childhood home of Maria do Carmo Miranda da Cunha, who would grow up to become Hollywood's "Brazilian Bombshell," Carmen Miranda (1909–1955).

### Espaço Cultural da Marinha:

Across busy Avenida Alfred Agache from Rio Minho (be careful of the buses careering by at top speed) is the Espaço Cultural da Marinha. The collection of nautical paraphernalia at this museum celebrating the imperial and Brazilian navies will interest boating and maritime history buffs. One of the main attractions is the *Dom João VI*, a splendid royal barge in which the imperial family often went boating around the bay. Kids will enjoy investigating the World War II–era torpedo destroyer and 1970s submarine, both moored outside the main building. The Espaço Cultural da Marinha is the departure point for boat trips that take you around Guanabara Bay as well as to nearby Ilha Fiscal.

## INSIDER TIP:

**Take a stroll along what was Rio's fashionable colonial street, Rua do Ouvidor. Despite its very narrow dimensions, the street was the first host of the now famous Carnaval.**

—SHAWN W. MILLER
*Scholar of Rio urban land use, Brigham Young University*

## Ilha Fiscal

Originally known as Ilha dos Ratos (Island of Rats)—the island was a refuge for rodents fleeing the hungry snakes of neighboring Ilha dos Cobras (Island of Snakes)—Ilha Fiscal (Fiscal Island) acquired its current name in the 1880s, following the construction of a customhouse. If the pistachio

green domed and turreted palace dreamed up by engineer Adolpho José del Vecchio (1848–1927) resembles a medieval fairy-tale castle more than an administrative building, it's because del Vecchio was inspired by a 14th-century castle from the French province of Auvergne. Once completed, the extravagant edifice was the talk of the town. An awestruck Pedro II referred to it as a "delicate jewel box" when he inaugurated the building in early 1889. In 1913, Ilha Fiscal was handed over to the Brazilian Navy, which administers the island to this day. Guided tours of the castle—which houses relics from the last imperial ball

### Ilha Fiscal
🅼 61 F2

**NOTE:** Boat trips (*$$*) around Guanabara Bay (1:15 p.m. & 3:15 p.m.) and to Ilha Fiscal (12:30 p.m., 2 p.m., & 3:30 p.m.) depart from the Espaço Cultural da Marinha, Thurs.–Sun. Arrive 15 min. in advance.

## The Last Imperial Ball

In 1889, Ilha Fiscal was the site of Brazil's last imperial ball. No sooner had host Pedro II sent out the invitations than Rio's aristocrats were invading tailors' shops, which sold out of imported fabrics in record time. Beauty salons were so booked up that many women had their hair done days in advance and then slept sitting up rather than risk messing up their elaborate coiffures. Finally November 9 arrived. More than 3,000 distinguished guests descended upon the island to waltz and polka the night away while indulging in fine food, spirits, and other appetite-satisfying pursuits (the subsequent discovery of intimate apparel left behind provoked much salacious commentary in the press).

The ball was the final hurrah for the emperor and his family. On November 15, Brazil was declared a republic. From the same docks that Pedro II had crossed the bay to Ilha Fiscal, he set sail to Europe, never again to return.

**Centro Cultural Banco do Brasil (CCBB)**

- 🅰 61 E2–F2
- ✉ Rua Primeiro de Março 66
- ☎ 21/3808-2020
- 🕐 Closed Mon.
- 🚇 Metrô: Uruguaiana

(see sidebar p. 79)—depart from the Espaço Cultural da Marinha.

## Cultural Centers

A highlight of the colonial center is the cluster of former administrative palaces that have been converted into some of the city's most dynamic cultural

Sunday Mass, Igreja e Mosteiro de São Bento

centers. Without a doubt, the largest and most magnificent is the **Centro Cultural Banco do Brasil (CCBB).** The former headquarters of Brazil's national bank, this eclectic-style edifice, built between 1880 and 1906, was designed by Francisco Joaquim Bethencourt da Silva (1831–1911).

A dome-shaped skylight dominates the column-studded, marble rotunda, a favorite meeting point for Cariocas, who sip *cafezinhos* in the café and browse for books and CDs in the Livraria da Travessa. Since Banco do Brasil is one of the country's major art patrons, the CCBB plays host to most of the major international and national art exhibits that pass through Rio de Janeiro. Additionally, the cultural center offers a high-quality selection of contemporary dance, theater, and music performances, along with film and video screenings, all of which are free or very affordable.

Behind the CCBB are two other important cultural centers. Completed in 1922, the **Centro Cultural dos Correios** served as the headquarters of Rio's postal service until 1980. From the lobby, a wrought-iron elevator creakily shuttles passengers between the three floors reserved for top-notch art exhibits. On the ground floor, a relaxing café spills onto the Praça dos Correios, an outdoor square where live musical performances often take place.

At the end of the same block, the **Casa França-Brasil** is Rio's earliest example of neoclassical architecture. Dating back to

## Hilltop Excess

The magnificent hilltop **Igreja e Mosteiro de São Bento** (*Rua Dom Gerardo 68, tel 21/2206-8100, Metrô: Uruguaiana*), a church and monastery that overlooks Centro, was inaugurated in 1649 by Benedictine monks, who arrived in Rio from Bahia earlier in the 17th century. In contrast to the church's austere facade is its gasp-inducing interior, featuring intricately carved columns and altars decorated with clouds of angels and cherubs, all drenched in gold. Instead of blinding, the excessive gold gives off a warm, burnished sheen, the result of the dim lighting used to

conserve precious artworks, including the 14 panels by Frei Ricardo do Pilar, a monk who was also one of Brazil's most acclaimed colonial painters.

To experience the church in all its glory, consider visiting during Sunday Mass (*10 a.m.*), when the monks chant Gregorian hymns accompanied by the church organ; arrive early to ensure yourself a seat.

English-language guided tours (*$*) of the church are available (*inquire at the bookstore*). To avoid the precipitous climb up the hill, take the elevator (*entrance at Rua Dom Gerardo 40*).

---

**INSIDER TIP:**

The Centro Cultural Banco do Brasil (CCBB) usually has interesting exhibitions and films. After taking one in, stop for snacks and a *chopp* (draft beer) or caipirinha at one of the sidewalk cafés near the CCBB.

—KELLY E. HAYES
*Scholar of Brazilian religion, Indiana University*

1820, it was designed by architect Auguste Grandjean de Montigny (1776–1850), one of many notable French artists imported to Brazil as part of an imperial plan to modernize (that is, European-ize) Rio. Featuring a prominent central cupola and trompe l'oeil Doric columns, this handsome construction served as a customs

building prior to its current incarnation as a compact cultural center emphasizing cultural ties between Brazil and France.

### Praça Pio X

Casa França-Brasil looks onto Praça Pio X, a traffic-surrounded square dominated by the **Igreja de Nossa Senhora da Candelária.** It's not surprising that this church is a coveted wedding venue for Rio's rich and famous. Awash in multicolored marble and crowned by an enormous cupola, visible for miles around, it's one of the city's largest and most ostentatious churches. Construction lasted from 1775 to 1889, which accounts for the fusion of Renaissance, baroque, and neoclassical elements. Ceiling panels depict the legend surrounding the site's original 16th-century chapel, erected by a devout sea captain whose ship was miraculously saved from a violent storm. ■

**Centro Cultural dos Correios**
- 🅰 61 F2
- ✉ Rua Visconde de Itaboraí 20
- ☎ 21/2253-1580
- 🕐 Closed Mon.
- 🚇 Metrô: Uruguaiana

**Casa França-Brasil**
- 🅰 61 F2
- ✉ Rua Visconde de Itaboraí 78
- ☎ 21/2332-5120
- 🕐 Closed Mon.
- 🚇 Metrô: Uruguaiana

**Igreja de Nossa Senhora da Candelária**
- 🅰 61 E2
- ✉ Praça Pio X
- ☎ 21/2233-2324
- 🚇 Metrô: Uruguaiana

# Walk: Following in João VI's Footsteps

On March 7, 1808, João VI arrived in Rio de Janeiro, accompanied by 15,000 royal followers. Now designated the capital of the Portuguese empire, Rio was transformed from a colonial backwater to a 19th-century world-class city. This walk cleaves a path through Centro, showcasing the most important architectural legacies of the imperial era.

The main rotunda of the Centro Cultural Banco do Brasil

Begin at Praça Floriano, also known as **Cinelândia.** In front of Cinelândia Metrô station is the **Biblioteca Nacional ❶** (see p. 68), the world's eighth largest library. The books, manuscripts, and maps that João VI carried with him from Portugal comprise the seed of the library's collection, which has expanded from 60,000 to more than 9 million volumes.

Next door, artworks from the Portuguese Royal Collection that João VI brought to Brazil form the core of the **Museu Nacional de Belas Artes' ❷** (see p. 67) European collection. Soon after arriving in Rio, João VI founded the Royal School of Sciences, Arts, and Crafts (later renamed the National School of Fine Arts). This grand building housed the school from 1908 until 1937, when it became the art museum.

**NOT TO BE MISSED:**

Paço Imperial • Centro Cultural Banco do Brasil

Continue north along Avenida Rio Branco to Rua da Assembléia and take a right. A five-minute walk will bring you to Rua Primeiro de Março. Formerly known as Rua Direita (Main Street), this wide avenue was the scene of major political and cultural happenings during Brazil's days of empire. Take a left, heading north on Rua Primeiro de Marco, and almost immediately you're at **Praça XV de Novembro.** This historic square is anchored by the

> 🅰 See also area map pp. 60–61
> ► Praça Floriano
> ↔ 1.7 miles (2.8 km)
> ⊕ 1.5 hours
> ► Espaço Cultural da Marinha

**Paço Imperial ❸** (see p. 75), where João VI lived with his family upon arriving in Brazil. This building complex was the seat of government throughout Brazil's imperial era.

## Churches & Cultural Centers

Across Rua Primeiro de Março from the Paço, the Cândido Mendes University occupies the former **Convento do Carmo ❹**, a Carmelite convent that dates back to the early 1600s. The convent was appropriated by João VI as a residence for his mentally ill mother, Queen Maria I, known as Maria a Louca (Mad Maria). A plaque on the corner notes that from this spot passersby could hear Maria's frequent screaming. Across Rua Sete de Setembro, the **Igreja de Nossa Senhora do Carmo da Antiga Sé ❺** (see pp. 76–77), which formerly belonged to the convent, functioned as the royal chapel during João VI's reign.

Continue along the right side of Rua Primeiro de Março. At No. 36 is the **Igreja de Santa Cruz de Militares,** a church whose original 17th century chapel was built by colonial soldiers as a place to bury their dead. The present incarnation dates to 1811 and was consecrated by João VI, shortly after his arrival in Brazil. Inside is a magnificent organ, frequently played for recitals. Farther along, at No. 66, lies the main entrance to the **Centro Cultural Banco do Brasil (CCBB) ❻** (see p. 80). Before becoming one of Rio's premier cultural centers, this palatial building housed the seat of the country's first national bank, created by João VI in 1808.

After roaming the CCBB, exit onto Praça Pio X and turn right to see the **Casa França-Brasil ❼** (see pp. 80–81) cultural center.

Commissioned by João VI, Rio's oldest neoclassical building was inaugurated on May 13, 1820, coinciding with his birthday. From here, follow cobblestoned Rua Visconde de Itaboraí and make a left onto Rua do Rosário, a charming old street lined with restaurants. Walk to the end and cross Avenida Alfred Agache to the **Espaço Cultural da Marinha ❽** (see pp. 78–79), where you can view João VI's namesake boat, in which the royal family cruised around Guanabara Bay. It was built in 1808, the same year the prince regent created the Royal Naval Brigade (today the Brazilian Marine Corps), whose headquarters is on adjacent Ilha das Cobras. Time your walk to end so that you, too, can get out on the bay, hopping on one of the tour boats that leave from the Espaço Cultural da Marinha.

# Praça Tiradentes & Around

Praça Tiradentes and the commercial streets around it are chaotic, lively, and noisy. Yet amid the movement and mayhem, surviving architectural, cultural, and culinary treasures allow you to get a sense of Carioca culture at its most vibrant and authentic.

The area surrounding Praça Tiradentes gained cachet among Rio's elite in the late 19th century.

**Praça Tiradentes**
 61 E1
🚇 Metrô:
Uruguaiana
or Presidente
Vargas

## Praça Tiradentes

In the 16th century, Praça Tiradentes was a marshy field on the edge of town where—much as they do today—merchants gathered to hawk their wares. For a long time, the region was known as Campo dos Ciganos ("field of the gypsies") due to the fact that, upon being banned from Portugal in the early 18th century, a community of gypsy exiles pitched their tents here. The square gained its present name in 1890, as an

homage to Joaquim José da Silva Xavier (1746–1792), a dentist who went by the nickname Tiradentes ("teeth puller").

Born in the state of Minas Gerais, Tiradentes was one of the leaders of an 18th-century independence movement that was foiled before it came to fruition. The only rebel who confessed to his involvement, Tiradentes was arrested and brought to Rio where he was executed (very close to the *praça*) by public hanging. After being drawn and quartered, his body parts were placed on display to dissuade future conspiracies against the Portuguese crown. With the declaration of the republic, Brazil resurrected the myth of Tiradentes and transformed him into a martyr of independence. Today, the anniversary of his death, April 21, is a national holiday. Meanwhile, the equestrian statue in the center of the square represents Emperor Pedro II as he declares Brazil's independence. The statue was the work of Parisian sculptor Louis Rochet (1813–1878), a professor of Auguste Rodin's whose specialty was equestrian monuments.

By the late 19th century, Praça Tiradentes had become a magnet for Rio's elite, as evidenced by the many grand (and formerly grand) neoclassical and eclectic-style buildings surrounding the square (many of which are under restoration in an attempt to revitalize the area). Two of Brazil's oldest theaters are located here. Inaugurated by João VI in 1813, the Teatro Real de São João saw such divas as Eleanora Duse and

Sarah Bernhardt walk across its stage. Following a fire in 1923, it was rebuilt—acquiring the name **Teatro João Caetano** *(tel 21/2332-9166)*—and decorated with murals by acclaimed modernist Emiliano Di Cavalcanti (1897–1976), depicting scenes from Carnaval. It remains one of Rio's premier theaters, hosting plays, shows, and musical performances, as does the smaller **Teatro Carlos Gomes** *(tel 21/2224-3602),* founded in 1888.

Just off the square, on Rua Luís de Camões, a striking building houses the **Real Gabinete Português de Leitura** (Royal Portuguese Reading Room). Dating back to 1837, the unusual facade, featuring stylized seashells, sailors' knots, and Moorish motifs, is a rare example of the Manueline style that was popular in Portugal during the reign of Manuel I

**Real Gabinete Português de Leitura**

🅰 61 E2
✉ Rua Luís de Camões 30
☎ 21/2221-3138
🕑 Closed Sat.–Sun.
🚇 Metrô: Uruguaiana or Presidente Vargas

---

## Don't Look on the Bright Side

Rio is one of the most photogenic cities on Earth, but there a few considerations to keep in mind when taking pictures. Foreigners, in particular, often fail to take into account the city's blinding light; as a result, areas of the photo may be "blown out," or lacking detail caused by overexposure. Ideally, try to photograph during the "golden hours" of early morning and late afternoon, when the light is softer (compared to high noon). Also keep in mind that even cloudy days in the tropics are luminous. Meanwhile, Brazilian filmmaker Luiz Carlos Barreto, who began his career as a photographer, advises shutterbugs to ignore the light altogether and instead focus on trying to photograph the shadows.

## EXPERIENCE: *Gafieiras* & Ballroom Dancing

If you're fond of cutting a rug—or watching others trip the light fantastic—head to Praça Tiradentes. This historic square is home to Rio's last true *gafieira*, the name given to traditional dance halls that were once magnets for Rio's dancing fools. When Gafieira Estudantina first opened in 1928, there were some 450 salons devoted to ballroom dancing in the city. Today, the **Centro Cultural Estudantina Musical** *(Praça Tiradentes 79, tel 21/2232-1149)* is considered the last one standing, a feat that earned it heritage status in 2012.

Despite some restoration, much of the original décor (including signs prohibiting "scandalous" kissing and women dancing together) remains the same. However, to keep up with changing tempos, the Estudantina—like the nearby **Elite** *(Rua Frei Caneca 4, tel 21/2232-3217)*, a 1930 gafieira that's now completely given over to alternative *festas*—features samba, hip-hop, funk, and *bailes de charme* as well as big band classics played by a live orchestra. If you're in a retro mood, Saturday nights are reserved for ballroom dancing.

### Centro de Arte Hélio Oiticica

- 🅰 61 E2
- ✉ Rua Luís de Camões 68
- ☎ 21/2242-1012
- 🕒 Closed Mon.
- 🚇 Metrô: Uruguaiana or Presidente Vargas

(1495–1521). Inside is one of the largest collections of Portuguese-language works in the world. It's worth stepping inside to gape at the jacaranda tables and delicately wrought shelves that climb 60 feet (18 m) toward the ceiling, from which a stained-glass skylight sends prisms of light spilling down in tinted hues of blue and red.

### Culture & Art

Directly across the Largo São Francisco from the Gabinete Português, a turn-of-the-20th-century, eclectic-style house shelters the **Centro Cultural Carioca** *(Rua do Teatro 37, tel 21/2252-6468)*. From the 1930s to the '60s, this cultural center went by the name Dancing Eldorado and was the most legendary of Rio's many dance halls, where gentlemen purchased dance cards and then spent the night sweeping able, if not always respectable, ladies across the parquet floors.

Today, the Centro Cultural Carioca is devoted to keeping Rio's musical traditions alive with a lively roster of musical shows, *festas,* and other events, along with performances by its own resident dance company. It also organizes percussion workshops and has its own dance school *(www.dancaccc .com.br)* where you can learn steps to everything from ballroom dancing to samba and *forró*. Stop by on a Saturday afternoon, when 82-year-old Tia Elza serves her famous *feijoada* to the strains of live samba.

Near the Largo São Francisco are two small but interesting art venues that are always worth visiting. Occupying Rio's former conservatory, the **Centro de Arte Hélio Oiticica** pays homage to one of Brazil's most revolutionary contemporary artists. A painter, sculptor, and performance artist, Hélio Oiticica (1937–1980) was born in Rio to a family of leftist intellectuals; his grandfather was an anarchist, and his father was an experimental photographer, an entomologist, and a math teacher. During his short but intense life,

Oiticica created a highly influential artistic oeuvre.

His earliest works consisted of Mondrian-like abstract compositions that explored notions of color and space. However, over time, he graduated to more transgressive "anti-art" sculptural objects and "habitable paintings." Among the most famous of these were *parangolés*. These brilliantly colored, flowing capes were intended to be worn while dancing to samba (Oiticica was famously expelled from Rio's Museum of Modern Art in 1965 when he arrived at an exhibition accompanied by parangolé-clad members of the Mangueira samba school). In addition to a small permanent collection focusing on the artist's earlier experiments, the center intermittently hosts provocative temporary exhibits.

Close by, located in the heart of the Saara district (see pp. 88–89), **A Gentil Carioca** is one of Rio's most important contemporary art galleries. Showcasing up-and-coming Brazilian artists, its provocative exhibits stress community as well as art, which results in art interventions such as painting neighborhood frescoes, creating "educational" T-shirts, and performances on the beach. ∎

### A Gentil Carioca

- 🅜 61 E2
- ✉ Rua Gonçalves Ledo 17
- ☎ 21/2222-1651
- 🕐 Closed Sun.– Mon.
- 🚇 Metrô: Uruguaiana or Presidente Vargas

**Artwork by Maria Nepomuceno adorns the side of A Gentil Carioca, one of Rio's most important contemporary art galleries.**

# Saara

"Saara" stands for Sociedade de Amigos das Adjacências da Rua da Alfândega (Society of the Friends of the Environs of Rua da Alfândega). It's also the Portuguese word for Sahara (as in the desert). The latter association is fitting given that this dense commercial district of pedestrian-only cobblestoned streets is reminiscent of a souk (a good number of businesses are in fact owned by Lebanese and Syrian immigrants, although more and more Chinese are moving in).

A bustling street in the Saara district, where wares spill out of storefronts to attract customers

Saara comprises the area bordered by Avenida Presidente Vargas, Praça da República, Rua da Constituição, and Rua dos Andradas. It dates to the 1800s, when Rua da Alfândega served as a route leading from Rio's main street of Rua Direita (now Rua Primeiro do Março) to the start of the long and treacherous road that wound through the mountains to the gold-mining state of Minas Gerais. By the end of the 19th century, this neighborhood had become an important commercial hub—and so it remains.

Saara's buzzing stalls and cramped discount shops are beloved by working-class Cariocas

seeking out all manner of bargain shoes, clothing, electronics, and falsified brand-name sporting gear, not to mention materials for the confection of Carnaval costumes. The shops lining Rua da Alfândega and Rua Senhor dos Passos, in particular, are where members of samba schools seek out the spangles, sequins, ribbons, and imported Australian ostrich feathers in which they sashay through the Sambódromo. In business since 1915, **Casa Turuna** (*Rua Senhor dos Passos 122, tel 21/2509-3908*) is one of the largest and most delirious of these shops.

Saara is also a good place to pick up cheap gifts and souvenirs, especially kitschy fridge magnets, of which there's an abundance of artisanally produced offerings made from plastic, paper, and plaster. Aside from tropicalia such as mangos, palm trees, and parrots, the miniature brand-name bottles of beer and guaraná along with Brazilian food products and laundry detergent will appeal to those with pop sensibilities. **CDLH Candelária Bazar** *(Rua Conceição 11, tel 21/2507-4294)* is one of many small stores with bins and bins of such magnets. Meanwhile, those who prefer authentic brand-name items to pirated ones can be assured that the flip-flops at the **Havaianas store** *(Rua da Alfândega 176, tel 21/2222-4634, www.havaianas.com)* are the real deal.

If you grow weary from all the commotion, duck into **Sîrio e Libanês** *(Rua Senhor dos*

Numerous vendors in Saara hawk colorful Carnaval paraphernalia.

**INSIDER TIP:**

**The narrow, pedestrianized streets of the downtown Saara District, just east of the Praça da República, offer a bustling, noisy, and colorful stroll among 19th-century shops that target locals rather than tourists.**

—SHAWN W. MILLER
*Scholar of Rio urban land use,
Brigham Young University*

*Passos 217, tel 21/2224-1629),* which has been serving Lebanese delicacies since 1965. The all-you-can-eat lunch *rodízio* is ideal if you're famished. Otherwise, munch on a crunchy *kibe* at the counter. Another classic eatery in the vicinity is the 19th-century **Casa Paladino** *(Rua Uruguaiana 226, tel 21/2263-2094),* a former emporium that houses a deli and a *botequim* drenched in belle epoque ambience. Popular with workers in search of a cheap lunch or happy hour *chopp* (draft), the *casa* is known for its omelets, made with such ingredients as shrimp, cod, and sardines.

## The "Crying" Game

A classic Brazilian bargaining technique is *chorar* (to cry). This doesn't necessarily entail bursting into sobs. Rather, it involves offering up a melodramatic tale of hardship capable of melting the hardest of hearts and persuading the seller that you truly deserve a discount (5–10 percent is standard). Don't be afraid of hamming it up. Although a command of Portuguese gives you a definite edge, you can do some effective *chorando* through a combination of facial gestures and sign language. Be prepared for the vendor to chorar as well. However, once the deal is done, both parties can bask in the cathartic satisfaction of having indulged in a good "cry."

# Port Zone

One of Rio's oldest and, until recently, most neglected areas, the Port Zone extending north from Praça Mauá embraces the overlapping neighborhoods of Saúde and Gamboa. Historically rich and increasingly cutting-edge, this area is in the throes of a major urban revolution in preparation for the 2016 Olympics.

An impromptu *roda de samba* (samba jam), Pedra do Sal

**Praça Mauá**
🗺 61 E2
🚇 Metrô:
     Uruguaiana

## The Port Zone's Past

The occupation of Saúde and Gamboa dates to colonial times. Back then, the busy Praça Mauá was known as Largo da Saúde, and Rua Sacadura Cabral, the neighborhood's main street, was called Rua da Saúde, in honor of the 17th-century chapel dedicated to Nossa Senhora da Saúde (Our Lady of Health). Instead of docks and warehouses, the waterfront

boasted picturesque beaches whose waters were dotted with fishing boats. Indeed, the area's bucolic aspect was a draw for local aristocrats and wealthy English shipping merchants, who, in the 1700s, built elegant villas on the hills overlooking the bay.

In the 1770s, the beaches disappeared to make way for the Cais de Valongo (Valongo Docks), which replaced Praça XV as the disembarkation point for African slaves. This became the port of entry for an estimated one million slaves who were brought to Rio. Those who didn't meet their demise on the miserable journey were washed, dressed, and taken to *casas de engorda* (literally "fattening houses") before being sold at the Mercado Valongo, located on what today is Rua Sacadura Cabral. For much of the 19th century, the Mercado had the dubious honor of being the world's largest slave market.

While waiting to be taken away to work in the gold mines of Minas Gerais and on the coffee plantations of Rio and São Paulo, homesick slaves gathered in the square known as Largo de São Francisco da Prainha. Sitting in circles, they sang and pounded out rhythms on improvised drums. Thus was born Carioca samba. Aside from music and dance, many elements of African culture were preserved, earning the neighborhood the nickname of "Little Africa."

## Decline & Development:

By the mid-1800s, this area began to decline as the port became increasingly industrialized. Well-to-do residents decamped to the up-and-coming neighborhoods of Catete, Glória, Flamengo, and Botafogo, while poor workers and migrants settled on the hilltops. It was on Morro do Livramento that one of Brazil's most celebrated writers of all time, Joaquim Maria Machado de Assis (see p. 44), author of such classics as *The Posthumous Memoirs of Brás Cubas* and

## The New (and Improved) Port

Rio's Porto Maravilha project promises to revolutionize the city's port. Aside from providing a modern docking space for cruise ships, it plans to bring businesses and residences to the area as well as green spaces, bike paths, and a light-rail transit system. A major focus will be on transforming the zone into a touristic and cultural attraction, both restoring historical buildings and converting warehouses into galleries and venues that house art exhibits, fashion shows, *festas*, and other events.

Great expectations also rest on two key elements of the project—a pair of brand-new, cutting-edge museums. Opened in March 2013 on the Praça Mauá, the **Museu de Arte do Rio** (whose acronym, MAR, means "sea") ingeniously fuses together an early 20th-century eclectic-style palace and a modernist former bus terminal into a museum featuring temporary exhibits devoted to Rio de Janeiro artists, past and present.

Slated to open in early 2014 is the futuristic **Museu do Amanhã** (Museum of Tomorrow). Located on the Mauá Pier, which juts out into Guanabara Bay, this space-age science museum features a design by Spanish architect Santiago Calatrava. Green solutions such as solar panels and the use of ocean water to keep the building cool highlight the museum's sustainable thrust, allowing visitors to both imagine and experience what their lives—and life on Earth—will be like in the future.

## Pedra do Sal

🅰 61 E2

✉ Rua Argemiro
  Bulcão

🚇 Metrô:
  Uruguaiana

*Quincas Borba,* was born to a mulatto housepainter and a Portuguese washerwoman. Meanwhile, in 1897, lured to Rio by land promised to them by the government (which was never delivered), freed slaves from Bahia began settling on the neighboring Morro da Providência. Today, the community known as Providência is considered Rio's very first favela.

### INSIDER TIP:

**The Port Zone has been undergoing an extensive renovation because of the 2016 Summer Olympics. It will be worth going there after the work is done!**

—LUIZ RENATO MALCHER
*Manager, Rio de Janeiro
Urban Adventures*

Despite its historical importance, until recently the Port Zone had been abandoned (and largely avoided). However, as part of a major US$33 billion city renovation project, the region is receiving a massive overhaul. Known as Porto Maravilha (a play on Rio's nickname as the Cidade Maravilhosa, or Marvelous City), this pharaonic revitalization project (see sidebar p. 91) plans to inject US$157 million into the area. Plans include upgrading existing communities and creating new ones via investment in ambitious residential, commercial, and cultural projects.

Already, land speculation is running rampant, which doesn't please the artists and other adventurous individuals who, in recent years, were moving to the cheap and spacious warehouses and run-down old houses and opening studios, galleries, and bars. Indeed, for a while now, the area—whose small but expanding number of bars and clubs have become a hot spot for those in search of authentic samba—has been dubbed the "new Lapa," a reference to Rio's former bohemian neighborhood par excellence, whose out-of-control success has blunted its once cutting edge.

### Port Zone Vibe

Due to ongoing construction, outside of visiting during a special event such as Rio Fashion Week or ArtRio, when converted warehouses are open to the public, it makes more sense to visit at night when the industrial spaces host *festas* and shows. After dusk is also when the bars and squares around Rua Sacadura Cabral throb with crowds who gather to listen to live samba—particularly those that take place at Pedra do Sal, a picturesque square surrounded by historic houses that lies at the foot of Morro da Conceição.

### Pedra do Sal & Around:

"Pedra do Sal" refers to the imposing hump of granite occupying the square, into which steps have been cut and whose name—literally, "rock of salt"—alludes to the heavy sacks of salt that slaves, who worked the docks, often carried up this steep hill.

In the 19th-century, Pedra do Sal was a gathering place for slaves and, later, immigrants from Bahia, as well as a sacred site where offerings were made to Afro-Brazilian *orixás* during festas that were both religious and profane. In the first decades of the 20th century, the earliest composers of samba—Donga (1890–1974), Pixinguinha (1897–1973), and João da Baiana (1887–1974)—gathered here along with the first of Rio's Carnaval groups (known as *ranchos carnavlescos*).

Today, the site's legacy as the cradle of samba is kept alive with free jam sessions, held on Monday and Friday nights, which draw residents and Cariocas who, fueled by the icy beer and potent caipirinhas hawked by street vendors, shake their stuff until late into the night. To get a sense of this historic neighborhood, wander up the winding Rua Jogo da Bola to the top of Morro da Conceição, which is crowned by the **Fortaleza da Conceição,** a fortress built in 1715 to protect Rio from French invaders (reservations are necessary to visit the fort).

To reach Pedra do Sal from Praça Mauá, follow Rua Sacadura Cabral for five minutes. Along the way, you'll pass **Largo da Prainha,** another traditional bohemian hangout where the neighborhood's Carnaval *blocos* (groups) hold rehearsals in the months leading up to the big

event. The square is dominated by the **Igreja São Francisco da Prainha,** a simple church dating to the mid-1700s. Shortly after the square, turn left on Rua Argemiro Bulcão, and you'll find yourself amid all the action.

It's also worth checking out the musical offerings at **Trapiche da Gamboa** (*Rua Sacadura Cabral 155, tel 21/2516-0868, closed Sun.*). Housed in an ingeniously restored 19th-century warehouse, this club is one of the city's top samba venues. Aside from the pulsing samba beat, the mixed crowd can rely on delicious appetizers and cocktails such as caipirinhas made with *cupuaçu*, an ambrosial fruit from the Amazon. ∎

**Fortaleza da Conceição**
- 61 E2
- Rua Major Daemon 81
- 21/2223-2177
- Closed Sat.–Sun.
- Metrô: Uruguaiana

**Street art in the Port Zone**

# São Cristóvão

Close to Centro, this traditional working-class Zona Norte neighborhood is not a tourist lure in itself, but its imperial past—and palace—combined with the most legendary soccer stadium on the planet justify a detour.

A statue of Pedro II stands in front of the Palácio da Boa Vista, a former imperial residence.

**São Cristóvão**
🗺 60 A2–B2

Historically and culturally, the vast poor and working-class neighborhoods that comprise the area known as the Zona Norte have some worthwhile—and refreshingly untouristy—sights to see.

Immediately to the north of Centro, São Cristóvão is one of the Zona Norte's oldest *bairros*. Its origins date back to a 16th-century chapel built by Jesuits in honor of St. Christopher. Following the Jesuits' expulsion from Brazil, their properties were sold and many were transformed into farms. One of the largest of these, Quinta da Boa Vista, came to be owned by a wealthy slave trader named

Elias Antônio Lopes, who used his considerable lucre to build a palatial estate known as the Palácio da Boa Vista. When Dom João VI and the royal family arrived from Portugal in 1808, they were less than enamored with the royal accommodations at the Paço Imperial. Officials were dispatched to seek out possible alternatives. Promising homes were branded with a large "PR" (prince regent), although Cariocas translated the initials as "*Ponha-se na rua*," an allusion to the fact that the residents of the future royal abode would inevitably find themselves "Put out into the road."

As one of the finalists, Lopes decided to be proactive and offered up his lavish palace to João VI in the hopes of gaining royal favors. João VI happily accepted his offer. Despite its relative distance from Centro, the **Palácio da Boa Vista** was one of the most sumptuous residences in Rio, with the bonus of lots of green space in which the royals could enjoy leisure activities. As the official royal, and then imperial, residence, the *palácio* spurred the development of São Cristóvão. The surrounding mosquito-filled swamps were drained and paved with streets upon which homes sprang up as aristocrats flocked in droves to live within proximity of João VI, Pedro I, and Pedro II. São Cristóvão was one of the first areas in the city to receive electricity, and Pedro II had the first telephone line in South America installed in the palace.

São Cristóvão was also the birthplace of Rio's nascent industry. New factories mushroomed, drawing immigrants, and by the early 20th century, São Cristóvão was the city's most densely populated neighborhood. It was also becoming increasingly noisy and polluted—facts which, combined with the end of the empire and the destruction of old mansions, drove wealthier Cariocas out of the area to the Zona Sul. In search of jobs, working-class Brazilians took their place, transforming many of the remaining old buildings into stores and restaurants, some of which have been around for decades.

## Quinta da Boa Vista

Now a public park, the former estate of the royal family, Quinta da Boa Vista, is one of São Cristóvão's main draws. Quiet during the week (security can be sketchy), on the weekends its sweeping lawns (more arid than verdant)

### Quinta da Boa Vista

 60 A1–A2

✉ Av. Pedro II

☎ 21/2234-5341

🚇 Metrô: São Cristóvão

---

## Pedro I's Mistress

Following Pedro I's coronation as emperor of Brazil, a woman named Domitila Castro de Canto e Melo moved into a small palace directly in front of the Palácio da Boa Vista. Domitila, aka the Marquesa dos Santos, was the emperor's lover, and he installed her in a mansion whose purposely enormous windows allowed him to literally keep an eye on her (a tunnel running between the mansion and the palace facilitated face-to-face rendezvous).

The lavishly appointed **Solar da Marquesa dos Santos** (*Av. Pedro II 293*) once housed a museum dedicated to the history of Pedro I's reign. However, renovations are under way to transform it into Rio's first Museu da Moda. Scheduled to open in 2014, this fashion museum will pay homage not only to the emperor's well-dressed lover but also to São Cristóvão as the birthplace of Brazil's textile industry.

---

are blanketed with picnicking residents of the Zona Norte, who chill out in the company of icy beers; *cachorros quentes* (hot dogs), stuffed to overflowing with matchstick potatoes; and quails' eggs. Reaching the park is easy by public transportation: Merely take any bus marked "São Cristóvão" or the Metrô to São Cristóvão station, located just across the street from the park.

## Museu Nacional da História Natural

🗺 60 A2

✉ Quinta da Boa Vista

☎ 21/2562-6901

🕓 Closed Mon.

💲 $

🚇 Metrô: São Cristóvão

## Jardim Zoológico

🗺 60 A2

✉ Quinta da Boa Vista

☎ 21/3878-4200

🕓 Closed Mon.

💲 $

🚇 Metrô: São Cristóvão

The park was created by French landscaper Auguste Glaziou, who arrived in Rio in 1858 to become parks and gardens director of the imperial house. In 1869, he designed the gardens of the Quinta da Boa Vista in English Romantic style, with rolling lawns and shady trees punctuated with lagoons, grottoes, and neoclassical marble and bronze statues. A grand alleyway lined with native *sapucaia* (monkey nut) trees leads up to the Palácio da Boa Vista, where the royal family lived from 1817 until the declaration of the republic in 1889.

### INSIDER TIP:

**Do not miss the *sapucaia* tree alley leading up to the main Museu Nacional building. The tree's purplish flowers have a hood that covers a ring of stamens, and the woody fruits the size of a child's head look like Indian pottery.**

—SCOTT A. MORI
*National Geographic grantee*

**Museu Nacional da História Natural:** Following its initial construction in 1803 by Elias Antônio Lopes, the palace underwent numerous renovations before assuming its current fin de siècle neoclassical facade. Sadly, none of the opulent furnishings remain (Pedro II took many of them with him upon his final exile to Europe). Instead, since 1892, it has housed the Museu Nacional da História Natural, which is simply referred to as the Museu Nacional. Brazil's oldest scientific museum and the largest natural history museum in Latin America, its origins stem from the collection of the Royal Museum created in 1818 by João VI.

Spread over two floors, the somewhat musty collection is nothing if not eclectic. The ethnographic section displays some compelling Brazilian indigenous objects and artifacts, while the archaeological collection dabbles in everything from Latin American prehistory (some creepy shrunken Jivaro heads) to ancient Egyptian artifacts (including some mummies that Pedro I got at auction). At the front entrance is the pièce de résistance of the mineral collection: a chunk of the Bendigo meteorite. The largest metallic mass known to have crashed through the Earth's atmosphere, it made a big impact when it landed in the state of Bahia in 1888.

**Jardim Zoológico:** A second highlight of the park is the Jardim Zoológico, also known as the RioZoo, which is home to more than 2,000 mammals, birds, and reptiles, many of them native to Brazil. Some of the most rare and distinctive beasts on display are the *tamanduá bandeira* (giant anteater), *urubu rei* (king vulture), and *mico leão dourado* (golden lion tamarin), a tiny monkey with a

The golden lion tamarin, an endangered primate species, is native to the Atlantic Forest.

surprisingly leonine face. Felines, which range from native ocelots and jaguars to imported Siberian and Himalayan tigers, number among the most popular displays. In keeping with the zoo's mission to rescue animals in danger, visitors will also find penguins, sea lions, and giant turtles, which find temporary refuge here after being washed up on Rio's coasts.

## Feira de São Cristóvão

Exiting the park onto Avenida Rotary Internacional, follow the perpendicular street, Avenida do Exército, for ten minutes until you reach the gigantic circular pavilion that houses the Feira de São Cristóvão. Also known as the Centro Luiz Gonzaga de Tradições Nordestinas, this vast open-air *feira* (market) is a gathering point for Rio's residents from the Brazilian Northeast, many of whom migrated to the city in search of work but get homesick for the food, culture, music, and sheer vibrancy of their home states.

They find it in spades at the 700 stalls hawking everything from bottles of herb-infused cachaça and bricks of *coalho* cheese to hand-woven hammocks and CDs and DVDs of typical *brega* and *forró* music. From Tuesday to Thursday, restaurants serve up typical fare for lunch, such as *bode assado* (roasted kid) and *carne de sol com aipim* (sun-dried beef with manioc). However, on weekends (the feira stays open nonstop from 10 a.m. Friday to Sunday night), the place really gets stomping. Aside from music shows on two main stages, there are smaller venues where *repentistas* (Northeastern versions of medieval troubadours) recite their improvised verses and couples waltz and dip to the strains

### Feira de São Cristóvão

- 🅜 60 B2–B3
- ✉ Campo de São Cristóvão
- ☎ 21/2580-5335
- 🕐 Closed Mon.
- 💲 Sat.–Sun. $
- 🚇 Metrô: São Cristóvão

## EXPERIENCE: The Beautiful Game

More than Brazil's national sport, soccer is a passion so fervent it borders on religion. For this reason, taking in a *jogo de futebol* can be an intensely emotional experience. When their team is losing, despairing fans rage, tear out their hair, implore saints, and hurl death threats (not to mention their drinks) at coaches and players. And yet, score a goal, and it's as if Carnaval has erupted, with fans sobbing and hugging each other for joy, as whistles blow, drums pound, and flares and fireworks in team colors light up the firmament.

*Torcedores* (supporters) of Rio-based Flamengo number more than 33 million, making the soccer team the most popular in Brazil.

Officially, Brazilians' love affair with soccer dates from 1894. That year, Charles Miller, the Brazilian-born son of a Scottish railroad employee, returned home to São Paulo from studying in England, armed with two balls, a pair of cleats, and a book of soccer rules. The next year, Miller organized Brazil's first official game, which pitted him and his colleagues from the São Paulo Railway against employees of the São Paulo Gas Company.

Rio hosted its first official game in 1901, when players from the Rio Cricket and Athletic Association played against members of Niterói's English Club. A year later, one of the cricket club's players, Oscar Cox, formed Rio's first soccer team, the Fluminense Football Club, and the game promptly took off.

### Taking in a Game

Today, **Fluminense** along with **Flamengo, Botafogo,** and **Vasco da Gama** comprise Rio's largest and most traditional teams, each boasting its own loyal band of fervent followers. Whenever any of these fab four butt heads, the games—known as *clássicos*—tend to be emotionally charged. The most hard-core rivalry is between Flamengo and Fluminense, affectionately known as "Fla–Flu."

You can usually purchase tickets to games—played year-round, several times a week—at the ticket office in front of the stadium on game day. But to be sure of getting a ticket, visit one of the official ticket outlets before game day: on Rua Xavier Curado, Laranjeiras; on Rua Haddock Lobo, Tijuca; or on General Severiano, Botafogo. If you want to experience a game in the company of some real Cariocas, **Be a Local** (http://bealocal.com) offers outings to games in the company of English-speaking Cariocas.

Seating is on a first-come first-served basis, so arrive early. Inside, vendors sell snacks and drinks (but no alcohol). The **Engenhão** (home to Botafogo) and **São Januário** (home to Vasco da Gama) stadiums, both in the Zona Norte, are best reached by taxi. **Maracanã** (home to both Flamengo and Fluminense) is more easily reached by public transit, but to steer clear of rabid fans, it's still better to take a taxi.

**INSIDER TIP:**

Take a taxi on a weekend to the Feira de São Cristóvão. Savor *muqueca de peixe* (fish stew) at any of the small restaurants before dancing the *forró* to live music.

—PRISCILLA GOSLIN
*Author of* How to Be a Carioca

of forró played by fiddlers and accordionists. Numerous buses to Centro pass by the main entrance.

## Maracanã

Taking the Metrô one stop past São Cristóvão to Maracanã brings you to the most famous soccer stadium on the planet.

Maracanã was originally built to host the 1950 World Cup, which Brazil had high hopes of winning. Instead, fans that crowded the stadium during the final game witnessed the tragic defeat to Uruguay (a loss that still weighs on the Brazilian psyche). In the hopes that history won't repeat itself, the stadium has been undergoing a massive renovation in preparation for the 2014 FIFA World Cup. It's possible to take a guided tour of the stadium, highlights of which include the panoramic view from the sixth-floor glass tower, memorabilia such as Garrincha's World Cup–winning jersey, and the Calçada da Fama, a soccer equivalent of the Hollywood Walk of Fame, in which 100 *futebol* superstars from Pelé to Ronaldo have left their footprints. ■

**Maracanã**

- 60 A1
- Rua Professor Eurico Rabelo, Portão 18
- 21/8871-3950
- $$$ (guided tour)
- Metrô: Maracanã

The Maracanã soccer stadium undergoes renovations in preparation for the 2014 FIFA World Cup, when the stadium will host seven games, including the final.

Historic neighborhoods rich in architecture and atmosphere that range from louche to lovely and mix urban grit with bucolic charm

# Lapa & Around

The neighborhood of Santa Teresa sprawls across a hilltop

# Lapa & Around

Lapa, Santa Teresa, Glória, and Catete were once posh residential neighborhoods fanning out from Centro. During the 20th century, some lost their luster, while others tumbled toward decadence. Steeped in history, they all boast a surplus of atmosphere; Lapa and Santa Teresa, in particular, have become bohemian hot spots.

**Chatting and chilling on a terrace at Santa Teresa's Parque das Ruínas**

## Lapa

Rio's bohemian *bairro* (neighborhood) par excellence, Lapa entered into the realm of Carioca myth in the early 20th century when its streets, bars, and brothels were haunted by some of the city's most illustrious samba composers and journalists, painters and poets, underworld figures and lowlifes, all seeking to live as if there were no tomorrow.

When tomorrow came—in the 1970s—the area fell into decay. It wasn't until the new millennium that the Lapa of myth was revived and dusted off, and its old houses, renovated and refurbished, were once again occupied by bars, clubs, and live musical venues showcasing some of Rio's (and Brazil's) best music, particularly samba. Originally edgy and alternative, today Lapa is safer and more democratic, but also on the cusp of being overblown. On weekends, Cariocas of all stripes, from beggars to Zona Sul beauties—along with an increasing number of tourists—flock to the streets riddled with

caipirinha stands and samba jammers and pack their way into dozens of clubs.

## Santa Teresa

Lapa's most iconic landmark is the Arcos da Lapa, a Roman-style aqueduct that stretches across the main square of Largo da Lapa on its way to the hilltop neighborhood of Santa Teresa. Easily one of the most charming neighborhoods in Rio, "Santa"—as it is fondly referred to by residents—is often compared to Paris's Montmartre due to the fact that its atmospheric old houses have long been home to artists and intellectuals.

Despite its central location, Santa Teresa's relatively difficult access has allowed the neighborhood to remain removed from the urban fray below. Strolling along its winding cobblestoned streets is akin to meandering through a bucolic village, albeit a cosmopolitan one where local artists' ateliers and funky boutiques share sidewalk space with chic but understated bars and restaurants.

### NOT TO BE MISSED:

Listening—and dancing—to live music all night long in Lapa's streets, bars, and clubs **104–109**

The exquisite art collection at the Museu da Chácara do Céu **113**

A stroll along the cobblestoned streets of Santa Teresa **114–115**

Being awestruck by the over-the-top opulence of the former presidential palace, the Palácio do Catete **118–121**

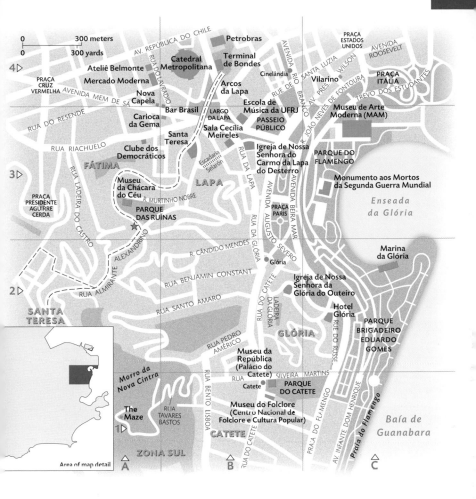

## Glória & Catete

The adjacent, compact neighborhoods of Glória and Catete extend south from Lapa along Guanabara Bay. In the 19th century, both areas were inhabited by Rio's elite, who built grand houses, and later equally grand apartment buildings, before moving to the Zona Sul in the mid-20th century. Quite a few of the buildings from these glory days remain (albeit in altered or dilapidated state), imbuing these bairros with the flavor of Rio of yesteryear. That said, traffic and commercial activity on the main drag of Rua da Glória, which segues into Rua do Catete, somewhat mar the effect.

Although Catete has some lively little bars, gastronomic and cultural offerings are scant, as are tourist-worthy attractions in these two neighborhoods—with a couple of notable exceptions. Glória's hilltop Igreja da Nossa Senhora da Glória do Outeiro—from which the bairro takes its name—is one of the earliest and most beautiful baroque churches in Rio. In Catete, don't miss the Museu da República. Housed in the Palácio do Catete, the seat of Brazil's government and official presidential residence from 1897 to 1960, the museum's substance—the history of the Brazilian republic—is trumped by style in the form of a lavishly appointed dream palace built by a 19th-century coffee baron. ■

# Lapa

Synonymous with Carioca culture and identity, not to mention nightlife, Lapa is somewhat seedy and constantly sizzling. Here legends of bohemia past and present collide in bars and clubs and on sidewalks where the musical offerings—*forró, pagode,* samba, and every other Brazilian melody ever invented—are off the charts.

Traffic motion on busy streets of famous night life area—Lapa

**Lapa**
🔼   103 B3

Lapa has lived through its share of ups and downs. In colonial times, much of the region was covered by swampland and framed by a beach known as the Areias da Espanha (Spanish Sands). The swamps were drained in the 19th century and transformed into a wealthy residential neighborhood. In the early 20th century, Lapa's well-to-do families moved south and were replaced by a colorful crew of tricksters, gangsters, prostitutes, *sambistas* (samba dancers), artists, and intellectuals, who created a vibrant and legendary underground scene. However, as the decades rolled by, the neighborhood fell on hard times. Increasingly dilapidated, it became disreputable and dangerous as crime levels escalated.

It wasn't until the late 1990s that a spontaneous and unexpected revival began to take hold of Lapa. Samba jams took place beneath the arches of the colonial aqueduct. Antiques shops opened along Rua do Lavradio. And Cariocas from all walks of life began flocking to new and decades-old restaurants and clubs to eat, drink, and dance the night away.

Today, Lapa is the undisputed nightlife hot spot of Rio de Janeiro, and nighttime is truly the right time to visit. Keep in mind, however, that Sundays and Mondays can be fairly dead. The movement really picks up from Thursday onward, but starts late (that is, after 10 p.m.) and really reaches a boil only after midnight. Despite the crowds (and police presence) on the main streets surrounding the Largo da Lapa, such as Avenida Mem de Sá and Rua Riachuelo, the dimly lit, emptier side streets can be as dangerous as they feel. Exercise caution.

By day, Lapa can be a little sketchy on the weekends, when its streets are devoid of traffic. If you're curious to explore this compact area (which can be easily combined with walks through Centro and/or Santa Teresa), it's best to do so on a busier weekday.

## Largo da Lapa

Lapa's nexus is the vast square known as Largo da Lapa. On the corner of Rua da Lapa sits the **Igreja de Nossa Senhora do Carmo da Lapa do Desterro,** whose origins date back to the 18th century and whose name—honoring Our Lady of Lapa—became that of the *bairro* (neighborhood) that grew up around it. The current church dates back to the 1820s, when João VI donated it to Carmelite friars. Inside, a statue of Our Lady of Mount Carmel sits upon a throne carved by master sculptor Mestre Valentim,

who is also responsible for the figures of the Apostles.

On the other side of Rua da Lapa, the **Sala Cecília Meireles** is a concert hall reputed to have the finest acoustics in the city. Dating to 1896, the building itself was originally the Grande Hotel da Lapa before its conversion, in 1965, into a music hall named in honor of celebrated Carioca poet (and amateur pianist) Cecília Meireles (1901–1964). To this day, some of the city's finest performances of classical music take place here.

**Largo da Lapa**
103 B3

### A Token of Love

Inaugurated in 1783, the **Passeio Público** was Rio's first public park. According to local legend, the impetus behind the park was state governor Vasconcelos e Sousa's desire to win the affections of a young woman who lived in the neighborhood. The original commission was awarded to master planner and sculptor Mestre Valentim, whose surviving works include a granite obelisk and the Chafariz dos Jacarés, a fountain adorned with bronze alligators (subsequent interventions were carried out by French landscaper Auguste Glaziou in the 1860s). Sadly, in recent times, the gardens have suffered from abandonment.

Another fine eclectic-style building, directly across from the Sala Cecília Meireles, houses the **Escola de Música da UFRJ** *(Rua do Passeio 98).* Brazil's oldest and most traditional music school, it is operated by the Federal University of Rio. The school overlooks the **Passeio Público** (see sidebar this page), a European-style
(continued on p. 108)

# Bohemians & *Malandros*

For Cariocas, and Brazilians, the mere mention of Lapa conjures up a mythical Rio populated by bohemians and *malandros* (rogues). While bohemians certainly existed in Rio prior to Lapa's 1930s heyday, the figure of the malandro was born in the narrow alleyways of early 20th-century Lapa.

Perennial Lapa hot spot Carioca da Gema is notable for the quality of its live music performances.

Quintessentially Carioca, the archetypal malandro was a charming, seductive, mildly dangerous, wily trickster (usually poor and mulatto, to boot) who lived by his wits as opposed to holding down a job. A glamorous and marginal figure whose classic accessories were a white suit, a panama hat, and a knifelike razor blade, he was usually an expert at breaking hearts as well as the law.

With its bars and brothels, ritzy dance halls and gambling casinos, Lapa was a hotbed for *malandragem* (basically, the art of the malandro) in the 1920s and '30s. Quite a few of the most colorful of these romantic antiheroes achieved lasting fame, among them Edgar, Miguelzinho Camisa Preta, and Meia Noite (Midnight).

The most notorious of all, however, was João Francisco dos Santos Sant'Anna (1903–1976). An illiterate, black, homosexual transvestite from the northeastern state of Pernambuco, Sant'Anna became known as Madame Satã after appearing in a Carnaval parade in which he dressed up as the title character from *Madame Satan*, a 1930 film directed by Cecil B. DeMille. Madame Satã was as notorious for his homosexuality and flamboyance as he was for his tough virility. As a nightclub security guard, he frequently got into brawls defending prostitutes from physical aggression and rape. A nimble practitioner of capoeira, he often tangled with the police—especially when they picked upon defenseless "marginals" such as beggars, transvestites, and blacks. As a result, he spent several periods in prison.

## A Popular Antihero

Like all Lapa habitués, malandros loved to listen and dance to samba. Indeed, many great samba composers of the day paid homage to malandros and their exploits in the lyrics they wrote. Later, the figure of the malandro also made its way into literature, film, popular song, and theater. One of the most famous examples, *Opéra do Malandro* (1985), was a Carioca reworking of *The Threepenny Opera* by Bertolt Brecht (1898–1956) and Kurt Weill (1900–1950). Set in 1940s Lapa, it featured music and lyrics by renowned Brazilian composer Chico Buarque (see p. 53).

Acclaimed singer-composer Chico Buarque, known for writing songs that offer social commentary, especially on Rio's culture

The malandro has also been tattooed onto the popular imagination of Brazil. Today Cariocas are often viewed by other Brazilians (with a mix of both admiration and disapproval) as being genetically prone to malandragem. Cariocas, however, largely view this mythical figure—savvy, quick-witted, romantic, and nobody's fool—as a positive archetype, which they embrace with a certain measure of pride.

## EXPERIENCE: Samba-ing the Night Away

While Lapa's famed brothels and gambling palaces are long gone, the neighborhood has kept alive its reputation as a hotbed of samba. Located in historic old houses, most of them on Avenida Mem de Sá and Rua do Lavradio, the following are some of the best places where you can hear and dance to samba. Be aware that Fridays and Saturdays can get very busy; it's recommended you show up early or make reservations.

**Carioca da Gema** (*Av. Mem de Sá 79, tel 21/2221-0043, www.barcariocadagema .com.br*) is one of the pioneers of Lapa's revival movement and offers high-caliber samba and *choro* performances. To avoid crowds, come early in the week. Delicious pizza is served upstairs.

**Clube dos Democráticos** (*Rua do Riachuelo 91, tel 21/2252-4611, closed Sun.– Tues.*) originally opened in 1867 as a social club for the abolitionists and republicans who were members of the Democráticos Carnaval society. Rescued from oblivion in 2004, its humongous ballroom lures Carioca dancers of all stripes.

**Rio Scenarium** (*Rua do Lavradio 20, tel 21/3147-9000, closed Sun.–Mon.*) is one of Rio's most stunningly beautiful venues; its three floors cluttered with antiques ensure the place is packed (with lots of gringos as well as locals).

**Arcos da Lapa**
🅼 103 B3–B4

**Escadaria
Selarón**
🅼 103 B3

garden that, with some imagination, conjures up what 19th-century Lapa must have been like when its fashionably upscale residents promenaded beneath its leafy trees.

## Arcos da Lapa

Lapa's most iconic landmark is the Arcos da Lapa, a two-tiered, 42-arch aqueduct that stretches across Largo da Lapa. Built during the first decades of the 18th century with the aim of supplying water to Rio's residents, the 885-foot-long (270 m) Aqueduto da Carioca (its original name) carried fresh water from the source of the Rio Carioca, in Santa Teresa, to a fountain located in Centro's Largo da Carioca. In 1896, its original services no longer required, the aqueduct was transformed into a viaduct upon which *bondes* (trams; see sidebar p. 111) transported

passengers from Centro to Santa Teresa. Come dusk, on weekends, throngs gather beneath the ghostly white arches to listen and dance to improvised samba jams.

## Escadaria Selarón

Behind the Sala Cecília Meireles, follow Rua Teotônio Regadas to the corner of Rua Joaquim da Silva, where a steep staircase ascends to Santa Teresa. What makes the 215 rising steps so eye-catching is that they're paved in a multihued mosaic of ceramic tiles. Baptized the Escadaria Selarón, this glittering Gaudí-esque piece of street art is the work of Chilean artist Jorge Selarón, who began this obsessive undertaking in 1994 as a gift to his adopted city.

Whenever the work approached completion, Selarón would break off old tiles and add new fragments from dishes

Bronze alligators embellish the Chafariz dos Jacarés fountain in Lapa's Passeio Público.

and ceramics sent to him by eager collaborators from all four corners of the planet. The artist vowed that his constantly evolving oeuvre would only truly be finished on the day of his death—which occurred in January 2013, when his lifeless body was discovered lying on the steps of his masterpiece.

Aside from a passageway to and from Santa Teresa, the stairway is a popular hangout for young people, who gather at night to sip beer and listen to music spilling out of adjacent bars.

## Rua do Lavradio

One of Lapa's most atmospheric old streets, Rua do Lavradio's secular houses shelter a number of antiques and furniture stores. Particularly worth checking out are **Ateliê Belmonte** (Rua do Lavradio 34, tel 21/2507-0934, closed Sun.), a combination atelier/boutique that sells exclusive restored Brazilian furniture and accessories, and **Mercado Moderno** (Rua do Lavradio 130, tel 21/2508-6083, closed Sun.), which specializes in mid-20th-century furnishings and decorative objects by local designers such as Joaquim Tenreiro, Sérgio Rodrigues, and Zanine.

If you happen to be around on the first Saturday of the month, don't miss the **Feira do Rio Antigo,** an outdoor fair where Rua do Lavradio's dealers set up shop in the street alongside independent exhibitors. Apart from eyeing all the intriguing wares on display, it's pleasant to wander amid the colorful crowd and take in the free music performances, fortified by icy beer and freshly grilled skewers of barbecued meat.

Near the intersection of Rua do Lavradio and Avenida Mem de Sá are two of Lapa's—and Rio's—oldest and most traditional *botequins*. Open since 1907, **Bar Brasil** (Av. Mem de Sá 90, tel 21/2509-5943, closed

## INSIDER TIP:

**There is no better place than Rio's samba clubs to experience the thrill of the dance. Most of Rio's samba dance clubs are congregated in the bohemian district known as Lapa.**

—SCOTT A. MORI
*National Geographic grantee*

Sun.) is renowned for its German specialties, such as *eisbein* (pigs' cheeks) and sauerkraut as well as tap beer that is reputed to be the best in the city. The art covering the walls is by Selarón, creator of Lapa's famous mosaic staircase. Farther along, **Nova Capela** (Av. Mem de Sá 96, tel 21/2252-6228) dates back to 1903. Open until dawn, it's a classic after-hours stop for those seeking sustenance after a night of drinking and/or samba-ing. The house specialty is the *cabrito com arroz-de-brocolis* (roasted kid goat with broccoli rice). ∎

**Rua do Lavradio**

🅰 103 A4–B4

# Santa Teresa

Picturesque hilltop Santa Teresa has always served as a lofty refuge from the city at its feet. In earliest colonial times, it functioned as an escape route and temporary shelter for Tamoio Indians and runaway slaves.

The Arcos da Lapa, one of Rio's few extant colonial landmarks, once carried water to Santa Teresa.

**Santa Teresa**
103 A2

Later, as Rio grew and became increasingly crowded and polluted, plagued by diseases and the stench of mosquito-infested swamps, the slopes of Santa Teresa, bathed by fresh, cooling breezes, beckoned. Despite the difficulty of navigating its steep hills, many began to move to the bucolic *bairro* named for the 18th-century Carmelite convent devoted to Saint Teresa. Then as now, a good number of these migrants were foreign expats.

Seduced by the magnificent views, they built rural estates, a few of which survive.

The catalyst for the urbanization of Santa Teresa was the arrival of the electrical tram *(bonde)* in 1896, which facilitated access and led to the arrival of a wealthy, cultivated class of Cariocas who set to work constructing mansions and miniature palaces. Throughout the late 19th and early 20th centuries, an illustrious group of poets, politicians, artists, and intellectuals flocked to the neighborhood, infusing it with a spirit of creativity and bohemianism that has held sway ever since.

While Rio's moneyed class abandoned Santa Teresa in the mid-20th century, its artistic class never deserted their beloved bairro. In the 1960s and '70s, a new generation of *alternativos* arrived, snatching up crumbling villas for a song and converting them into ateliers. In the past few years, a second wave of revitalization has taken hold, led by foreigners who have been busy transforming the historic houses into intimate boutique hotels, guesthouses, and charming bistros. At the same time, security has improved (surrounded by favelas, Santa Teresa used to have a sketchy reputation)—but visitors should still take precautions to prevent thefts.

Despite the transformations taking place, Santa—which possesses an active residents association—remains an idyllic and charming haven that seems worlds away from the city beneath it. While it has few specific attractions, the bairro itself, with its twisting streets, handsome old houses, and languorous rhythms, is an enticing place to while away at least part of a day.

## Getting to Santa Teresa

There are several ways to access Santa Teresa. One is to take a minibus that departs from Largo da Carioca (next to the Carioca Metrô station) in Centro. Another is take a taxi (recommended at night), although be

### The *Bonde*

For more than a century, and until quite recently, the favored—not to mention most picturesque—means of getting to and from Santa Teresa was via the cheery yellow, open-air *bondes*, which have become a neighborhood symbol. Regularly, the bonde departed from Centro and clattered over the top of the Arcos da Lapa before winding its way through the neighborhood. However, in 2011, a tragic accident occurred in which 6 people died and 57 were injured. As a result, service has been discontinued until further notice (despite pressure from residents who demand the return of their beloved bonde). The hope is that the bonde will be up and running sometime in 2014.

forewarned that many cabs will balk at having to climb the steep streets (without the certainty of a return fare). A third means is to walk, although the climb, full of switchbacks, can prove scalding under the sun and dangerous after dark. By foot, the easiest routes are via the Escadaria Selarón in Lapa and via Rua Cândido Mendes, which leads from Largo do Curvelo down to Glória Metrô station. One other option, the bonde, is, alas, not available right now (see sidebar this page).

## Parque das Ruínas

One of the high points of Santa Teresa—quite literally—is the lofty Parque das Ruínas. From its multiple terraces, one is treated to fantastic views of the city. At the height of Santa Teresa's early 20th-century heyday, two influential women reigned supreme over

### Terminal de Bondes (Bonde Station)

- 103 B4
- Rua Professor Lélio Gama (behind the Petrobras building on Av. República do Chile)
- 21/2215-0621
- Metrô: Carioca

### Parque das Ruínas

- 103 A3
- Rua Murtinho Nobre 169
- 21/2215-0621
- Closed Mon.
- Bus: 006, 007, 014 to Largo do Curvelo

**The renovated ruins of Laurinda Santos Lobo's house form the centerpiece of Parque das Ruínas.**

the bairro's artistic and social scene. Júlia Lopes de Almeida (1862–1935) was a pioneering Brazilian feminist and the first woman to make a living as a professional writer in Brazil. Her most acclaimed novel, *A Viúva Simões (The Widow Simões)*, was one of many set in Santa Teresa. She was equally famed for her literary salons frequented by intellectual luminaries.

A more flamboyant presence was Laurinda Santos Lobo (1878–1946), a patroness of the arts whose parties—packed with presidents and protégés—were as legendary as Santos Lobo herself. Known as "the princess of 1,000 skirts," Santos Lobo's hostess outfits were imported from Paris and considered (by disapproving aristocratic matrons) as more suitable for the stage (in other words, vulgar) than for cruising around the neighborhood in one of three imported Chryslers (although Santos Lobo wasn't above traveling by bonde, either). She was known for her generosity and extravagance; her birthdays were celebrated by the entire bairro. Following Santos Lobo's death, her mansion was abandoned for years and stripped of its contents by looters. In the 1970s and '80s, the crumbling structure was home to squatters and drug traffickers before finally being transformed into a municipal park.

Santa Teresa's Parque das Ruínas offers one of the best views of the central city—a 360-degree panorama of bay and mountains, skyscrapers and favelas.

—SHAWN W. MILLER
*Scholar of Rio urban land use,*
*Brigham Young University*

Indeed, the highlight of the Parque das Ruínas are the ruins of Santos Lobo's house, whose exposed red brick and stone contrasts with the glass-and-metal structure added in 1996. In keeping with its original role, the *casa* functions as a cultural center, playing host to local exhibits and performances.

## Museu da Chácara do Céu

Next door to the Parque das Ruínas lies another splendid house—and this one is intact. Built in 1954 by modernist architect Wladimir Alves de Sousa (1908–1994), the Chácara do Céu is the former home of wealthy industrialist Raymundo Castro Maya (1894–1968). Now a private museum, the streamlined elegance of its modernist lines provide an ideal backdrop for contemplation of Castro Maya's impressive art collection, which refreshingly mingles individual paintings, drawing, and engravings by European masters such as Seurat, Degas, and Miró with Brazilian modernists such as

Alberto Guignard, Di Cavalcanti, and Portinari.

Of particular interest is Castro Maya's collection of Brasiliana: precious images of Brazil dating back to its days of "discovery." Alongside rare 17th- and 18th-century maps are 19th-century drawings and paintings carried out by awestruck foreign artists such as German Johann Moritz Rugendas, Englishman Henry Chamberlain, and Frenchman Félix Émile Taunay. Of particular value are the anthropologically detailed engravings by Jean-Baptiste Debret, which document the lives of 19th-century Cariocas from all walks of life.

As enticing as the art is Castro Maya's home—furnished with an exquisite selection of antiques and furnishings from Brazil and around the world—along with the beautifully landscaped gardens. ∎

**Museu da Chácara do Céu**

- 103 A3
- Rua Murtinho Nobre 93
- 21/3970-1126
- Closed Tues.
- $. Free Wed.
- Bus: 006, 007, 014 to Largo do Curvelo

## EXPERIENCE:
## Carioca Living

If you're hankering for a taste of Carioca home life, check out **Came e Café** *(tel 21/2225-4366, www.camaecafe.com.br),* a bed-and-breakfast network that allows you to temporarily move in with locals, many of whom are artists and liberal professionals with some command of English and lots of knowledge of their hometown. The service is the brainchild of three Brazilian friends in Santa Teresa who felt there was a dearth of accommodation options for foreign visitors who came to Rio seeking a more intimate experience with the city and its inhabitants. Although most homestays you can choose from are in Santa Teresa, other locations are available. Prices range from R$150 to R$300 a night, but cheaper packages exist for long-term stays.

# Walk: Following the Tram Tracks

Even though Lapa's iconic yellow *bonde* (tram) is temporarily out of commission (see sidebar p. 111), it's possible to follow its scenic route through Santa Teresa's sinuous streets on foot. Consider doing this walk in the mid- to late afternoon in order to beat the heat and take advantage of the twin allures of twilight and happy hour at the end of the journey.

Chácara do Céu, a house turned art museum

This walk begins at the **Largo do Curvelo** ❶. Coming from Centro, by bus or by bonde (if it's working), get off at the Largo do Curvelo stop, located in front of a striking, saffron-colored villa crowned by an onion dome. Built in 1938, the neighborhood's first "modern" house is known as the Casa Návio due to its design being inspired by the shape of a ship *(návio)*.

A charming square with multiple panoramic lookouts, the *largo* is a magnet for residents, who congregate in late afternoons to gossip, quaff beer, and play chess. From here, take a left on Rua Dias de Barros and then another left up the steep and curving Rua Murtinho Nobre to the entrance of the **Parque das Ruínas** ❷ (see pp. 111–113). The glassed-in top terrace of this cultural center offers fantastic 360-degree views of the city. Next door, the **Museu da Chácara do Céu** ❸ (see p. 113) is definitely worth a visit for its artworks; if you don't have an hour to spare now, come back another time.

Return to Largo do Curvelo, and this time follow the bonde tracks as they weave along

## NOT TO BE MISSED:

Parque das Ruínas • Museu da Chácara do Céu • Largo dos Guimarães

Rua Almirante Alexandrino. At No. 54B, the **Ateliê Pedro Grapiuna** ❹ *(tel 21/9276-7097, closed Sun., irregular hours, so call ahead)* can initially be mistaken for a carefully curated scrap heap. However, the mess of hinges, car and bike parts, and other metallic flotsam are all recycled into art by Pedro Grapiuna, a native of the Bahian interior who draws on images and memories of his childhood to create the surreal sculptures on display (and for sale).

Farther along, **La Vereda** ❺ *(Rua Almirante Alexandrino 428, tel 21/2507-0317)* is one of the best places in Rio to shop for folk art and artifacts from all over Brazil as well as by local Santa Teresa artists. At No. 501, a somewhat dilapidated, turn-of-the-20th-century mansion shelters **Largo das Letras,** a bookstore and café. Take a seat outside to down a quick espresso and a Portuguese pastry while keeping an eye on **Largo dos Guimarães,** an attractive square that is Santa's nerve center.

## Largo dos Guimarães & Beyond

On Largo dos Guimarães, it's worth peeking into **Gamar Brinquedos** ❻ *(tel 21/2208-1744),* which sells beautifully crafted wooden toys, mobiles, and kaleidoscopes, all made from sustainably harvested materials. Here, the bonde tracks split and follow two roads. Take the path going straight down Rua Paschoal Carlos Magno, to the right of Santa's

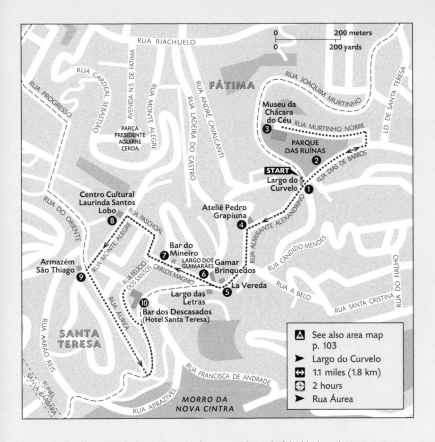

RUA RIACHUELO

RUA CARDEAL SEBASTIÃO

RUA PROGRESSO

AVENIDA N.S. DE FÁTIMA

RUA MONTE ALEGRE

RUA ANDRÉ CAVALCANTI

RUA LADEIRA DO CASTRO

FÁTIMA

RUA JOAQUIM MURTINHO

LD. DE SANTA TERESA

Museu da
Chácara
do Céu
**3**    RUA MURTINHO NOBRE

PARQUE
DAS RUÍNAS
**2**

RUA DIAS DE BARROS

**START**
Largo do
Curvelo **1**

PARÇA
PRESIDENTE
AGUIRRE
CERDA

Centro Cultural
Laurinda Santos
Lobo
**8**    RUA PASCHOAL

Ateliê Pedro
Grapiuna
**4**

RUA ALMIRANTE ALEXANDRINO

RUA CÂNDIDO MENDES

RUA DO ORIENTE

RUA MONTE ALEGRE

Bar do
**7** Mineiro
LARGO DOS
GUIMARÃES

Gamar
Brinquedos
**6**

RUA CARLOS MAGNO

RUA FELÍCIO DOS SANTOS

Armazém
São Thiago
**9**

La Vereda
**5**

RUA A. BELO

RUA SANTA CRISTINA

RUA DO FIALHO

Largo das
Letras

RUA ÁUREA

**10**

Bar dos Descasados
(Hotel Santa Teresa)

RUA AARÃO REIS

SANTA
TERESA

TUNEL
SANTA BÁRBARA

RUA FRANCISCA DE ANDRADE

RUA APRAZIVEL

MORRO DA
NOVA CINTRA

0        200 meters
0        200 yards

See also area map
p. 103

Largo do Curvelo

1.1 miles (1.8 km)

2 hours

Rua Áurea

tiny art-house cinema, which passes several charming restaurants and bars. **Bar do Mineiro 7** *(Rua Paschoal Carlos Magno 99, tel 21/2221-9227, closed Mon.)* is a traditional old *boteco* that has long been a favorite hangout for neighborhood artists (many of whose works hang on the walls). Accompanying delicious food from the state of Minas Gerais are some of Minas's finest cachaças.

After a couple of curves in the road, you'll find yourself on Rua Monte Alegre, a leafy street lined with gracious old mansions. The faded coral affair at No. 306 is one of the most noteworthy; it was built in 1907 by a local baroness. Today, it houses the **Centro Cultural Laurinda Santos Lobo 8** *(tel 21/2215-0618, closed Mon.),* a cultural center that hosts art exhibits, as well as dance and musical performances.

The end of the block, at the intersection with Rua Áurea, is a good place to end your walk and reward yourself with a cool drink at **Armazém São Thiago 9** *(Rua Áurea 26, tel 21/2232-0822, www.armazemsaothiago.com.br),* Santa's coolest neighborhood bar, whose interior betrays its 1919 origins as a corner general store. Alternatively, walk up Rua Áurea, which curves and turns into Rua Felício dos Santos, to the back entrance of the Hotel Santa Teresa for a (more expensive) drink at the **Bar dos Descasados 10.** The luxury Hotel Santa Teresa *(Rua Almirante Alexandrino 660, tel 21/2222-2755, www.santa-teresa-hotel.com)* occupies a 200-year-old coffee plantation, and this romantic lounge (housed in the former slaves' quarters) at the far end of the estate is a bewitching place from which to watch the sun set.

# Glória & Catete

Largely overlooked by tourists, the traditional Carioca neighborhoods of Glória and Catete have lost some of their original splendor, but it's worth visiting the Igreja de Nossa Senhora da Glória do Outeiro and the Palácio and Parque do Catete.

Parque do Catete, the former gardens of the Palácio do Catete, serves as a peaceful retreat.

**Glória**

⚠ 103 B2–C2

Up until the mid-19th century, the adjacent neighborhoods of Glória and Catete were considered to be on the outskirts of the city. Yet their proximity to Centro and Guanabara Bay lured Rio's growing upper middle classes and led to their transformation into one of the city's poshest residential areas. By the mid-20th century, Rio's elite had decamped farther south and these neighborhoods became increasingly commercial. The most interesting sights are within close proximity and can be easily visited in several hours on foot.

## Glória

An extension of Centro whose hilly residential streets twist their way up to Santa Teresa, Glória's main attraction is the photogenic church perched upon the steep Morro da Glória. In 1567, Estácio da Sá succeeded in taking this strategic hilltop from French invaders (and dying shortly afterward from the arrow wound he received from France's Tamoio allies), thus sealing Portuguese control of Rio de Janeiro. However, it wasn't until the 18th century that this dazzling white church overlooking Guanabara Bay was built.

### INSIDER TIP:

**You can get a great view of downtown and Guanabara Bay from the hilltop Nossa Senhora da Glória do Outeiro church in Glória.**

—KELLY E. HAYES
*Scholar of Brazilian religion, Indiana University*

**Igreja de Nossa Senhora da Glória do Outeiro:** Completed in 1739, the Igreja de Nossa Senhora da Glória do Outeiro—which lent its name to the surrounding *bairro*—is one of Rio's earliest baroque churches, not to mention one of its most unusual due to a floor plan consisting of two intersecting octagons (viewed as innovative at the time). Considered one of the finest baroque churches in Brazil, it was also a favorite of the royal family; various princes and princesses were baptized here, among them Pedro I and his daughter Isabel.

From the Glória Metrô station, it's a short but very steep walk up the Ladeira da Glória to the church. A less challenging

alternative is to ride up the free 1945 funicular *(entrance at Rua do Russel 300, on the Guanabara Bay side)*. The church exterior is a striking exercise in contrasts, with the gleaming white of its facade set off by somber stone pillars. Inside, covering the lower portions of the walls, splendid frescoes in traditional Portuguese blue-and-white azulejos depict biblical scenes. At the back of the church, a small museum *($)* displays a collection of sacred art along with some royal paraphernalia; a surprising portrait of Pedro I falling off his horse, painted by French artist Félix Émile Taunay (1795–1881), offers an unexpected dose of slapstick.

**Igreja de Nossa Senhora da Glória do Outeiro**

🅰 103 B2

✉ Praça Nossa Senhora da Glória

☎ 21/2557-4600

🕐 Closed Mon.

🚇 Metrô: Glória

### Keep Tabs on Your Tab

Upon entering many Carioca bars, nightclubs, and even some restaurants (particularly per-kilo eateries), you'll be handed a *comanda,* a slip of paper upon which all your food and drink orders are tallied over the course of the meal, or the night. Feel free to spill or splatter upon your comanda, or even fold it into an airplane, but *não perca* (don't lose) it or you'll end up paying an exorbitant *multa* (fine), the specific value of which will be noted in tiny print. Although such fines are actually illegal, many establishments will detain you unless you pay up (and suing them later will only add to your headache).

**Wending Toward Catete:** Glória is a Metrô stop north of Catete, but you can easily walk to the neighboring bairro instead—either by going south along Rua da Glória, which

**Catete**
🅼 103 B1

turns into Rua do Catete, or by following Rua do Russel, which segues into Avenida Beira Mar. This latter route not only offers captivating views of Guanabara Bay backed by Sugar Loaf but also passes a handful of buildings of architectural note. On Rua do Russel—named after Englishman John Russel who created Rio's sewage and drainage system—the **Ipu** *(No. 496),* **Itacolomy** *(No. 680),* and **Itatiaia** *(No. 694)* apartment buildings are all fine examples of art deco, which was all the rage in the 1930s.

**INSIDER TIP:**

**Catete has an excellent buffet called Estação República (Rua do Catete 104) that offers a wide selection of dishes (great for vegetarians).**

—KELLY E. HAYES
*Scholar of Brazilian religion, Indiana University*

These edifices pale in comparison, however, to the neoclassical facade of the **Hotel Glória** *(Rua do Russel 632).* Rio's oldest—and one of its grandest—luxury hotels, the Glória was inaugurated with great pomp by then president Epitácio Pessoa in 1922. It reigned supreme for all of one year before being eclipsed by the Copacabana Palace (ironically, also designed by French architect Joseph Gire). Still, the Glória

hardly lacked for illustrious guests. It was while gazing out at Guanabara Bay from his room in 1925 that German physicist Albert Einstein was inspired to complete his theory of light (he even jotted down notes on hotel stationary). More infamous was Hollywood starlet Ava Gardner, who checked in during a 1954 press junket for *The Barefoot Contessa,* only to be evicted after getting drunk and trashing her room. Having lost its former cachet, the hotel was snatched up in 2008 by local billionaire Eike Batista (considered the seventh richest man in the world in 2012). After a complete overhaul in which little more than the original facade will remain, the revamped hotel is slated to reopen in 2014 as the Glória Palace.

## Catete

Catete—an indigenous term meaning "large leaf"—was originally swampland fed by a branch of the Rio Carioca as it wound its way down from Corcovado to Flamengo Beach. The abundance of fresh water led to the creation of farms that sprouted in the 18th century along the Caminho do Boqueirão da Glória, a road that connected Glória to the Lagoa Rodrigo de Freitas. In the 19th century, affluent Cariocas began building mansions along this increasingly urban thoroughfare, which took the name Rua do Catete.

**Palácio do Catete:** The most magnificent residence of all was a palace constructed by the Baron de Novo Friburgo

(1795–1869). An imperial crony and wealthy coffee planter, he owned a vast plot of land stretching from Rua do Catete down to Praia do Flamengo. In 1854, the baron spared no expense when he contracted German architect Carl Friedrich Gustav Waenheld to construct an eclectic-style building, inspired in part by the aristocratic palaces of Venice and Florence. Completed in 1867, the grand residence was known as the Palácio do Catete.

Following the baron's death, there were plans to convert the palace into a luxury hotel. Instead, it was purchased to serve as the seat of government of the new republic as well as the official residence of the president. To underscore its aura of authority,

in 1906 President Afonso Pena (1847–1909) hired sculptor Rodolfo Bernardelli to create the seven cast-iron eagles that glare down austerely from the roof, earning it the nickname Palácio das Águias (Palace of the Eagles). Between 1897 and 1960, when the capital moved to Brasília, 17 Brazilian presidents occupied the palace. It was the 18th president, Juscelino Kubitschek, who came up with the idea of transforming it into the **Museu da República.**

The museum occupies three floors. The main floor traces the history of the palace itself and also hosts temporary exhibits that focus on various aspects of the Brazilian republic. Ascending a dramatic staircase brings you to the second floor, where wandering from opulent room to room,

**Museu da República**
- 103 B1
- Palácio do Catete, Rua do Catete 153
- 21/3235-5236
- Closed Mon.
- $. Free Wed. & Sun.
- Metrô: Catete

Palácio do Catete's opulent decorative scheme, completed in 1867, features a mix of artistic styles.

you're treated to the full force of the Baron of Novo Friburgo's over-the-top extravagance. The **Banquet Room,** with its lavishly arrayed table, seems to be waiting with bated breath for the imminent arrival of the president and his VIP guests.

Also quite jaw-dropping are the exotically adorned **Pompeiian and Moorish Rooms,** in which ladies and gentlemen, respectively, retired after dinner to gossip, play chess, and smoke pipes and cigars (in the early 1900s, smoking Brazilian cigars—as opposed to those from Cuba—was considered a patriotic act).

The highlight of the third floor is the fascinating and eerily macabre, fully furnished **bedroom in which President Getúlio Vargas lived**—and died, at 9 a.m. on August 24, 1954, after shooting himself through

the heart in response to mounting opposition to his government and charges of corruption. The 1940s-style room resembles a film noir crime scene. Along with the immaculately made bed and retro telephone are Vargas's suicide note and the smoking gun as well as his bloodstained, striped pajama top. Somewhat anticlimactically, the remaining

## EXPERIENCE: Jazz With a View

The pacification of Rio's favelas has resulted in the creation of myriad alternative events held in areas that were once strictly off-limits to tourists. You should make time to enjoy one of the first—and still one of the best—of these: the bimonthly jazz performances held at the **Maze** (*Rua Tavares Bastos 414, Casa 66, Catete, tel 21/2558-5547, http://jazzrio.com, cash only*), a pioneering inn created by former journalist, artist, and storyteller supreme Englishman Bob Nadkarni.

It's hard to dispute *Downbeat* jazz magazine's hyping of the Maze as "one of the world's best jazz venues." Held on the first and third Friday evening of every month, these singular, hours-long sessions take place on the hilltop of Tavares Bastos, where a series of bars and terraces afford magnificent views of Guanabara Bay. Although many of the musicians, as well as the attendees, are foreign, the event itself has become thoroughly entwined with the larger community.

Prices—a R$40 cover charge and beer costing beyond usual favela levels—have increased in proportion to the event's popularity; arrive unfashionably early (well before 9 p.m.) in order to nab a table with a view. Despite the crowds, however, the vibe and setting continue to cast a bewitching spell. You can reach the Maze by taxi or by hopping a van or *moto-taxi* (recommended for thrill seekers), which depart from the corner of Rua Tavares Bastos and Rua Bento Lisboa, in Catete.

A temporary exhibition at the Museu do Folclore, which focuses on Brazilian folklore and culture

rooms on this floor recount the history of the Brazilian republic. Illustrated by period artifacts and objects ranging from the interesting to the arcane (lots of presidential spectacles and fountain pens), this section will appeal more specifically to amateur Brazilianists and political junkies.

Behind the museum, extending down to Praia do Flamengo, the former palace gardens now form the **Parque do Catete.** The park was designed by French landscape artist Paul Villon (1841– 1905) during the palace's conversion from private to presidential residence and features an artificial lake complete with a cascade and grotto and serpentine pathways punctuated with 19th-century French sculptures. Very welcome

shade Is provided by native fruit trees bearing mangos, avocados, and tamarinds. Various cultural events are often held here. There is also a small art-house cinema along with a pleasant outdoor café.

**Museu do Folclore:** Next door to the Palácio do Catete, on Rua do Catete, the Museu do Folclore, dedicated to popular Brazilian folk art and culture, is in the throes of a long renovation project with no specific completion date beyond "maybe sometime in 2013." In the meantime, near the entrance, small temporary exhibits devoted to individual folk artists provide a taste of the rich diversity of Brazilian *artesanato.* ∎

**Parque do Catete**
- 🅰 103 B1–C1
- ✉ Rua do Catete 153
- 🚇 Metrô: Catete

**Museu do Folclore (Centro Nacional de Folclore e Cultura Popular)**
- 🅰 103 B1
- ✉ Rua do Catete 179–181
- ☎ 21/2285-0441
- 🕐 Closed Mon.
- 🚇 Metrô: Catete

**www.cnfcp.gov.br**

Traditional *bairros* that are eclectic, vibrant, and rife with history—
as well as home to the mountains Corcovado and Pão de Açúcar

# Corcovado &
# Pão de Açúcar

Cable cars provide the easiest means of ascending iconic
Morro Pão de Açúcar (Sugarloaf)

# Corcovado & Pão de Açúcar

**Although they contain two of Rio's most iconic and visited natural landmarks—Corcovado and Sugarloaf—the largely residential neighborhoods of Flamengo, Laranjeiras, Cosme Velho, Botafogo, and Urca are all too often overlooked by foreigners. Yet they offer a textured slice of middle-class Rio life at its least touristy and most authentic.**

## Flamengo

Wedged between Catete to the north and Botafogo to the south, once fashionable Flamengo impresses with its wealth of eclectic-style, art deco, and modernist palaces, hotels, and apartment buildings. Cutting-edge cultural centers such as Oi Futuro share sidewalk space with decades-old restaurants and bars. Meanwhile, its long waterfront is flanked with a wide ribbon of green known as the Parque do Flamengo. Stretching all the way from Centro to Botafogo, this favorite Carioca playground embraces attractions as varied as walking and bike paths, playing fields, and skateboard ramps; a yacht-stuffed marina; and one of Rio's finest museums, the Museu de Arte Moderna (MAM).

## Laranjeiras & Cosme Velho

To the west of Flamengo, the elegant neighborhoods of Laranjeiras and Cosme Velho climb up toward the heights of Rio's most famous peak: Corcovado, where the famous granite statue of Cristo Redentor stands, arms akimbo, embracing the entire city at its feet. Cosme Velho has lesser, unsung gems, too, such as the Museu Internacional de Arte Naïf and the cinematic square of Largo do Boticário.

## NOT TO BE MISSED:

Brazilian modern art at the Museu de Arte Moderna **128–129**

Experiencing, up close, the embrace of Cristo Redentor **135–138**

Live *choro* played at Laranjeiras's weekend street markets **136**

The Museu Internacional de Arte Naïf's vibrant canvases **138–139**

The community of Santa Marta and the view from the Espaço Michael Jackson **141–142**

Being hypnotized by the sun setting over the city from the top of Pão de Açúcar **143–145**

## Botafogo & Urca

Many of Botafogo's smaller, tree-lined streets leading inland are occupied by gracious mansions, some of which were built by 19th-century coffee barons and subsequently converted into museums such as the Casa de Rui Barbosa and the Museu do Índio. Botafogo is also home to Santa Marta, one of the area's largest favelas, with stunning views from the top. Botafogo's pretty bay is separated from the open Atlantic by a peninsula of land that comprises the charming neighborhood of Urca. Urca's most compelling attraction by far is the monumental, mystical, and primitive chunk of sculpted granite known as Sugarloaf, which is synonymous not only with the neighborhood, but with Rio de Janeiro itself. ■

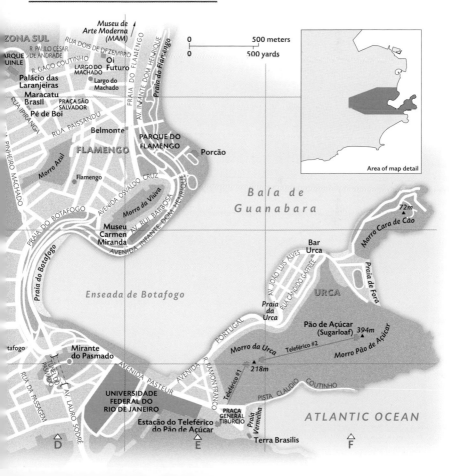

# Flamengo

Flamengo is an attractive neighborhood of wide avenues and leafy side streets, lined with art deco apartments and palaces that once sheltered embassies. Its most notable, and popular, feature is Parque do Flamengo, a vast green park that runs along Guanabara Bay.

Skateboarders love to cruise the wide paths of Parque do Flamengo.

**Flamengo**
📍 125 D3

**Parque do Flamengo**
📍 125 E3
Ⓜ Metrô: Cinelândia (northern extreme) to Flamengo (southern extreme)

According to competing legends, the *bairro* of Flamengo earned its name either from the *flamengo* (Dutch) prisoners held captive here by the Portuguese in the 17th century or from the pink flamingos that (poetically, but improbably) frequented its long, curvaceous shoreline. In the early to mid-20th century, Flamengo was one of Rio's most fashionable addresses, and to this day it retains a certain cachet.

## Parque do Flamengo

In the 1950s, the hill known as Morro de Santo Antônio, in Centro, was decimated and its earth was used as landfill along the waterfront extending from Glória to Botafogo. The main purpose of this Aterro (landfill) project was to construct a series of expressways that would facilitate traffic between Centro and the Zona Sul.

It was the inspired idea of Maria Carlota de Macedo Soares (1912–1967) to reduce the number of proposed thoroughfares from four to two and create a green space dedicated to leisure, culture, and recreation (see sidebar this page). The daughter of a prominent Carioca family and a self-taught architect with a passion for modernism, "Lota" was hired by then governor (and friend) Carlos Lacerda to head the vast project. She recruited visionary figures such as architect Affonso Eduardo Reidy, who oversaw construction of all buildings, and landscape artist Roberto Burle Marx, who shared her view that the park should feature only native flora (a novelty at the time).

The park contains more than 4,400 palm trees representing 50 species, including the rare *Corypha umbraculifera*, which flowers only once and then dies.

Inaugurated in 1964, the Parque do Flamengo completed the cycle of landfills that had razed the hills of Centro and used the earth to urbanize the shoreline of Guanabara Bay, a process that dated back to the creation of Lapa's Passeio Público in the 18th century. Having miraculously resisted the onslaught of developers and speculators, today this sweeping green ribbon is one of the city's most popular playgrounds for Cariocas of all ages, with jogging, biking, and skateboard paths; numerous playing

## Lota & Elizabeth

In 1951, Carlota "Lota" de Macedo Soares, an aesthete who dressed in jeans, tore around town in a Jaguar, and hobnobbed with artistic and intellectual luminaries, found herself tending to celebrated American poet Elizabeth Bishop (1911–1979). Docked in Rio while on a cruise around South America, Bishop had eaten the fruit of a cashew, which caused her head and limbs to swell up horribly.

Bishop never resumed her cruise. She and Macedo Soares fell in love and spent the next 16 years together in Brazil, alternating between an apartment in Leme and a modernist house in the mountains of Petrópolis. It was in Rio that Bishop wrote many of her most famous poems—and received the news that she had won the 1956 Pulitzer Prize for poetry.

While Bishop struggled with her writing, Macedo Soares struggled with the construction of Parque do Flamengo.

A gigantic undertaking, it was especially so for a woman without a university degree who was also a lesbian. Battling bureaucracy and machismo, for five years Macedo Soares worked obsessively, putting in 12- to 14-hour days. Her battles with Roberto Burle Marx were epic. The legendary landscaper was particularly galled by her desire to install tall lampposts to illuminate the park's many playing fields (to this day, their light allows teams of taxi drivers and doormen to engage in all-night-long soccer matches).

The park took its toll on both women. Increasingly lonely, Bishop struggled with depression, alcoholism, and writer's block. In 1965, Macedo Soares was abruptly removed from the project and had a nervous breakdown. Their relationship never recovered. But the park spearheaded by Macedo Soares forever transformed the landscape of Rio de Janeiro—for the better.

The Museu de Arte Moderna is considered one of Rio's most important modernist landmarks.

### Museu de Arte Moderna (MAM)

🅼 103 C3

✉ Av. Infante Dom Henrique 85—Parque do Flamengo

☎ 21/3883-5600

🕐 Closed Mon.

💲 $. Free Wed. after 3 p.m.

🚇 Metrô: Cinelândia

fields; a children's park; and an area for flying model planes, as well as two museums, the Museu de Arte Moderna and the Museu Carmen Miranda. It is also home to the Marina da Glória, from which yachts and schooners depart for points up and down the state of Rio de Janeiro. The park is especially packed on Sundays and holidays, when Avenida Infante Dom Henrique is closed to traffic and activities such as sporting events take place.

#### Museu de Arte Moderna (MAM): Located across from Cinelândia square, the MAM occupies a somewhat bleak but

beguiling modernist structure, whose glass-and-concrete exterior offers a striking contrast to the soft colors and organic forms of Guanabara Bay and the surrounding gardens by Burle Marx. Completed in 1958, the monumental building is supported by thrusting V-shaped columns and is considered to be the masterpiece of architect Affonso Eduardo Reidy (1909–1964).

Inside is one of Brazil's most significant collections of 20th-century art, with choice works by such international artists as Alberto Giacometti, Henry Moore, and Jackson Pollack sprinkled amid key pieces by important national figures such as Tarsila do Amaral (1886–1973) and Anita Malfatti (1889–1964) (look for the former's "Urutu" and the latter's "O Farol"). The permanent collection on display provides an excellent overview of Brazilian modernism. That the works are framed in such spacious, light-suffused galleries—in which there is constant interplay with the scenery—enhances the viewing experience.

Apart from hosting top-notch temporary exhibitions, the museum possesses a cinémathèque, a design shop, a café, and a pricey but elegant restaurant, **Laguiole** (tel 21/2517-3129), which is open during the week for lunch. On summer evenings, DJ-hosted festas sometimes take place on the rooftop terrace.

## INSIDER TIP:

**Riding a bike is the best way to experience the Parque do Flamengo and the different vistas created by landscape artist Roberto Burle Marx.**

—KELLY E. HAYES
Scholar of Brazilian religion,
Indiana University

### Enseada da Glória & Beyond:

From the museum, it's possible to walk (or cycle) through the park all the way to Botafogo beach (which will take close to an hour). Heading south along the small bay known as the Enseada da Glória, you'll pass by the **Monumento aos Mortos da Segunda Guerra Mundial.** This monument featuring a granite sculpture by noted modernist Alfredo Ceschiatti (1918–1989) honors Brazilian soldiers who fought for the Allied forces in Italy during World War II. Completed in 1960, the simple and sober ensemble includes a small armed forces museum as well

---

### Doormen vs. Waiters

Rio's beaches play host to *peladas*—amateur soccer games in which players often exhibit feats of prowess that put pros to shame. Among the most classic are the midnight games held in the Parque do Flamengo, which pit off-duty *porteiros* (doormen) against *garçons* (waiters). These all-night games lure faithful fans, not to mention the requisite vendors of icy beer and barbecued meat, and even samba bands. Afterward, victors and vanquished cool off with the aid of showerheads attached to motorized pumps that suck up fresh water from beneath the sand.

---

as an underground mausoleum where the bodies of 462 Brazilian soldiers were laid to rest.

The Monumento aos Mortos is located adjacent to the **Marina da Glória.** Aside from being a point of departure for cruises, this picturesque harbor backed by Sugarloaf often hosts events such as the Rio Music Conference. From the marina, daily boat trips operated by **Saveiros Tour** (tel 21/2225-6064, www.saveiros.com.br) whisk tourists around Guanabara Bay. Departing in the morning, the two-hour voyage takes in the

**Museu Carmen Miranda**

🗺 125 E2

✉ Av. Rui Barbosa 560

☎ 21/2334-4293

🕐 Closed Mon.

🚇 Metrô: Flamengo

beaches of Flamengo, Botafogo, and Urca and offers seaside vantage points of Sugarloaf and Oscar Niemeyer's spaceship-like Museu de Arte Contemporânea in Niterói.

After the marina, the park continues along Flamengo Beach, passing playing fields and tennis courts. At the southern tip lies **Porcão** (*Av. Infante Dom Henrique, tel 21/3389-8989*), the largest and most scenic outpost of a chain of *churrascarias* (barbecue houses). Apart from its high-quality cuts of meat—which range from beef to ostrich—and banquet-worthy all-you-can-eat buffet, the aptly named "Big Pig" is famed for being a pioneer of the *rodízio* system, in which waiters circle (*rodar*) from kitchen to dining room and ply diners with an endless array of meat. Due to the lofty prices and tantalizing number of choices, go only on a very empty stomach.

**Museu Carmen Miranda:** Rounding the tip of Flamengo Beach brings you to the end of the park and the beginning of Botafogo. Amid the traffic racing

along Avenida Infante Dom Henrique sits a squat concrete building that resembles a bomb shelter. This less-than-inspiring design by Affonso Eduardo Reidy is truly at odds with the extravagance of the "Brazilian Bombshell" (see sidebar this page) to whom the Museu de Carmen Miranda pays homage. Due to its small size, there isn't enough space within the cramped interior to display all 3,000 artifacts that belonged to one of the most internationally famous—not to mention surreal—Brazilian performers of all time. Fans of

**INSIDER TIP:**

**The Porcão restaurant at the southern tip of Parque do Flamengo serves up amazing views of Sugarloaf and Guanabara Bay along with its terrific barbecue.**

—BRUNO LFITE
*Embassy of Brazil diplomat*

## Carmen Miranda

Although she was born in Portugal, Maria do Carmo Miranda da Cunha (1909–1955) was raised in Rio, where her rise to fame as a singer in the 1930s coincided with the birth of Brazil's recording industry and explosion of radio. In 1939, she was discovered by impresario Lee Schubert while performing in the Urca Casino and whisked off to Broadway. After taking New York by storm (the windows of Saks Fifth Avenue displayed

Carmen-inspired platform shoes and turbans), the 5-foot-tall (1.52 m) "Brazilian Bombshell" went to Hollywood, where she starred in 14 movies between 1940 and 1953. At the time, her over-the-top celluloid "Brazilian-ness" was met with ambivalence by Brazil's elites, but today Carmen is beloved in Rio, particularly when Carnaval rolls around and Carmen look-alikes take to the streets.

**The Museu de Carmen Miranda showcases costumes worn by the "Brazilian Bombshell."**

Hollywood's golden age and lovers of kitsch can get a quick glitz fix by ogling the appetizing tutti-frutti hats and sky high platform shoes worn by the diminutive Carmen in the Technicolor musicals that made her Hollywood's top-earning female star in the mid-1940s.

There are plans to move the museum's collection to the soon-to-be-opened Museu da Imagem e do Som (see sidebar p. 151) in Copacabana. Not only would this provide Carmen's legacy with a worthy showcase, but it would also prove more convenient than this somewhat isolated location.

## Oi Futuro

A block up from the Parque do Flamengo and a block over from bustling Largo do Machado, Oi Futuro is one of Rio's most dynamic cultural centers. Operated by Oi, a major Brazilian telecommunications company, this cutting-edge multimedia center takes the future seriously. Within the cleverly renovated, early 20th-century phone company building, multiple floors play host to exhibits of contemporary visual art, many of which incorporate technology. There are also spaces for concerts, film screenings, and dance performances.

Having Oi in charge explains the free Wi-Fi access as well as an interactive telecommunications museum that recounts the history of telephones in Brazil (design aficionados will salivate over some of the retro residential and public phones). On the top floor is a cyber café whose chairs were once used by phone operators. The rooftop terrace offers good views. ■

**Oi Futuro**

- 🅜 125 E4
- ✉ Rua Dois de Dezembro 63
- ☎ 21/3131-3060
- 🕐 Closed Mon.
- 🚇 Metrô: Largo do Machado

# Rio's *Botequins*

**Just as Paris has its cafés and London its pubs, Rio de Janeiro has its *botequins*. Descendants of Spanish *bodegas* and Portuguese *boticos*—stores that sold fresh produce, dry goods, and basic necessities—Rio's first botequins appeared in the 19th century, springing up in the port district warehouses of Saúde and Gamboa.**

The retro interior of the Belmonte *boteco,* a favorite watering hole for Flamengo residents

After shopping for provisions at street markets, Cariocas would inevitably stop by their favorite *boteco* (an abbreviation of *botequim,* the singular form of botequins) to complete their purchases and relax among friends. To gain customer loyalty, many botecos began serving wine and food—a strategy that proved so successful that many botequins became second homes to the Carioca men who haunted them (it was a while before women joined the boteco fray).

## Homes Away From Home

Today botequins are veritable social and cultural institutions, as sacred to Cariocas as soccer and samba. The neighborhood boteco is where one goes to get away from it all, to meet up with friends, family members, and complete strangers; to unwind after work (or after the beach); to tie one on; to nibble on *petiscos* (tapas-like bar food) and/or stuff one's face; to flirt, *fofocar* (gossip), and razz one's favorite waiter. Most importantly, it's where Cariocas breezily, yet vigorously, discourse on every important topic under the sun—from sports and politics to soap operas and sex lives. The euphemistic premise is to "*tomar uma*" (that is, "drink just one"), but any Carioca who dares to call it quits after a sole libation risks being stripped of his or her citizenship. Similarly, when it's finally time for the *saideira,* know that this seemingly final "last call" is invariably only the first of many.

What's amazing about Rio's botequins is how democratic they are. Although distinctions are made between *pé sujo* (dirty foot)—that is, a hole-in-the-wall—and *pé limpo* (clean foot), which tends to be a little more gleaming and upscale, the classic boteco is proudly simple and immune to changes in fashion; many have been around for decades. Regardless of whether you happen to be high up in a favela or in the depths of Leblon, the decor

(or absence thereof; most botecos possess coveted terraces and/or sidewalk space that are ideal for watching the world parade by), drinks, and *comida caseira* (home cooking) are similar (although there will be a difference in price). Ultimately, the most fundamental considerations are the iciness of the beer, the crunchiness of the *bolinhos de bacalhau* (codfish balls), and the friendliness of the service.

## EXPERIENCE: *Boteco* Hopping

Rio has hundreds of *botequins* where you can cool your heels, quench your thirst, fill your belly—*botecos* serve some of the most authentic, not to mention tasty (and nicely priced), Brazilian cuisine in town—and soak up the local atmosphere. Here are a few classics (not otherwise listed in this book):

**Bar Lagoa** *(Av. Epitácio Pessoa 1674, Lagoa, tel 21/2523-1135)* The terrace tables overlooking Lagoa Rodrigo de Freitas at this bar dating back to 1934 are as coveted as the hearty German fare.

**Belmonte** *(Praia do Flamengo 300, Flamengo, tel 21/2552-1399)* This 1950s Flamengo favorite gets so packed on late afternoons that regulars balance their cups on the beer barrels. The *empadas* (empanadas) here rule.

**Bip Bip** *(Rua Alimirante Gonçalves 50, Copacabana, tel 21/2267-9696)* Just off the beach, this tiny hole-in-the-wall hosts live samba jams *(Thurs.–Fri. & Sun.)* and choro *(Mon.–Tues.).*

**Bracarense** *(Rua José Linhares 85B, Leblon, tel 21/2294-3549)* Leblon's favorite sidewalk boteco is famed for *petiscos* (tapas-like bar food) such as the *bolinhos de aipim com camarão,* crunchy manioc balls stuffed with shrimp and Catupiry cheese.

**Jobi** *(Av. Ataulfo de Paiva 1166, Leblon, tel 21/2274-0547)* Since 1956, this clubby boteco has been a classic haunt of Zona Sul artists, journalists, and intellectuals.

**Pavão Azul** *(Rua Hilário de Gouveia 71, Copacabana, tel 21/2236-2381)* This laid-back neighborhood Copa bar is famed for having the best *bolinhos de bacalhau* (codfish balls) in town.

**Vilarino** *(Av. Calógeras 6, Centro, tel 21/2240-9634, closed Sat.–Sun.)* A sacred bossa nova hangout with plenty of retro charm, this is where Tom Jobim and Vinícius de Moraes first met.

# Laranjeiras & Cosme Velho

Two of Rio's oldest residential neighborhoods, Laranjeiras and Cosme Velho are low-key, verdant, and pretty *bairros* that are agreeable to stroll around. By far the most significant attraction is Corcovado, accessible by the train that departs from Cosme Velho station.

At nighttime, the view from Corcovado reveals Guanabara Bay ringed by glittering neighborhoods.

**Laranjeiras**
🚂 125 C3

**Cosme Velho**
🚂 125 B2–B3

Laranjeiras dates back to the 17th century, when early settlers built farms along the banks of the Rio Carioca as it swept down from Corcovado to Praia do Flamengo. Aside from the fruits and vegetables grown to feed Rio's growing populace, the area was known for the cultivation of the *laranjeiras* (orange trees), which earned the bairro its name. In the 19th century, the rural estates and orange groves gave way to elegant apartment buildings. Off the main tourist track, Laranjeiras retains a pleasant neighborhood atmosphere. Its main thoroughfare, Rua das Laranjeiras, spools its way up from Largo do Machado before turning into Rua Cosme Velho, the main street of the more bucolic (and wealthier) residential neighborhood of Cosme Velho, which leads all the way up to Corcovado.

## Palácio das Laranjeiras & Around

From Largo do Machado, follow Rua das Laranjeiras for two blocks. To the right, you'll find the majestic Palácio das Laranjeiras. Built at the turn of the 20th century in the eclectic style, it was the residence of wealthy industrialist Eduardo Guinle (1846–1914), who modeled it on the Monte Carlo Casino. Falling on hard times, the Guinle family was later forced to sell their opulent abode. It was purchased in 1947 by the state of Rio de Janeiro and transformed into the official governor's residence.

The palace is not open to the public, but the surrounding gardens—**Parque Guinle**—are *(main entrance on Rua Gago Coutinho)*. Curving paths, a lake strewn with swans, and wrought-iron gates guarded by winged lions and sphinxes add European accents to the tropical shrubbery planted by Roberto Burle Marx in the 1950s. Overlooking the park from Rua Paulo César de Andrade is an ensemble of residential buildings designed by architect Lúcio Costa (who later planned Brasília) in the 1940s. Apart from the slender columns supporting the structures, other remarkable modernist features include the geometrically patterned ceramic sunshades in pastel hues of coral, lemon, and powder blue.

**Shopping:** Emerging back onto Rua das Laranjeiras, crossing the street and following **Rua Ipiranga** leads to a pair of interesting stores for those in search of authentic "Brazilianisms." At No. 49, **Maracatu Brasil** (see sidebar this page) is a drummers' paradise. It boasts an impressive selection of traditional handcrafted and modern Brazilian percussion instruments that can be purchased new or used. Acclaimed musicians often drop by to give happy hour shows in the courtyard.

For those interested in folk art, next door at No. 55, **Pé de Boi** *(tel 21/2285-4395, www.pedeboi .com.br, closed Sun.)* boasts one of the city's most prolific and carefully culled selections of *artesanato* from around Brazil, ranging from naïf canvases, ceramics, and wooden sculptures to silver jewelry and vintage photos of Rio.

## Corcovado

The **statue of Cristo Redentor** (Christ the Redeemer) hovering gloriously atop Corcovado

---

**EXPERIENCE:**
# Drumming With the Pros

If you've ever dreamed of playing drums in a Carnaval samba school or slapping a *pandeiro* in a Lapa bar, your wish could come true at **Maracatu Brasil** *(Rua Ipiranga 49, tel 21/2557-4754)* in Laranjeiras. Behind its front room filled with *cuicas, maringas,* and *berimbaus* for sale (and rent) is a soundproof recording studio where professionals offer private lessons on whatever instrument you want to pound away on. Apart from individual lessons *(four hours cost R$220)*, frequent group workshops in a multitude of homegrown styles (samba, *maracatu,* candomblé, *cocô, afoxé*) are also offered on a longer term basis.

---

**Palácio das Laranjeiras**
- 🅜 125 D4

**Cristo Redentor (Corcovado)**
- 🅜 124 A2
- ✉ Rua Cosme Velho 513 (train station)
- ☎ 21/2558-1329
- 💲 $$$$$
- 🚇 Metrô: Largo do Machado. Bus: 422, 498

**www.corcovado .com.br**

mountain is to Rio what the Statue of Liberty is to New York and the Eiffel Tower is to Paris. However, unlike these other landmarks, the statue is remarkable in that no matter where you happen to be in a 360-degree circle—from the swankiest Zona Sul enclave to the poorest Zona Norte favela—the 98-foot (30 m) Christ, his arms outstretched in a welcoming embrace, can be seen watching benignly over the city.

Rio's earliest Portuguese settlers ascribed spiritual significance to the mountain they referred to as the Pico da Tentação (Peak of Temptation), an allusion to a biblical passage in which Jesus, atop a mountain, was tempted by the devil. It wasn't until the 19th century that the 2,330-foot

INSIDER TIP:

**The train ride to the top of Corcovado is very enjoyable. The best time to take it during the high tourist season is before the tour buses arrive, so try to catch the 8:30 a.m. train.**

—LUIZ RENATO MALCHER
*Manager, Rio de Janeiro Urban Adventures*

(710 m) granite pinnacle acquired the more secular, but no less poetic, name of Corcovado (Hunchback). By then, aristocrats had begun constructing estates on its refreshingly cool heights while plantation slaves often found shelter amid its tangled green canopy of Atlantic Forest.

Emperor Pedro II was fond of making the arduous journey to Corcovado's summit by donkey. Wanting to share the sublime experience (and magnificent views) with his subjects, he authorized the construction of a steam train that could whisk nature-worshipping pilgrims up to the top. Inaugurated in 1884, the railway was a remarkable feat of engineering due to the length and steepness of its route.

Originally commissioned to coincide with the commemoration of Brazil's independence centennial in 1921, the statue of Cristo Redentor wasn't completed until 1931. Designed by French sculptor Paul Landowski, the

## EXPERIENCE:
## Going to Market

For an authentic slice of laid-back Carioca neighborhood life, while away a weekend afternoon at one of the city's two most atmospheric street markets, both in Laranjeiras. Just five blocks from the Cosme Velho train station, on Saturday the **Feira da General Glícerio** lures local families seduced by live *choro*—a 19th-century Carioca style of instrumental music played with a flute, *pandeiro* (tambourine), and the ukulele-like *cavaquinho*—as well as piping hot *pastéis* served with *caldo de cana* (sugarcane juice). Choro also reigns at Sunday's *feira* at **Praça São Salvador,** which features handicrafts as well as fresh produce. At both markets, a refreshing presence is Luizinho, whose caipirinhas—made with Minas cachaça and inspired mixtures such as ginger and tangerine in addition to classic lime—are a neighborhood institution.

individual parts of the art deco monument, whose exterior was sculpted out of resistant soapstone, were created separately. Only after they had been shipped from France were they assembled for the first time on a 26-foot (8 m) pedestal.

**Ascending Corcovado:**

Apart from being iconic and photogenic, the statue—whose head alone weighs 30 tons, the

Rua Cosme Velho at 30-minute intervals. The slow ride up Corcovado takes 17 minutes and includes a stop at Paineiras station, where you can get off and walk around, admiring the Tijuca Forest and the views. For the best vantage points during the ascent, fight for a space at the back or on the right-hand side of the train.

An alternative way of reaching the statue is to travel by taxi or

People flock to the top of Corcovado to marvel at the Cristo Redentor, an art deco Rio icon.

outstretched arms 80 tons—is mesmerizing when seen up close where one can contemplate Christ's serene yet forceful gaze. There are two principal means of reaching the Cristo Redentor. The most traditional, and most popular, is to take the electric *trenzinho* (little train) that departs from the station on

car to Paineiras station (there is no vehicle access to the statue itself), where vans operated by IBAMA (the Brazilian environmental agency) offer transportation farther up the hill. If you choose to take a taxi, get one from your hotel or another departure point and not from the vicinity of the Corcovado train station, where

## Solar dos Abacaxis—House of Pineapples

Near the Largo do Boticário, at Rua Cosme Velho 857, sits one of Rio's most significant examples of neoclassical architecture. Constructed in 1843, the Solar dos Abacaxis owes its unusual name to the wrought-iron pineapples adorning the front balcony. Rare and exotic pineapples (whose origins are thought to be Brazilian) were a status symbol among colonial elites throughout the Americas. Those who couldn't afford to buy (or rent) them for table arrangements, showcased the fruit—a symbol of hospitality—via art and architecture.

True to its name, the Solar das Abacaxis was famous for welcoming artists and intellectuals. From the 1940s to the 1980s, owner Anna Amélia de Queiroz (1896–1971), a poet, and her husband, Marcos Carneiro de Mendonça (1894–1988), a historian who himself made history as the first goalkeeper of Brazil's national soccer team, hosted some of the city's most dazzling parties and salons. Unfortunately, despite being declared a state cultural heritage site, the Solar—on the market for more than a decade—has been neglected in recent times.

**Museu Internacional de Arte Naïf**
- 🅼 124 B3
- ✉ Rua Cosme Velho 561
- ☎ 21/2205-8612
- 🕒 Closed Mon.
- 💲 $$$
- 🚇 Metrô: Largo do Machado. Bus: 422, 498

you'll be overcharged. Arrange for the same driver to pick you up again at a specific time from Paineiras station. From where the IBAMA vans drop you off, you can walk or take an elevator or escalator to the top of Corcovado.

However you reach the summit, expect it to be cluttered with vendors hawking souvenirs and tourists, arms akimbo in redemptive poses, being photographed beneath the statue.

**When to Visit:** If you're concerned about crowds, be aware that lines—for tickets and to board the train—can be long. Consider arriving early to make the first train (8:30 a.m.). If you do have to wait, kill time at the station's small cultural center, where photos and press clippings reveal famous faces—from Pedro II to Princess Diana—who made the ascent before you.

The early morning also coincides with favorable lighting conditions, while before sunset is

a good time to come, to see the city below dappled in gold before dusk falls and the lights twinkle on. After dark, the illuminated statue takes on a ghostly presence, floating magically against the night.

Regardless of the hour, check the weather forecast before investing time and money in this outing; if it's overcast or rainy, visibility will be poor and the experience will be disappointing.

## Museu Internacional de Arte Naïf

Two minutes by foot from the Corcovado train station sits a handsome 19th-century mansion that houses the Museu Internacional de Arte Naïf. This museum is home to the world's largest single collection of art naïf, defined as works created by artists with no formal training. Comprising more than 6,000 works from Brazil and 100 countries around the globe, the collection was started by a jeweler named Lucien Finklestein. At 16, he left his native France in the aftermath of World War II and came to live with two uncles in Rio. He subsequently fell in love with the city and the "anarchist poets" who painted it with such verve on the canvases he avidly began to purchase.

Although Brazil is considered to have one of the richest art naïf traditions in the world, neither the art nor the artists had ever been taken seriously, which was a large motivation in Finklestein's decision to open the museum. Among the highlights on display is **"Brasil, Cinco Séculos."** Dense with vibrant detail, the 92-foot (28 m) mural by Aparecido Azevedo depicts five centuries of Brazilian history. Also noteworthy is the room of paintings devoted entirely to Carioca landmarks—from Corcovado to the Confeitaria Colombo.

Should you wish to start your own collection, contemporary works are available for purchase in the small boutique.

## Largo do Boticário

From the Museu Internacional de Arte Naïf, continue walking up Rua Cosme Velho. Be sure to stop and marvel at No. 857, the faded-pink **Solar dos Abacaxis,** a 19th-century mansion with unusual design elements on its facade (see sidebar opposite).

A little farther along and across the street, a narrow alley leads to the Largo do Boticário. Engulfed in jungly foliage, this charming square framed by pastel-colored houses resembles the set of a period movie. The bucolic ambience is enhanced by the rushing waters of

the Rio Carioca, in whose waters the local Tamoio bathed with the aim of increasing their beauty and virility. The square was named after one of its original residents, Joaquim Luís da Silva Souto, who served as *boticário* (apothecary) to the Brazilian royal family. While the seven houses were built in the early 1800s, their neocolonial facades are from the 1920s. ■

**Largo do Boticário**
📍 124 B3

**Atmospheric Largo do Boticário had a cameo in the 1977 James Bond film *Moonraker.***

# Botafogo & Urca

Botafogo's most defining characteristic is the sweeping cove of its bay, as picturesque as it is polluted. However, its tranquil side streets are stuffed with small museums, cinemas, restaurants, and bars that offer a multifaceted taste of a traditional Carioca neighborhood. Meanwhile, although adjacent Urca is most famous for sheltering Sugarloaf, this beach *bairro* (neighborhood) is one of Rio's most idyllic and charming.

Gazing down at the city from Morro Pão de Açúcar, with Morro da Urca in the foreground

**Botafogo**
 124 C2

**Fundação Casa de Rui Barbosa**
🅰 124 C2
✉ Rua São Clemente 134
☎ 21/3289-4600
🕐 Closed Mon.
💲 $. Free Sun.
🚇 Metrô: Botafogo

## Botafogo

For many tourists, Botafogo is the sprawling bairro they inevitably pass through en route to somewhere else. The area closest to the waterfront is built-up and commercial. However, heading inland, one encounters tree-lined streets flanked by mansions—a few sheltering small but interesting museums—that hint at the neighborhood's aristocratic past.

**Fundação Casa de Rui Barbosa:** One of Botafogo's principal avenues is Rua São Clemente, which cuts through the bairro from the beach all the way to Humaíta and still possesses a good number of stately mansions built by Rio's coffee barons. Take the Rua São Clemente exit from Botafogo Metrô and walk for two blocks until you reach the Fundação Casa de Rui Barbosa. One of Brazil's most important public figures, Rui Barbosa (1849–1923) was an influential journalist, jurist, and statesman whose writings on abolition played a key role in the passage of the Lei Áurea that finally ended slavery in

## EXPERIENCE: Sustainable Santa Marta

Although pacified Santa Marta is safe, like many favelas, its steepness, density, and lack of street names—or streets, for that matter—can make for tricky navigating, particularly if you don't speak Portuguese. To explore the community in depth, take a tour with local resident Thiago Firminio, who operates **Favela Santa Marta Tour** *(tel 21/9177-9459, www.favelasantamarta tour.blogspot.com.br, $$$$$)*. The basic two-hour tour takes you through the ins and outs of the community, weaving in facts and colorful neighborhood anecdotes. Optional extras include hikes through the nearby Tijuca Forest, kite flying (a favorite sport among favela kids, who try to cut each other's kites down with glass shards glued to the strings), capoeira classes, and joining the funk and samba *festas* that take place at Quadra da Santa Marta, home to the community's Mocidade Unida samba school.

Brazil. A staunch republican, he also made important contributions to the nation's first constitution.

In 1893, Barbosa purchased this handsome mid-19th-century neoclassical mansion. He lived here with his wife and five children until his death, after which it became the first private home in Brazil to be converted into a museum. Furnished with period pieces, the gracious bedrooms, ballrooms, and salons (not to mention bathrooms and kitchen) are so immaculately preserved that it feels as if the family has only just stepped out for a brief jaunt. The ensemble—which includes a garage with Barbosa's beloved Benz—offers a rare glimpse into (upper) middle-class Carioca domestic life at the beginning of the 20th century.

In addition to the museum, the foundation possesses a vast library, containing 37,000 volumes and a valuable archive of historical manuscripts that are an important source for researchers. The surrounding gardens are a favorite refuge of neighborhood children, who play in the shade of fruit-laden mango, pitanga, and lychee trees.

**Santa Marta:** Continue west along Rua São Clemente a few blocks. To the right, you'll see a mountainside covered with a dense cubist swatch of houses that rises up to Corcovado. This is the favela of Santa Marta. Formerly one of Rio's most notoriously dangerous and drug-ridden favelas, it was the first to receive its own UPP (Pacification Police Unit) in 2008. That same year, a *plano inclinado* (elevator) was inaugurated to shuttle residents up and down the crazily steep hill—a welcome alternative to tackling the 788 stairs.

Grab a free map (and free advice) from the well-trained guides at the Rio Top Tour kiosk, located at the entrance to the favela on **Praça Corumbá.** Then jump aboard the free elevator, which makes stops at five stations as it slowly glides up the hill. From Estação 3, you can walk to **Praça Cantão,** where fabulous Day-Glo colors have been splashed across

**Museu do Índio**

- 🏛 124 C1–C2
- ✉ Rua das Palmeiras 55
- ☎ 21/3289-4600
- 🕐 Closed Mon.
- 💲 $. Free Sun.
- 🚇 Metrô: Botafogo

dozens of homes as part of a project by two Dutch artists, Dre Urhann and Jeroen Koolhaas, who teamed up with local residents and a major Brazilian paint manufacturer to bring new vibrancy (literally) to the favela.

At Santa Marta's summit sits the UPP headquarters as well the **Mirante Dona Marta,** a lookout point that offers magnificent vistas of Botafogo Bay, Sugarloaf, and the Zona Sul, while Cristo Redentor hovers above your shoulder. For view junkies who don't want to brave the lines or fork out the money to ascend Corcovado, this lookout is a worthy alternative. A short walk through twisting alleyways brings you to an open

plaza known as **Espaço Michael Jackson.** A mosaic fresco and a life-size bronze statue of the "gloved one" mark the spot where Jackson filmed the Spike Lee–directed video to his controversial 1995 hit song "They Don't Care About Us."

**INSIDER TIP:**

**At the top of Morro da Urca, station No. 2 of the Sugarloaf complex, a trail leads to a little-visited area in the woods that offers a different perspective of Guanabara Bay.**

—LUIZ RENATO MALCHER
*Manager, Rio de Janeiro Urban Adventures*

## EXPERIENCE:
## Scaling Sugarloaf

**Apart from walking to—and on top of—Sugarloaf, you may also walk around it, following the 1.5-mile (2.4 km) Pista Claudio Coutinho, an easy paved trail that wraps its way around the *morros* of Urca and Pão de Açúcar and provides colorful birds and chattering monkeys as company. If you want something more challenging, this route passes more difficult trails, such as Bem-te-vi, which those spry of limb follow to Morro da Urca, and Costão, which rises to Pão de Açúcar, although climbing experience is necessary to ascend the vertical rock. For outings—and rock courses for beginners—contact Climb in Rio (tel 21/2245-1108, www.climbinrio.com) and Companhia da Escalada (tel 21/2567-7105, www.companhiadaescalada.com.br), both of which offer numerous scaling experiences on more than 1,000 breathtaking routes throughout the city, including Corcovado, Pedra da Gávea, and Dois Irmãos.**

**Museu do Índio:** Directly across the street from Praça Corumbá, on Rua das Palmeiras, is the Museu do Índio. Occupying a gracious house dating back to 1880, this museum was founded in 1953 by renowned anthropologist Darcy Ribeiro and is operated by the National Indian Foundation (FUNAI), a government agency responsible for the welfare of Brazil's more than 220 indigenous ethnic groups. Only some of them are represented by the modest but compelling ensemble of artifacts on (somewhat sad) display, which range from war, hunting, and cooking implements to religious objects and traditional costumes. Particularly noteworthy are the exquisite headdresses.

Fashioned from the jewel-hued feathers of Amazonian toucans and parrots, they would leave any Parisian couturier gasping with envy. Written explanations offer some insight into the social, economic, and spiritual lives of many groups—but only if you read Portuguese. In addition to the permanent collection, temporary exhibits also occur.

In the garden surrounding the house is a model *oca* (indigenous home) as well as a small boutique selling a nicely priced selection of authentic handicrafts. You can also relax in the café.

## Urca

Tucked away on a promontory facing Botafogo Bay—and backed by the über-iconic Pão de Açúcar—Urca has managed to stay mercifully secluded from the rest of Rio's mayhem. Unscathed by developers and ignored by tourists, it's a pleasant place to while away a few hours.

Urca was the birthplace of Rio. It was at its tip—at the Morro Cara de Cão (whose unlyrical literal translation is "dogface hill")—that Estácio de Sá landed on March 1, 1565, and that the tiny settlement of São Sebastião do Rio de Janeiro was founded before later being uprooted to Morro do Castelo in Centro. It was only in the 1920s, however, that Urca began to emerge as a residential neighborhood. In the 1930s, the opening of the famous Cassino da Urca (see sidebar p. 144) lured artists, celebrities, and bon vivants to the area and spurred the construction of chalets, villas, and apartments,

**More than 50 climbing routes snake up Pão de Açúcar.**

many in art deco and modernist styles, which have survived to this day.

**Pão de Açúcar:** The 1,293-foot-high (394 m) block of granite known as Morro Pão de Açúcar (Sugarloaf) is a natural marvel one never tires of gazing upon. Standing guard at the entrance to Guanabara Bay, this primitive sentry, cloaked in native Atlantic Forest, was called *pau-nh-acugua* (high pointed mountain) by Rio's original Tupi inhabitants. Both the

**Urca**
🅼 125 F2

**Pão de Açúcar**
🅼 125 F2
✉ Av. Pasteur 520
☎ 21/2546-8400
💲 $$$$$
🚇 Metrô: Botafogo. Bus: 511, 512, 513

## Cassino da Urca

The 1930s and early '40s were Rio's golden age of casinos. During these years, champagne-swilling Cariocas and jet-setters descended on swank gambling palaces overlooking the ocean, not just to test their luck at roulette but also to dance, dine, and take in shows by some of Brazil's hottest new radio and recording stars. Although the Atlântico and Copacabana Palace casinos were both the rage in Copa, the most glamorous of them all was the Cassino da Urca.

This dazzling white edifice was originally built in the 1920s to house a luxury hotel on Praia da Urca before morphing, in 1933, into Rio's most famous casino. Its stage welcomed the international likes of Josephine Baker and Maurice Chevalier, and homegrown talent Carmen Miranda was an exclusive performer between 1937 and 1940 (a plaque at Avenida São Sebastião 131 indicates the house in which the star lived while under contract).

In 1946, the casino era came to an abrupt end with the prohibition of gambling venues in Brazil, and the Cassino da Urca fell into decline. With the building recently restored, there are plans for the casino to get a new lease on life as a Rio outpost of the European Design Institute.

Tupi term and the mountain itself reminded early Portuguese settlers of a *pão de açúcar* (sugar loaf), a cone-shaped mound of sugar produced by pouring the juice from crushed cane into a mold where it solidifies. The name stuck—and today Pão de Açúcar is a symbol of Rio de Janeiro that is instantly recognizable around the world.

Pão de Açúcar actually consists of twin hilltops: Morro da Urca and Morro Pão de Açúcar. Both can be visited by taking the famous *bonde* (cable car) that departs from beside Praia Vermelha beach. Inaugurated in 1912, the cutting-edge bonde—which relied on German parts and Brazilian workmanship—was the first cable car in Brazil and only the third in the world. The original cars were elegant all-wood affairs with curtains. They were replaced in 1972 by more modern models, which in turn were replaced in 2008.

The trip to the top is divided into two parts. The first involves a ride from the bonde station at Praça General Tibúrcio up to the summit of **Morro da Urca.** Here, passengers can get out and walk around, taking in the views (particularly of Morro Pão de Açúcar, staring one straight in the face) and preparing for what's next to come. Aside from the surprisingly comfy wooden chaise longues that invite you to sit and contemplate, there's a small museum where interactive screens cover various themes related to Pão de Açúcar's geology, history, and celebrity status.

Hang out as long as you want—it's possible to avoid the crowds by wandering down the trails that weave through the forest and down the mountainside—before taking a second cable car up to **Morro Pão de Açúcar.** From here, the views are truly sublime, taking in Niterói and the entrance to Guanabara Bay; the beaches of Copacabana, Ipanema, and Leblon backed by the twin heads of Dois Irmãos; and Botafogo framed by Corcovado. Here, too, there are numerous facilities, including a bar where you can toast the sunset with champagne. Speaking of sunset, that is the most magical time to come. Attempt to arrive a couple of hours before dusk in order to catch Rio bathed in golden light before the sun descends behind the mountains and the city lights start to twinkle like millions of tiny fireflies.

The vision is bewitching. A close second to sunset is early in the morning; avoid the middle of the day when both the sun and crowds are at their apex. Also avoid cloudy and rainy days in which visibility will be poor.

If you want to interact with nature (and save some money), it's possible to follow steep, but short and not too difficult, trails from Praça General Tibúrcio up to the Morro da Urca (from where you can purchase a ticket to Morro Pão de Açúcar at a reduced fare).

**Praia Vermelha & Praia da Urca:** In the shadow of Pão de Açúcar, the small, picturesque beach of Praia Vermelha served as a defensive outpost during colonial times, and later a naval school and military engineering institute were built there. It wasn't until the 1930s that civilians could set foot in the soft sand here. Although the waters aren't the cleanest, the beach is a charming Côte d'Azur look-alike. To admire the view, nab a table on the terrace of **Terra Brasilis** (tel

21/2275-4651), a simple restaurant housed within the Círculo Militar military club (civilians are welcome, although the drinks come more recommended than the basic grub). On some evenings, live music is performed.

From Praça General Tibúrcio, turn right on Rua Ramon Franco

**Praia Vermelha**
   125 E1

**Praia da Urca**
   125 E2

Scenic Praia Vermelha sits in the shade of Pão de Açúcar.

until you reach Avenida Portugal, which runs along the waterfront. Turn right again, passing Praia da Urca. During the week, the rampart-like stone walls overlooking Guanabara Bay are haunted by fishermen and friends balancing beers from nearby bars. On weekends, young Cariocas gather here to drink, flirt, and listen to impromptu samba jams. One of the oldest and best places is **Bar Urca** (Rua Cândido Gaffrée 205, tel 21/2295-8744). Dating back to the 1930s, it serves delicious snacks such as empadas and turnover-like pastéis as well as a popular feijoada on Saturday afternoons. ∎

Shimmering white-sand beaches, splayed between the open blue
Atlantic and a sea of high-rises backed by jungle-clad mountains

# Zona Sul Beaches

The iconic "wave" *calçadão* (promenade) lining Copacabana
beach was created by Roberto Burle Marx in the 1970s.

# Zona Sul Beaches

The legendary Zona Sul beaches of Copacabana, Ipanema, and Leblon are what most people conjure up when they think of Rio. Long and languorous, they are the source of a compelling beach culture that radiates throughout these neighborhoods, casting a spell that is cool, carefree, and quintessentially Carioca.

Their very names, sonorous and sensual, slip off one's tongue like magical incantations: the exotically indigenous Copacabana and Ipanema, tied up with the elegant French twist of Leblon. And they comprise some of the most drop-dead gorgeous urban beaches on the planet. However, Copacabana, Ipanema, and Leblon offer far more than just sun, surf, and sand. These perennially fashionable neighborhoods are vibrant and extremely cosmopolitan, wedding a relaxing beach vibe with world-class sophistication in terms of hotels and restaurants, cafés and clubs, bars and boutiques. They are also Rio's most tourist-infested neighborhoods. However, once you get off the main beachfront *avenidas* and onto the shady side streets, you'll discover neighborhoods brimming with indelible Carioca charm and flavor.

## Copacabana

Stretching from Botafogo to Ipanema, and hemmed in by the *morros* of Babilônia, São João, Cabritos, and Cantagalo, Copacabana is the largest and longest, and the most vibrant and democratic, of the Zona Sul neighborhoods. Much of the glamour of its mid-20th-century heyday has faded, but despite the

**NOT TO BE MISSED:**

Savoring seafood *feijoada* (and seafood croquettes) along with live *pagode* at Bar do David **155**

A stroll along the glorious length of Copacabana beach **158–159**

Renting a chair and parasol from a *barraca* and then chilling out on Ipanema beach **160–161**

View of the sunset from the Pedra do Arpoador **161**

Hiking to the top of Morro Dois Irmãos **165–166**

Drinking an antioxidant-filled concoction at a juice bar **166**

onslaughts of decay, rampant verticalization (Copa is the densest of Rio's neighborhoods), and overblown tourism, it still has an undeniable charisma. Its 2.5-mile-long (4 km) beach—which includes the 0.6-mile (1 km) expanse of Leme—is majestic in its sweep, but it's also astonishingly full of life from dawn, when power-walking seniors take their poodles for strolls, to long after dark, when workers gather for midnight soccer in the sand.

A pair of picturesque fortresses—Forte de Copacabana and Forte Duque de Caxias—bracket the beach, while its center is ruled over by the regal Copacabana Palace Hotel. A wealth of art deco buildings line Copa's streets, which are bustling, vital, and suffused with a deliciously laid-back atmosphere that extends from the *quiosque* bars lining Avenida Atlântica to the *botecos* (bars) of Morro da Babilônia.

## Ipanema

"Tall and tan and young and lovely," the opening lyrics to the bossa nova classic "The Girl from Ipanema," also aptly describe the eternally sun-drenched, carefree hedonistic beach *bairro* of the same name. Idyllically situated between Copacabana, Leblon, the open Atlantic, and the Lagoa Rodrigo de Freitas, Ipanema is unsurprisingly Rio's most sought-after (and extravagantly

priced) neighborhood. With nonchalant ease, it evokes a highly seductive form of Carioca living that easily contaminates those intent on whiling away a morning on its famous beach, an afternoon in its chic boutiques, or an evening at its fashionably casual restaurants and bars.

## Leblon

Separated from Ipanema by the narrow Jardim de Alah Canal, Leblon is a little more chic, staid, and residential than Ipanema. Although lovely, its narrow beach—above which loom the twin peaks of Dois Irmãos and the favela of Vidigal—is less magnificent than its neighbors'. Both Leblon's sands and its shady streets tend to draw more locals than tourists, as do its urbane yet easygoing bars, boutiques, and delicatessens. Leblon also shelters some of Rio's most innovative—and expensive—restaurants. ∎

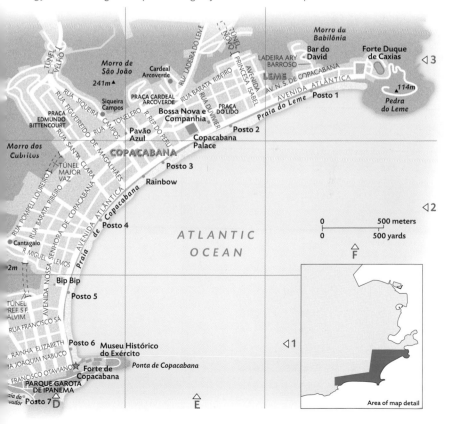

# Copacabana

Its splendid curve of a beach is a galaxy unto itself, but it's well worth exploring the rest of this vibrant and varied, somewhat dissonant, but compelling *bairro* (neighborhood) that in so many ways captures the essence of Rio de Janeiro. Despite its dissipated mid-20th-century glamour, unpretentious and unrepentant Copa still seduces.

### Copacabana's Growth

It's hard to imagine, but until the late 19th century, Copacabana's sweeping sands were practically deserted. The only

Late afternoon on Copacabana Beach

signs of civilization were a small 17th-century church built in honor of Nossa Senhora da Copacabana—from which the bairro takes its name—and a few simple fishermen's cottages huddled in the shade of cashew trees. Due to the steep, forested mountains encircling the beach, access was extremely difficult.

At the end of the 19th century, however, Copacabana literally exploded onto the scene. In 1892, an initial tunnel (Túnel Velho) was blasted through the mountains between Botafogo and Copacabana. In 1906, a second, wider tunnel (Túnel Novo) linked Botafogo's bay with Leme (to this day, the "New Tunnel" is still the main access route to Copa). Shortly afterward, the first electric streetcars began running up and down the newly laid oceanfront thoroughfare of Avenida Atlântica.

In the early 1920s, Copa really took off, following the construction of the Copacabana Palace. One of the city's first beachfront hotels, the Copacabana Palace was also by far its most luxurious. Period photos reveal a magnificent edifice set amid an untamed landscape of sand and mountains. Such splendid seclusion, however, would prove ephemeral.

The opening of the Copacabana Palace was the catalyst

for a major revolution in Rio. Suddenly, healthy beach living—with exposure to sun and sea breezes—became all the rage. The fishermen's bungalows lining the beach gave way to swanky summer homes, which in turn were replaced by elegant, ultra-modern apartment buildings. This translated into the streamlined curves of art deco in the 1930s and '40s, followed by the pared-down lines of modernism in the 1950s and early '60s. To this day, Rio boasts the greatest number of art deco buildings of any city in the Southern Hemisphere, a large number of which are preserved in Copacabana.

Mid-20th-century Copa was a magnet for hedonism loving jet-setters from around the world. Yet, as the century wore on, the neighborhood's glamour began to pale and decadence set in. Gargantuan chain hotels increasingly elbowed out many of the deco palaces on Avenida Atlântica. Meanwhile, along the busy, commercial thoroughfare of Avenida Nossa Senhora de Copacabana, blocks of concrete high-rises packed residents into closet-size apartments. Occupied by poor migrants and workers, the hills of Cantagalo, Cabritos, São João, and Babilônia gradually grew into some of Rio's most notorious favelas.

Happily, after years of its reputation being tarnished by street crime, beachfront prostitution, and general neglect, today Copa is cleaner and safer, but still as textured and eclectic as ever. Its former beauty may be chipped and worn, but it hasn't lost any of its vitality.

## Leme

Emerging from the Túnel Novo, Avenida Princesa Isabel divides Copacabana from the tranquil

**Cobacabana**
🅐 149 D2–D3

**Leme**
🅐 149 F3

---

## Museu da Imagem e do Som

Avenida Atlântica will welcome in late 2013 the Museu da Imagem e do Som (Museum of Image and Sound) at No. 3423. The contemporary building—inspired by Copa's sidewalk of alternating black and white waves—will feature three floors devoted to images and music created in, and about, Rio, as well as a movie theater, concert hall, café, restaurant, and rooftop terrace (which will screen films en plein air).

Most funding for this museum comes from the Roberto Marinho Foundation. Founder of the Globo media empire, Marinho (1904–2003) was one of Latin America's richest and most powerful men. To get a sense of Globo's pop cultural clout, visit the kiosks across the street where all sorts of Globo paraphernalia is sold.

---

and largely residential beachside neighborhood of Leme. Leme's short, palm-lined stretch of beach is a favorite of local families due to the fact that its waters are warmer (and sometimes cleaner) than those of Copacabana. At the end of the beach, beneath the gigantic looming rock known as Pedra do Leme, high waves lure adventurous surfers.

From the sprinkling of kiosk bars hugging the base of **Pedra do Leme,** one has a terrific view of Copacabana Beach's majestic sweep in its entirety. A short trail, (continued on p. 154)

# Rio's Beach Culture

**Copacabana, Ipanema, and Leblon are sun-drenched testaments to an indisputable Rio flair for living it up and chilling out. Not just for show, these beaches are an integral part of Carioca lifestyle and character, contributing to a population that is extroverted, outdoorsy, and fiercely proud of their tan lines.**

Sand sculpting has become a career for entrepreneurial local Cariocas.

Far more than magnificent open-air tanning salons, the Zona Sol beaches are microcosms in which a vast amount of living goes on. From sunrise Pilates classes for seniors and early morning *Vogue* swimsuit shoots to early afternoon teenage volleyball practices and midnight prowling by prostitutes in search of randy foreigners, there is always something happening (particularly on Copacabana's beach, where the sands are illuminated all night long). On Sundays and holidays, things get especially busy (and crowded) with the partial closing to cars of the beachfront avenues of Atlântica, Vieira Souto, and Delfim Moreira.

Endless activities aside, many people are content to rent a beach chair (residents bring their own) or take a seat at one of the many sidewalk kiosk bars. While some are passionately loyal to the traditional, family-owned *quiosques,* which serve simple grub and cans of beer at plastic tables and chairs, others gravitate to the more recent, modern structures, many of which boast more sophisticated (and expensive) offerings, along with amenities such as bathrooms, showers, and diaper stations.

The Zona Sul beaches are as fascinatingly varied as off-sand society. Over time, different patches of sand have been appropriated by different "tribes." Territorial reference points

## Beach Behavior

Keep these customs and codes in mind to blend in and stay safe on Rio's beaches:

• Invest in Carioca beachwear. This means a *biquini* for women (forget about a one-piece suit, or going topless, which is illegal) and *sunga* (trunks) for men (Speedos are for competitive swimmers, while surf shorts are for surfing or wearing *over* your sunga). For feet, only flip-flops (preferably Havaianas) will do.

• Nobody takes a towel to the beach. Instead, purchase a lightweight, colorful *canga* from a beach vendor, which can also double as a sarong.

• Leave valuables at the hotel. Take only enough money for renting chairs and buying food and drink. Opt for a beach bag with a secure closure. If you take a dip, ask a distinguished-looking neighbor, or the *barraca* owner, to keep an eye out.

• Don't swim if a red flag is flying, and enter the water only where locals are bathing.

• Stay out of the noonday sun and slather on the sunscreen. A sunburn can result in excruciating pain and possible skin cancer. Worse: It will brand you as a clueless gringo.

---

are the 12 lifeguard *postos* (posts) stretching from the beginning of Leme (Posto 1) to the end of Leblon (Posto 12). Visible due to their height and clearly indicated numbers, these postos function as social as well as geographical markers. Posto 1, for example, attracts seniors and families; Posto 4 is a mecca for *futebol*-loving jocks; and Posto 10 (in front of Rio's posh country club) is where well-bred millionaires hang out.

Reigning over the sands are a host of *barracas* (rustic beach bars), whose employees rent beach chairs and umbrellas to loyal customers and keep them supplied with chilled beers, caipirinhas, and *água de coco* (coconut water). Picking up any slack are legions of *ambulantes*, itinerant vendors who hawk everything from henna tattoos and transistor radios to *comidinhas* (little meals; see sidebar p. 161).

Sunset soccer on Ipanema Beach

**Forte Duque de Caxias (Forte do Leme)**

🏛 149 F3

✉ Praça Almirante Júlio de Noronha

☎ 21/3223-5076

🕐 Closed Mon.

💲 $

🚇 Metrô: Cardeal Arcoverde

the **Caminho dos Pescadores**—named after the *pescadores* (fishermen), professional and amateur, who come here to cast off—leads partway around the base of the hill.

### Forte Duque de Caxias

At the summit of Pedra do Leme sits the Forte Duque de Caxias,

## EXPERIENCE:
## Reveling in Réveillon

Copacabana Beach is the stage of one of the biggest and best **New Year's Eve** (Réveillon) blowouts on Earth. As dusk falls, millions of people descend upon the beach clad in white, symbolizing peace and new beginnings. White is also the color of Iemenjá, the popular Afro-Brazilian *orixá* (deity) who is known as the "queen of the seas." To ensure a happy year, at the stroke of midnight, many Cariocas wade into the Atlantic and toss perfume, champagne, and flowers into the waves as offerings to Iemanjá. White gladioli are the most popular, but those hoping for riches opt for yellow, while the lovelorn invest in red.

Midnight also heralds a spectacular **fireworks display** followed by **live music performances** held at stages erected along the beach. Then it's dancing and drinking until dawn, at which point revelers rinse off the night's excesses with a dip in the sea.

**Morro da Babilônia**

🏛 149 F3

also known as the Forte do Leme. Built in 1779 (but most recently renovated in the 1920s), this fort—and the Morro do Leme, a designated nature reserve—is protected by the Brazilian Army. To reach the top via a winding trail, you must pass through the military complex—and the many young, muscled recruits going about their

business—before beginning the steep, 25-minute ascent through tropical foliage. Along the route, brilliantly hued butterflies and chattering monkeys are frequent companions. Constructed like a bunker, with thick walls of stone, the fort's cool subterranean passages shelter a control center and munitions storehouse. From the vast rooftop—sprinkled with Krupp cannon—there are terrific views, particularly of Copacabana and Pão de Açúcar, whose lush backside is practically in one's face. Bring a bottle of water to quench your thirst, since the fort's fountain and snack bar are not always in service.

### Morro da Babilônia

Also visible from Morro do Leme is the adjacent hilltop of Morro da Babilônia, occupied by two of Rio's oldest favelas, Babilônia and Chapéu Mangueira. In 1959, Morro da Babilônia earned international renown when it served as the backdrop for a Carioca shot-on-location retelling of the myth of Orpheus in Marcel Camus's celebrated film *Black Orpheus*. In more recent times, even when the favelas were considered dangerous due to drug trafficking, the *feijoadas* served by residents enticed a bohemian crew of musicians, artists, and intellectuals.

Since 2009, both communities have received UPP forces, making security far less of an issue for the intrepid gringos who often venture up the hill to join the regular stream of residents, cab drivers, and cops who swear by the celebrated cooking at **Bar do David** *(Ladeira Ary Barroso 66, tel 21/7808-2200, closed Mon.),* a simple bar overlooking a square, accessible via the steep Ladeira Ary Barroso from Rua General Ribeiro da Costa, in Leme. The charismatic owner, David, is a former fisherman and serious *sambista*. Aside from sublime *petiscos* such as *croquetes de frutas do mar* (seafood croquettes), the Saturday seafood feijoada (made with white, instead of dark, beans), accompanied by live samba, attracts a loyal following.

## Forte de Copacabana

The tip of Copacabana Beach closest to Ipanema is guarded by the Forte de Copacabana. Newer than it appears, this low-slung, whitewashed fortress was built in 1914 on the site of the Igreja de Nossa Senhora de Copacabana, a church that sheltered the image of the neighborhood's patron saint. Today, much of the fort is occupied by the **Museu Histórico do Exército,** where a permanent exhibition provides some mildly interesting insights

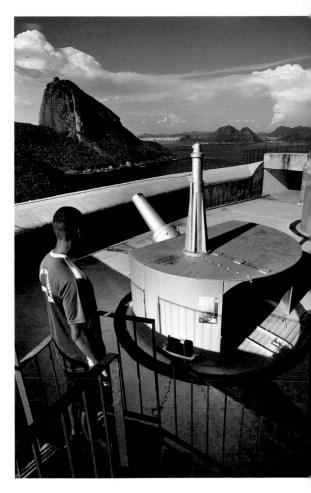

Krupp cannon on the roof of Forte Duque de Caxias

into the workings of a military fortress. More worth the entrance fee are the mesmerizing views of Copacabana from the fort's rooftop and the seaside outpost of Confeitaria Colombo, where you can easily while away an hour beneath some shady almond trees.

## Praia de Copacabana

One of the most instantly recognizable and splendid

**Forte de Copacabana**

🅰 149 D1

✉ Av. Atlântica, Posto 6

☎ 21/2521-1032

🕐 Closed Mon.

 $

🚇 Metrô: Ipanema/ General Osório or Cantagalo

**www.fortede copacabana.com**

**Praia de Copacabana**

A  149 D1–E3

**Marius Degustare**

✉  Av. Atlântica 290

☎  21/2104-9000

urban beaches on the planet, Copacabana's sweeping arc of white sand is one of Rio's biggest tourist attractions. Aside from Cariocas and tourists soaking up the sun in rented beach chairs, an astounding number of activities take place on the beach—from early morning yoga classes and private Pilates training sessions

## Beco das Garrafas

Although the bossa nova is associated with Ipanema, it actually all started in Copa, in a tiny alley off Rua Duvivier: Beco das Garrafas. Here, in the late 1950s, an avant-garde group of composers, musicians, and singers gathered to play the pioneering music in venues such as Bottles Bar and the Don Juan Night Club. Known as *fumaceiros* due to their *fumaça* (smoke)-filled interiors, these clubs were so cramped that much of the action took place outside. The merry-making (and mayhem) incited the wrath of sleepless neighbors, who regularly hurled *garrafas* (bottles) down at the offenders—hence the alley's name. While today none of the clubs (or risks) remain, it's worth visiting **Bossa Nova e Companhia** (*Rua Duvivier 37, tel 21/2295-8096, www.bossanovaecompanhia.com.br*), a treasure trove of books, recordings (CDs and LPs), and souvenirs that pay homage to this famous era.

to all-day and all-night games of *futebol*, *volei* (volleyball), and even *futevolei* (a Brazilian version of volleyball in which players can lob the ball over the net using every body part under the sun except their hands). The beach is also the stage for sporting events (during the 2016 Olympics, it will host the beach volleyball and triathlon competitions), major

**INSIDER TIP:**

For an unforgettable dining experience, check out Marius Degustare at the northern end of Copacabana's beach. The decor is over the top (don't miss the restroom!) and the seafood spectacular.

—BRET WHITNEY
*National Geographic grantee*

concerts, and events such as free film screenings.

Separating the sand from Avenida Atlântica is the iconic **black-and-white mosaic *calçadão*** (promenade), designed by Roberto Burle Marx in the 1970s. Resembling a psyche-delic sea of white (limestone) and black (basalt) waves, this boardwalk constitutes the biggest public mosaic in the world (the op art effect is particularly trippy when viewed from above). Aside from walking and jogging along the calçadão, Cariocas are fond of hanging out at the many *quiosque* (kiosk) bars that line the beach.

If you plan to swim or body-board at Copa's beach, keep in mind that the currents here are strong and potentially dangerous. Due to the open sea, the quality of the water is usually good; however, following intense rains, washed-up debris and runoff can be a problem.

## Copacabana Palace

Copacabana Beach was virtually deserted when wealthy industrialist Otávio Guinle hired French architect Joseph Gire to design a grand hotel modeled after the Negresco in Nice and the Carlton in Cannes. The Copacabana Palace first opened its doors in 1923, and international fame arrived a decade later when a duo of hoofers named Fred Astaire and Ginger Rogers danced on the hotel's terrace in the 1933 film *Flying Down to Rio* (in reality, the couple performed against a backdrop of filmed-on-location footage).

The glossy Hollywood musical not only catapulted Astaire and Rogers to stardom but also put the Copacabana Palace—and Rio de Janeiro—on the map as a romantic and glamorous destination. Over subsequent decades, moguls and movie stars, presidents and princesses, have checked in and out of this elegant hotel (Orson Welles famously tossed an entire sofa out of his window—and into the pool—after a heated dispute with actress Dolores Del Rio).

The easiest way to inspect the interior (aside from being a guest) is by eating at one of the hotel's two restaurants, the refined **Cipriani,** which serves northern Italian cuisine, and the more contemporary poolside **Pérgula,** which serves drinks, afternoon tea, and a mean Sunday brunch. Otherwise, call ahead to reserve a guided tour. ■

**Copacabana Palace**

🅰 149 E3
✉ Av. Atlântica 1702
☎ 21/2545-8790
🚇 Metrô: Cardeal Arcoverde

**www.copacabana palace.com.br**

The Copacabana Palace hotel has been a favorite among the rich and famous since the 1930s.

# A Walk Along Copacabana

Strolling along Copacabana's black-and-white *calçadão* (promenade) should be done in leisurely fashion, with plenty of sunscreen and some small change available to purchase a restorative *água de coco* (coconut water) or icy beer (yes, you can walk and drink at the same time). Early morning and late afternoon are ideal times.

Copacabana's famous mosaic *calçadão* has become a part of everyday Carioca life.

Start at the tip of Avenida Atlântica, in front of the **Forte de Copacabana ❶**. Almost immediately, near the lifeguard station Posto 6, is a patch of sand littered with brightly painted boats, shaded by almond trees and featuring a small fish market. Since 1923, members of this traditional **Colônia de Pescadores ❷** (Fishermen's Colony) have been setting out at the crack of dawn and hauling in their catch at around 9 a.m. To earn extra income, some make and repair volleyball nets. In the morning, you'll see them untangling nets and carrying glittery fish to the tiled market stalls to be snapped up by locals.

A few steps away, seated upon a bench overlooking the beach, a **statue of poet Carlos Drummond de Andrade** (1902–1987) poses alongside numerous tourists who drape

**NOT TO BE MISSED:**

**Colônia de Pescadores • Copacabana Palace • Pedra do Leme**

their arms around his stooped bronze shoulders. One of Copa's most illustrious residents, the renowned 20th-century modernist poet often spent afternoons at this spot, gazing out to sea in search of inspiration.

## Art Deco Gems

Across the street, at Avenida Atlântica 3940, **Edifício Ypiranga ❸** (1935) is one of the oldest and most aerodynamic of Copa's glamorous art deco buildings. Indeed, its voluptuous curves earned it the nickname "Mae West." Prior to his death in 2012, the building housed the studio and offices of internationally acclaimed architect Oscar Niemeyer.

At Avenida Atlântica 3170, the **Edifício Embaixador** ❹ (1935) is another fine deco building. Its exterior was inspired by the transatlantic cruise ships of the time.

Continue strolling down Avenida Atlântica until you reach No. 1880. Here it's possible to peek through the massive front doors of the **Edifício Labourdette** ❺ (1937) to confirm the opulence of its marble foyer. Nearby, at **No. 1782,** the complex of four luxury residential buildings (the Chopin, Prelúdio, Balada, and Barcarola) was considered revolutionary for the manner in which it appropriated the "crate-like" facades normally reserved for 1950s office buildings. These huge apartments are also famed for the lavish *festas* thrown by residents, particularly for Réveillon (see sidebar p. 154). Enormous windows overlook the legendary

**Copacabana Palace** ❻ (see p. 157), as well as Copa's gayest beach kiosk, the **Rainbow,** known for its Sunday night drag shows.

Two blocks farther along, you'll come to **Praça do Lido,** a small square frequented by seniors and toddlers. On weekends, it hosts a lively outdoor market. Many of the surrounding buildings are deco gems, including **Edifício Ribeiro Moreira** ❼ *(Rua Ronald de Carvalho 21).* When completed in 1928, it was the tallest residential building in town and was referred to as "Rio's Empire State Building."

## Toward Leme

Soon after Posto 2, Avenida Princesa Isabel marks the beginning of Leme Beach. The sight of **Pedra do Leme** ❽ (see pp. 151, 154) looming closer and closer is hypnotic. At its base, stop for a cold drink—and a plate of fried fish—at a kiosk. Then relax and contemplate the magnificent length of Copacabana that you've just navigated.

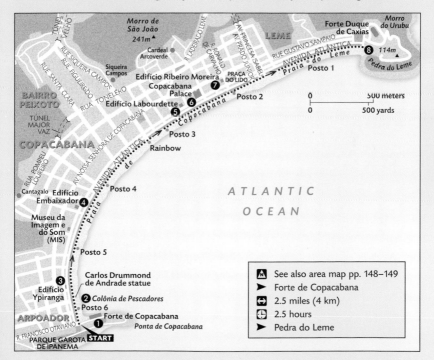

See also area map pp. 148–149
► Forte de Copacabana
↔ 2.5 miles (4 km)
⊕ 2.5 hours
► Pedra do Leme

# Ipanema

Apart from the natural allure of its famous beach, Ipanema packs a disarming quantity of laid-back charm into its tree-shaded avenues and side streets. Although it's easily Rio's most fashionable *bairro* (neighborhood), stylishness is rarely done with such appealing and understated languor.

Crowds gather daily at Pedra do Arpoador to watch the sun set, and sometimes rise.

**Ipanema**
🅰 148 B1

**Praia de Ipanema**
🅰 148 B1–C1

It's ironic to discover that, in Tupi-Guarani, Ipanema means "bad waters." Although the reference is believed to allude to strong ocean currents, it's difficult to succumb to any negative thoughts whatsoever when confronted with the cobalt waters and white sands of Ipanema's glorious beach.

The only Brazilian beach that comes close to rivaling Ipanema's in terms of pure iconicity is that of Copacabana. Indeed, for decades Copa's magnetism helped preserve Ipanema's seclusion. In the 1960s, however, artists, musicians,

hippies, and intellectuals began converging upon its sands, not to mention its burgeoning restaurants and bars. Set to a lulling bossa nova sound track, it wasn't long before its fame as Rio's coolest yet most cosmopolitan bairro had been cemented.

## Praia de Ipanema

It's not surprising that Ipanema Beach is the source of so many myths and so much music. Fringed by palm trees, framed by the gleaming hotels and residences that line Avenida Vieira Souto, and bookended by Pedra do Arpoador and Morro Dois Irmãos, it's quite an arresting sight.

At Ipanema's eastern extremity (closest to Copacabana) is **Praia do Arpoador,** a narrow 500-yard (457 m) strip of sand that is a mecca for surfers. To see them in action, join the fishermen, lovers, favela kids, and other habitués who gather along the rocky promontory of **Pedra do Arpoador** (which separates Ipanema from Copacabana) to admire the sweeping views and ritually applaud the sunrise and sunset (the latter in summer, when the sun sets over the ocean). *Arpoador* is Portuguese for

**INSIDER TIP:**

## Sunrise is the best time to take a walk along Ipanema Beach.

—JORGE DIAZ
*Professor of architecture,
Universidad Autônoma del Estado
de Morelos*

"harpoon," and the *pedra* (rock) proved an ideal spot from which to spear the many whales that populated these waters prior to the late 1800s.

Like many of Rio's beaches, Ipanema is punctuated by lifeguard *postos* (posts), around which very different clans traditionally congregate. After Posto 7 at Arpoador's extremity, Posto 8 lures parents with small children and their nannies. The area to the left of Posto 9, at the foot of Rua Farme de Amoedo, is a magnet for gays, lesbians, and *simpatisantes* (sympathizers), while

the portion to the right draws an alternative crowd of students, artists, and neo-hippies that gather round the Coqueirão ("big coconut palm"—actually the tallest on Ipanema). The beach also has its share of kiosks serving snacks and drinks and another mosaic *calçadão* (promenade) designed by Roberto Burle Marx. While Ipanema gets packed during the day—on summer weekends, one must often squint to catch sight of any exposed sand—at night all the action moves inland.

## Rua Visconde de Pirajá

Parallel to Avenida Vieira Souto and two blocks inland, Rua Visconde de Pirajá is Ipanema's main commercial thoroughfare. Aside from trees, it's lined with banks, bookstores, juice bars, chic boutiques, and innocuous-seeming *galerias,* micro-malls sheltering hundreds of other chic boutiques.

**Rua Visconde de Pirajá**
🖼 148 B1–C1

### Beach Bites

Inseparable from the Zona Sul beach experience are several edible offerings made available by roving vendors. In existence since the 1950s, Globo *biscoitos de polvilho* are crunchy, light-as-air biscuits made of manioc flour that melt in your mouth. Equally beloved are Mustafá's *esfihas*—delicious meat- and cheese-stuffed pastries of Middle Eastern origin, sold by a crew dressed up as sheiks. *Picolés* (popsicles) are particularly popular in the summer; on weekends, Nuvem sells fruity flavors such as açai and *maracujá* (passion fruit). Wash these delicacies down with *cha-maté,* a chilled version of the traditional gaucho beverage made from the *erva-maté* plant.

**Praça General Osório**

🅰 148 C1

🚇 Metrô: Ipanema/ General Osório

**Complexo Rubem Braga**

🅰 148 C1

🚇 Metrô: Ipanema/ General Osório

At the beginning of Rua Visconde de Pirajá lies **Praça General Osório** (also the site of the southernmost Metrô station, Ipanema/General Osório). At the square's center is a pyramidal fountain guarded by a quartet of *saracuras* (wood rails) sculpted by Mestre Valentim in 1795. On Sundays ever since the 1960s, the square has hosted the Feira Hippie, where vendors (some of them, in fact, aged hippies) hawk a colorful but somewhat ragtag collection of handicrafts, souvenirs, and flea market flotsam that lures tourists (and pickpockets).

## Complexo Rubem Braga

One block behind Praça General Osório, just behind the entrance to the Ipanema/General Osório Metrô station, rises the **Morro do Cantagalo.** Much of the hilltop is covered with homes belonging to residents of the

Cantagalo and Pavão/Pavãozinho communities, whose combined population numbers some 17,000 people. For years, these favelas were controlled by gangs and drug traffickers prior to the installation of a Police Pacification Unit in late 2009. Several months later, the Complexo Rubem Braga was inaugurated.

Comprising two towers, each with a pair of elevators capable of whisking residents to and from their precarious hilltop homes to the entrance of Ipanema/General Osório Metrô station, the complex represented a breakthrough as symbolic as it was logistical. Not only did it mean that favela residents would no longer have to climb hundreds of steep and precariously laid stairs to their homes but it also signified forging a link between the *morro* (hilltop) and the *asfalto* (asphalt, i.e., the city proper).

A secondary consequence was

Ipanema is squeezed between the Atlantic and the Lagoa Rodrigo de Freitas, a saltwater lagoon.

## The Girl From Ipanema

One sunny afternoon in 1962, musicians Vinícius de Moraes and Tom Jobim were sitting in a favorite sidewalk *boteco*, Bar Veloso, when along walked a 17-year-old *garota* (girl). She swayed so much "like a samba" that it inspired the famous duo to reach for the nearest napkin and immediately start transcribing the lyrics to what would become one of the greatest bossa nova classics, and the second most recorded song in the world (after the Beatles' "Yesterday")— "A Garota da Ipanema." Located on Rua Vinícius de Moraes 49A, the bar—now called Garota de Ipanema—still exists, even though more tourists than locals fill its tables. As for the girl—Helô Pinheiro— she is nearing 70 and lives in São Paulo, where she works as a television host.

Those nostalgic for bossa will find it alive and well at the **Vinícius Show Bar** *(Rua Vinícius de Moraes 39, tel 21/2287-1497, www.viniciusbar.com.br)*, where daily live performances of classic bossa nova compositions are given by noted musical artists. Nearby, **Toca de Vinícius** *(Rua Vinícius de Moraes 129, tel 21/2247-5227)* is bossa nova central, featuring a wealth of books, music, and souvenirs dedicated to the genre as well as a "walk of fame." On Sundays, live performances sometimes take place.

that the Complexo has become a tourist attraction. Apart from the elevators' functionality, the two towers—measuring 79 feet (24 m) and 210 feet (64 m) (the equivalent of a 29-story building)—are visually arresting due to their bold colors and strong graphic elements. However, the real draw is riding up the first elevator, then walking up a flight of stairs to the **Mirante da Paz,** a glassed-in lookout whose 360-degree panoramic views of the morro, Lagoa Rodrigo de Freitas, and Ipanema, Leblon, and Copacabana framed by mountains are mesmerizing.

## Praça Nossa Senhora da Paz

One block west of Rua Vinícius de Moraes, along Rua Visconde de Pirajá, Praça Nossa Senhora da Paz is a lovely tree-shaded square where Ipanema's elderly and very young residents (usually accompanied by nannies) congregate to while away an hour or two. On Friday mornings, the square is home to a colorful outdoor market, with numerous stands hawking artfully arrayed fruits, vegetables, fish, and flowers.

Near the square are some of Ipanema's most chic boutiques, including **H. Stern** *(Rua Visconde de Pirajá 490, tel 21/2274-3447),* Brazil's premier jeweler. Specialists in the country's vast array of precious and semiprecious stones, their flagship store includes a small gem museum whose collection of 1,200 tourmalines is worth a quick gape. Also of note are **Galeria Forum Ipanema** *(Rua Visconde de Pirajá 351)* and **Galeria Ipanema 2000** *(Rua Visconde de Pirajá 547);* two of the neighborhood's swankiest micro-malls, they contain some of Rio's most fashionable beachwear labels, including **Blue Man, Lenny,** and **Salinas,** famed for their stylish *biquinis* and *sungas.* ■

**Praça Nossa Senhora da Paz**

- ⚑ 148 C1
- Ⓜ Metrô: Ipanema/ General Osório

**NOTE:** Much of the square is closed while a new Metrô station is being built. It is scheduled to reopen at the end of 2015 or in early 2016.

# Leblon

More sedate than neighboring Ipanema, swank Leblon is one of Rio's most coveted residential *bairros* (neighborhoods), with an appealing, old-fashioned neighborhood vibe and scores of cafés, bars, and restaurants that invite one to linger and lounge.

**Leblon**

148 A1

Fittingly for a bairro renowned for its sophistication and elegance, Leblon owes its French name to one Charles Le Blond, among the area's earliest landowners. In 1878, Le Blond sold his estate to José de Seixas Magalhães, a Portuguese merchant with abolitionist tendencies who allowed runaway slaves to take refuge on his land.

Up until the early 20th century, Leblon was still largely rural, developing much more gradually than neighboring Ipanema. Even today, its main commercial street, Avenida Ataulfo de Paiva (a continuation of Ipanema's Rua Visconde de Pirajá), and tree-lined side streets retain the feel of a village (albeit an upscale one), where bakeries, cafés, delis, and *botecos* (bars) are interspersed between attractive houses and low-slung apartment buildings. Meanwhile, like Ipanema, Leblon is also a shopper's mecca; although it has fewer boutiques and *galerias* (micro-malls), it's home to the Zona Sul's most upscale mall, **Shopping Leblon** (*Av. Afrânio de Melo Franco 290, www.shoppingleblon.com.br*).

## Praia do Leblon

Leblon's beach picks up where Ipanema's ends, at the point where the **Jardim de Alah Canal** drains into the sea (between lifeguard stations 10 and 11). It continues for 1.2 miles (2 km) before ending at the base of Morro Dois Irmãos (Posto 12). Less hip and happening than Ipanema, Leblon tends to be less crowded (especially during the week).

Crowds throng Leblon Beach in the summertime.

**Praia do Leblon**
⚿ 148 A1–B1

**Mirante do Leblon**
⚿ 148 A1

**INSIDER TIP:**

Foodies will be well served by strolling the 20-minute length of Leblon's Rua Dias Ferreira, the gastronomic strip where some of the city's best Brazilian, Japanese, Thai, and Italian restaurants can be found.

—DOUG GRAY
*National Geographic contributor*

a pair of primitive *irmãos* (brothers). Encircling the *morro* is **Avenida Niemeyer,** a spectacularly scenic (and traffic-infested) coastal road that leads from the end of Leblon to São Conrado and links the Zona Sul to the Zona Oeste. As astonishing as the view is the thought that between 1933 and 1954, this 7-mile (11 km) route was where Brazil's Formula 1 races played out (before they were moved to São Paulo's less harrowing Interlagos track).

While the stretch closer to Ipanema is better for bathing—the waters tend to be cleaner, except for the area immediately near the Jardim de Alah Canal—the area between Postos 11 and 12 is coveted by families, especially those with babies and young children. In fact, the patch in front of Rua General Venâncio Flores is popularly known as Baixo Bebê because its soft sands—raked, swept, and cleaned daily—offer everything a beachgoing baby (not to mention parents and nannies) could desire: from changing tables, diapers, and baby wipes to a vast collection of toys, slides, castles, and wagons. The latter can be pulled along the mosaic promenade, where numerous kiosks sell *água de coco* (coconut water) to the toned and tanned adult bodies walking, running, and cycling by.

## Morro Dois Irmãos

Instantly recognizable, the fraternal granite peaks of Morro Dois Irmãos really do conjure up

### Nature's Most Nutritious Nut

Although Brazil is the world's fourth largest producer of coconuts, there's a good reason why the country needs to import coconuts to keep up with the voracious popular demand for coconut meat, milk, and, especially, water. Sold natural and *gelada* (chilled), *água de coco* (coconut water) is not just refreshing but a vitamin-, mineral-, and antioxidant-packed health drink that's a natural isotonic. Teeming with electrolytes, it's the best rehydrating beverage in existence; for this reason, água de coco was injected into the veins of wounded and fatigued soldiers during both World Wars. It's also a sure-fire remedy for *ressacas* (hangovers).

At the beginning of Avenida Niemeyer, easily reached by foot, the **Mirante do Leblon** is a favorite lookout (and make-out) point that offers stunning views out over the beaches of Leblon and Ipanema. A couple of simple kiosks sell beer and água de coco, perfect accompaniments to watching the sunset.

### Parque do Penhasco Dois Irmãos

🅜 148 A1
✉ Rua Aperana
☎ 21/8909-2056
🕐 Closed Mon.
🚌 Bus: 382, 522, 557

### Vidigal

🅜 148 A1
🚌 Metrô Na Superfície: Vidigal. Bus: 382, 522, 557

A steep walk up Rua Aperana (take Avenida Visconde de Albuquerque to the end and then follow Rua Gabriel Mufarrej) leads to the entrance of **Parque do Penhasco Dois Irmãos,** a municipal park covering the lower flanks of Morro Dois Irmãos. Apart from playgrounds and soccer fields, nature trails lead to four lookout points. On weekends, the park is popular with families, while during the week it sometimes attracts New Age followers who like to meditate to the accompaniment of the crashing ocean waves.

## Vidigal

Rising above Leblon and covering the lower slopes of Morro Dois Irmãos is the favela of Vidigal. Prior to the arrival of a Police Pacification Unit in January 2012, Vidigal had a reputation for being both exceptionally dangerous and extremely beautiful. Happily, in recent times, only the latter source of notoriety still rings true—indeed, due to the community's newfound safety, Cariocas and tourists alike are now discovering what residents have long known: Vidigal's views are among the most stunning in Rio.

As a result, this community of 9,000 is quickly becoming somewhat of a hot spot, especially for foreigners who are not only shacking up at the mushrooming number of simple *pousadas* but

## EXPERIENCE: All Juiced Up

You'll find *bares de suco* (juice bars) all over Rio, but nowhere else are they as numerous or as succulently enticing as in the Zona Sul, where gleaming counters backed by a cornucopia of tropical fruits attract a steady stream of lithe, limber, health-conscious Cariocas. They drop by pre-beach or post-gym, sometimes 24/7, for everything from a freshly squeezed *suco de laranja* (orange juice) to a power-packed Amazonian açaí topped with granola, bananas, powdered milk, and honey.

You'll encounter fruits you've heard of—*goiaba* (guava), *mamão* (papaya), *abacate* (avocado, which Brazilians always eat sweet)—as well as a profusion of exotica from the Amazon *(cupuaçu, bacuri, murici)* and Brazil's Northeast *(cajá, siriguela, umbu)*. All of these and more can be imbibed solo (with filtered water), thickened with milk *(com leite)* into a *vitamina*, or mixed with other

fruits. They can also be made into fruity potions guaranteed to cure whatever ails you. *Energéticos*, for example, use guaraná powder and magnesium-rich chlorophyll to pump up your adrenaline levels, while *anti-estresses* rely on the pacifying powers of *maracujá* (passion fruit). If you don't want sugar and ice, request "*um suco sem açúcar e sem gelo.*"

In addition to juices, *bares de suco* offer a variety of healthy fare that can easily serve as a meal. Particularly good are the *sanduíches naturais*, hearty sandwiches made with multigrain bread and a wealth of nutritious fillings.

Although all Cariocas have their favorite bar de suco, two beloved juicy institutions in Leblon routinely rack up all the "Best of" awards: **Bibi Sucos** *(Av. Ataulfo de Paiva 591, tel 21/2259-0000)* and **BB Lanches** *(Rua Aristedes Espinola 64, tel 21/2294-1397).* Stop in for a delicious concoction.

The favela of Vidigal sprawls across the lower stretches of Morro Dois Irmãos.

**INSIDER TIP:**

**Lavanda Suissa, a favorite Carioca cologne, is available for a few dollars at most drugstores.**

—PRISCILLA GOSLIN
*Author of* How to Be a Carioca

also investing in real estate with exquisite views of their own.

Among the most talked about Vidigal expats is the Austrian owner of **Casa Alto Vidigal** *(Rua Armando de Almeida 2, tel 21/3322-3034, http://altovidigal .com),* a backpacker's hostel at the upper reaches of the morro that inadvertently became one of the hippest and most happening all-night-long spots in Rio when the owner started inviting DJs from all over Brazil and Europe to host outdoor parties that last until the sun rises over the blue Atlantic Ocean.

To get to Casa Alto Vidigal, take a van or *moto-taxi* to Arvrão ("big tree"—yes, there's only one and everyone knows where it is). From Arvrão, a gateway behind a soccer field opens onto a trail that allows you to ascend Dois Irmãos. The climb is easy at first, then becomes more strenuous during the last 20 minutes (the entire hike should take around 45 minutes)—however the breathtaking views at the (windy) summit are worth all the effort. An ideal time for this hike is the mid to late afternoon. ■

A sparkling lagoon ringed by residential neighborhoods rich in lushly vegetated public spaces, perfect for relaxing

# Around the Lagoa

Alley of Imperial Palms, Jardim Botânico

# Around the Lagoa

No mere lagoon, the Lagoa Rodrigo de Freitas (commonly called simply the Lagoa) is a fabulous plein air gym, relaxing refuge, and hypnotically beautiful spot ringed by some of the city's toniest residential areas and most sculptural mountain peaks. Awash in exuberant greenery—from the Jardim Botânico to the Tijuca Forest—it's the best place to immerse yourself in Rio's lush life.

**Cascatinha do Taunay, one of dozens of waterfalls in Parque Nacional da Tijuca**

Much of the area upon which Rio de Janeiro was constructed was originally swampland, riddled with saltwater lagoons. Over the centuries, many of these were filled in and built on. The largest, however, Lagoa Rodrigo de Freitas, survived and was transformed into a popular playground.

Although bereft of ocean views, the lush, upscale residential neighborhoods of Lagoa,

Jardim Botânico, and Gávea that surround the lagoon are among the most coveted in Rio.

## Lagoa Rodrigo de Freitas

Connected to the Atlantic by the narrow Jardim de Alah Canal that separates Ipanema from Leblon, the Lagoa Rodrigo de Freitas has a circumference of 4.5 miles (7.3 km). Lining its verdant shores is a series of parks sprinkled with piers, sports courts, private athletic clubs, and pathways along which buff Cariocas stay tanned and toned by walking, jogging, and cycling. Less athletically inclined residents enjoy kicking back at the numerous waterfront *quiosques,* whose drinks and culinary offerings range from simple to sophisticated. Contrasting with the luxury high-rises that gaze out over the lagoon is the 1930s residence that houses the Fundação Eva Klabin, one of the foremost private art collections in Brazil. The Lagoa neighborhood lies along the lagoon's northern and eastern edges.

## Jardim Botânico

Straddling the lagoon's western shore, and hemmed in by mountains, the affluent and intensely leafy *bairro* of Jardim Botânico sprang up around and takes its name from Rio's Botanical Garden, which, along with the nearby Parque Lage, is the neighborhood's main draw. Rio's Jardim Botânico is considered one of the most important botanical gardens in the world. It's 356 acres (144 ha) unite native tropical forest and some 10,000 carefully cultivated species in verdant harmony. Botanical treasures aside, the gardens provide a shady oasis in which to while away the hottest hours of the day in the company of brilliantly hued toucans, hummingbirds, and butterflies.

Jardim Botânico embraces patches of the Floresta da Tijuca. The largest urban woodland on the planet, the Tijuca Forest consists of 9,600 jungly acres (3,900 ha), much of which is protected within the boundaries of the Parque Nacional da Tijuca, the most visited national park in Brazil. One can easily spend a few hours—or days—navigating its many walking trails, scaling the heights of Pico da Tijuca, plunging into waterfalls, picnicking in glades, and marveling at the view below from countless lookout points.

## Gávea

Squeezed between Leblon, Jardim Botânico, and the favela of Rocinha, well-to-do Gávea is primarily residential. Its steep slopes are encrusted with mansions, among them the modernist dwelling that houses the must-see Instituto Moreira Salles cultural center and the 19th-century Solar de Santa Marinha, home to the Museu Histórico da Cidade. Hovering above are the twin peaks of Morro Dois Irmãos and the vast rock slab of Pedra da Gávea.

**NOT TO BE MISSED:**

Zip-lining through the foliage of Parque da Catacumba   173

Gliding around the Lagoa in a swan-shaped pedal boat   174

Chilling out in the Jardim Botânico, which is always slightly cooler than the rest of the city   176–177

Sipping a *cafezinho* beneath the arcades of the School of Visual Arts, in Parque Lage   177

A hike in Parque Nacional da Tijuca   180–183

The striking contrast between nurture and nature at the Museu do Açude   183

Creative art installations at the Instituto Moreira Salles   186–187

Fanning out from the lively Praça Santos Dumont, the traditional bars of Baixo (Lower) Gávea are a perennial lure for the area's young blood. Other nearby attractions include Rio's Planetarium and the Joquei Clube, surely one of the most scenic racetracks on Earth. ■

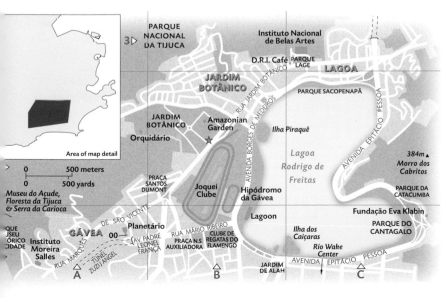

# Lagoa Rodrigo de Freitas

Lagoa Rodrigo de Freitas (commonly just called Lagoa) is proof that Rio's life aquatic transcends life along the Atlantic Ocean. The park-lined shores of this saltwater lagoon offer a limitless number of sporting, leisure, and cultural activities amid an indelible natural setting.

Green spaces and residential neighborhoods ring Lagoa Rodrigo de Freitas, a saltwater lagoon.

**Lagoa Rodrigo de Freitas**

🅰 171 B1–B2 &
C1–C3

Rodrigo de Freitas Carvalho was a Portuguese cavalry officer who, in 1702, married a sugarcane heiress twice his age. Carvalho's wife owned much of the land surrounding the lagoon—and when she left him a young widower, he became proprietor of the lagoon that today bears his name.

A practical way to reach the Lagoa is from Copacabana's Cantagalo Metrô station. From there, it's only a couple of blocks to the main thoroughfare of Avenida Epitácio Pessoa, which parallels the lagoon's eastern shore.

## Fundação Eva Klabin

One of the first houses built here—and one of its sole survivors—is a 1931 two-story Norman-style villa. Eva Klabin (1903–1991), the Brazilian-born daughter of a Lithuanian Jewish founder of Brazil's first paper and cellulose manufacturer, purchased it in 1952. A wealthy woman with a penchant for the finer things in life, Klabin, following her husband's death in 1957, channeled her energies (and considerable fortune) into amassing a fantastic collection of art that spans five centuries and four continents. To house the more than 2,000 paintings, sculptures, furnishings, and decorative objects she acquired, Klabin enlarged and remodeled the house in which she lived and entertained dignitaries, artists, and intellectuals in high style.

Upon her death in 1991, under the auspices of the Eva Klabin Foundation, the house was converted into a living museum. Visitors are guided through treasure-laden rooms that are perfectly conserved—from the golden baroque bed in which Klabin slept (beneath a Baccarat crystal chandelier) to the portraits by Thomas Gainsborough and Sir Joshua Reynolds that gazed down at her as she read her beloved Agatha Christie mysteries in the English Room.

Despite its disparate nature and vast scope, what ties the collection together is Klabin's unique sensibility and her life; she didn't just acquire objects, she lived with them. Apart from the permanent collection and thematic temporary exhibits, the foundation often invites contemporary artists to stage interventions using Klabin's artifacts.

## Parque da Catacumba

A ten-minute walk north along the shores of the Lagoa from the Fundação Eva Klabin brings you to the entrance of the Parque da Catacumba. *Catacumba* is

Portuguese for "catacomb," and it's believed that the Morro da Catacumba was once a burial ground for its original Tamoio inhabitants. For more than half of the 20th century, the hillside sheltered one of Rio's oldest favelas; then, in 1960, the favela's inhabitants were evicted and the *morro* was transformed into a natural park. While the upper reaches were reforested with native Atlantic vegetation, the lower swatches were landscaped as a lush sculpture garden.

## Park Thrills

**Those seeking a shot of adrenaline can take advantage of the Parque do Cantagalo's zip-lining circuits, which are tailored for adventurous adults as well as young children. These and other activities, such as tree canopy tours and rappelling down from the top of the 427-foot-high (130 m) Pedra do Urubu** *(reservations necessary),* **are organized by Lagoa Aventuras** *(tel 21/4105-0079),* **which operates a kiosk at the park's entrance.**

Among the 31 works dispersed amid the thick tropical shrubbery are pieces by noted Brazilian and international artists. A steep but well-marked 20-minute trail climbs up through the forest to a lookout point that offers a spectacular bird's-eye view of the Lagoa, Cristo Redentor, and the entire Zona Sul backed by mountains. ■

**Fundação Eva Klabin**

 171 C1

⊠ Av. Epitácio Pessoa 2480

☎ 21/3202-8550

🕐 Open Tues.–Fri. 2:30 p.m.–4 p.m. (guided tours only)

💲 $$

🚇 Metrô: Cantagalo

**www.evaklabin .org.br**

**Parque da Catacumba**

171 C2

⊠ Av. Epitácio Pessoa 3000

☎ 21/2247-9949

🕐 Closed Mon.

🚌 Bus: 157, 461

# The Lagoa's Life of Leisure

From the crack of dawn until long after dusk, there's always something happening in, on, and around the Lagoa Rodrigo de Freitas.

A paved path circles Lagoa Rodrigo de Freitas, attracting cyclists, skateboarders, runners, and more.

Before becoming one of Rio's favorite recreational havens, the Lagoa Rodrigo de Freitas was quite polluted. In recent times, however, the lagoon—measuring 2 miles (3.2 km) across at its widest point and 1,410 feet (430 m) deep at its nadir—has received a new lease on life. The infamous algae scourges that used to turn the lagoon a radioactive green are currently under control, much to the relief of the 30 species of fish, crabs, and shrimps that inhabit it—and those intent on catching them—not to mention the numerous Cariocas who windsurf, sail, row, and wakeboard its waters.

Located near Rua Garcia D'Ávila in Ipanema, the **Rio Wake Center** *(tel 21/2239-6976)*

offers wakeboarding lessons for everyone from neophytes to those seeking to perfect their 360s, as well as waterskiing courses. A more relaxing method of navigating the lagoon's placid waters is to rent one of the swan-shaped *pedalinhos* (pedal boats) moored near the Parque do Cantagalo, which lies in the shadow of Morro de Cantagalo. An equally Zen pursuit—albeit a landlocked one—is to bring a *canga* and partake in the free Sunday morning yoga classes offered once a month, near the pedal boats, by **Método DeRose.**

**Parque do Cantagalo** is outfitted with fields, courts, and diamonds dedicated to sports ranging from soccer and volleyball to the more imported likes of baseball and hockey. You can also rent a bicycle or quadricycle—a less perspiration-inducing means of touring the entire circumference of the Lagoa than jogging.

Bikes can also be rented at the **Espaço Victor Assis Brasil,** a park until recently called—and still commonly known as—Parque dos Patins. Located along the shores of Jardim Botânico (behind the Joquei Clube), this park has various sports facilities as well as a skate park, a playground, and an amphitheater that often hosts theater and performances for kids.

Nearby, an inspired metamorphosis recently transformed the bleachers and headquarters of the former Lagoa Rowing Club into the brand-new **Lagoon** (Av. Borges de Medeiros 1424).

## INSIDER TIP:

**Rent a bike and follow the road around the Lagoa, especially at the end of the afternoon; there are nice and relaxing views.**

—RAFAEL DUARTE
*Professor of microbiology,*
*Federal University of Rio de Janeiro*

Cruising the lagoon in a swan-shaped *pedalinho* (pedal boat) is a classic Carioca pastime.

Outfitted with a retractable roof and oodles of terraces, this high-end entertainment complex unites a handful of gourmet restaurants and bars, a concert hall, and a six-screen cineplex, all of which invariably boast stunning views.

## Lagoon-side *Quiosques*

While many Carlocas visit Lagoa Rodrigo de Freitas with the intent of sweating up a storm, an equal number do so with the intent of not breaking a sweat at all. Indeed, among the most idyllic places in the city to kick back and relax is any one of the 23 *quiosques* that line the lagoon's shores. Aside from cool cocktails and drinks, each kiosk bar specializes in a different kind of cuisine (from *churrasco* and sushi to Mineiro and Mediterranean), not to mention a different type of music (jazz, rock, bossa nova), sometimes performed live after dark.

Two quiosques in particular stand out. In the vicinity of Espaço Victor Assis Brasil, the immensely popular

**Arab** (tel 21/2540-0747) lures lovers of *choro* and MPB music (see pp. 48 & 53–54) as well as those who appreciate the Lebanese likes of *kibes* and *kaftas* served in a setting festooned with Middle Eastern accents. Even more exotic is **Palaphita Kitch** (tel 21/2227-0837). Located in the Parque do Cantagalo, this quiosque specializing in contemporary Amazonian fare has a decorative scheme best described as Tarzan nouveau, with rustic sofas carved out of wood and lots of jungly foliage. The menu is equally creative, with snacks such as wild boar carpaccio and camembert stuffed with açai chutney paired with drinks concocted from exotic Amazonian fruits.

# Jardim Botânico

Rio's most verdant neighborhood is framed by forested mountains and lush parks, among them its namesake Botanical Garden. Its leafy residential streets shelter some of the city's finest restaurants.

### Jardim Botânico

Whether it's a scaldingly sunny day or a cloudy nonbeach day, whiling away a few hours at Rio's Jardim Botânico offers welcome respite. The Jardim was created

Relaxing poolside at Parque Lage's D.R.I. Café

by João VI in 1808 as a place where he could cultivate his favorite native fruits along with spices from far-flung colonies such as Goa and Mauritius, which took months to arrive by boat. Among the initial plantings he introduced were nutmeg, cinnamon, and avocados—all of which subsequently grew rampantly throughout Brazil. In 1822, his son Pedro I opened the royal gardens to the public. Aside from introducing many new exotic species, he added lagoons, waterfalls, and alleyways along which members of Rio's elite, decked out in top hats and parasols, took languorous strolls.

Today, the Jardim Botânico contains some 10,000 different plant species and has been designated a UNESCO biosphere reserve. Apart from the garden's visual splendor, its heady fragrance of fruit and flower trees combined with the choir of insects, monkeys, and gaudily plumed parrots and toucans—the Jardim is one of the best birding spots in Rio—is a welcome assault on one's senses.

Particularly compelling attractions include the **Amazonian Garden,** the **Sensory Garden,** and the **Orquidário,** a hothouse that shelters more than 600 species of strangely beautiful orchids. Kids will find it difficult to resist the carnivorous plant collection, the lagoon topped with coffee-table-size *Victoria amazonica* water lilies, and the **Jardim dos Beija-Flores,** whose shrubs attract tiny, iridescent hummingbirds.

Near the main entrance, a boutique sells an assortment of eco-gifts (including seeds to start your own tropical garden) and **La Bicyclette Café** proffers delicious French pastries. The nearby **Espaço Tom Jobim,** a cultural center devoted to the Carioca composer for whom the Jardim Botânico was a second backyard, boasts a collection of photos and recordings; its theater often hosts performances of jazz, bossa nova, and MPB (see pp. 53–54) on Sunday afternoons. On weekends, Carioca families crowd the Jardim.

## Parque Lage

Only five minutes from the Jardim Botânico, Parque Lage is sadly overlooked by many tourists. The park was originally occupied by a 16th-century sugarcane plantation, which was carved out of the Atlantic jungle at the foot of Corcovado. In 1840, the site was purchased by a wealthy English nobleman, who hired compatriot landscaper John Tyndale to transform the "savage" forest into a Romantic garden replete with lakes, islands, bridges, and artificial grottoes (one of which is encrusted with 12 small aquariums). Aside from playgrounds and picnic areas, there are numerous serpentine paths that wind their way through the tropical foliage—including an arduous 1.4-mile (2.2 km) trail that leads straight up to the

outstretched arms of the statue of Cristo Redentor, a climb that takes about two hours (for information, ask at the Parque Nacional de Tijuca visitor center in Parque Lage).

**Lage Mansion:** In the 1920s, under the ownership of wealthy industrialist Henrique Lage (1881–1941), Italian architect Mario Vodrel was commissioned

### INSIDER TIP:

A day at the Jardim Botânico is the equivalent of a course in tropical botany. The garden is also a haven for birds, so don't forget to take along your binoculars.

—SCOTT A. MORI
*National Geographic grantee*

to construct the eclectic-style mansion, awash in marble, where Lage subsequently lived with his wife, Gabriela Bezanzoni, a noted Italian opera singer. Today, their palatial abode is occupied by Rio's School of Visual Arts.

Artworks often adorn the Alhambra-esque central patio, where stately arcades frame the **D.R.I. Café** *(tel 21/2226-8125).* Take time out to lounge with a drink or homemade ice cream, or to indulge in Sunday brunch at tables overlooking a turquoise swimming pool whose waters reflect a floating image of the Cristo Redentor. ∎

### Jardim Botânico
- 171 B2
- ✉ Rua Jardim Botânico 1008 & 920
- ☎ 21/3874-1808
- $ $
- 🚇 Metrô Na Superfície: Jardim Botânico. Bus: 161, 162, 570, 584

### Parque Lage
- 171 C3
- ✉ Rua Jardim Botânico 414
- ☎ 21/3257-1800
- 🚇 Metrô Na Superfície: Jardim Botânico. Bus: 161, 162, 570, 584
- www.eavparquelage.rj.gov.br

# A Walk in the Gardens

Strolling languidly through the tree-shaded *aléias* (alleyways) of the Jardim Botânico is perhaps the most relaxing and refreshing walk one can undertake in this sometimes busy, often sweltering city.

Due to the profusion of greenery, the Jardim Botânico is often cooler than other parts of Rio.

## NOT TO BE MISSED:

Alley of Imperial Palms
• Orquidário • Lago Frei Leandro

From the main entrance, turn right and start down Aléia Karl Glasl. You'll pass the **Japanese Garden ❶**, with its bamboo groves, cherry trees, and languid pond full of carp, and the **Rose Garden ❷**, which oddly doesn't feature any roses, before arriving at the **Amazonian Garden ❸**. Next to a typical palm-thatched hut, overlooking a lagoon, a seated statue of an Amazonian fisherman watches over native species, including an impressive *Bombax munguba* Mart. Planted in 1899, its thick trunk boasts a diameter of 66 feet (20 m).

At the end of the alley, take a left on Aléia Frei Leandro. Inside a former violet hot-house, the **Memorial Mestre Valentim ❹** houses works by the eponymous master sculptor, including "Eco" and "Narciso." The first metal sculptures forged in Brazil—in 1783

and 1785—these lyrical renderings of Greek mythological figures were created out of lead. Continue to the **Chafariz Central ❺**. One of the Jardim's most recognizable symbols, the wrought-iron fountain originally stood in the Largo da Lapa. To the right, look for the tree bearing a plaque; it pays homage to composer Tom Jobim (see p. 49).

Turn right on Aléia Barbosa Rodrigues to come face to face with the gardens' signature **Alley of Imperial Palms ❻**. Planted in 1842, the 137 lithe palms, averaging 82 feet (25 m) tall, are all descendants of a single imperial palm planted by João VI himself in 1809 with a seed imported from Mauritius.

Next, turn left onto Aléia Bento Pickel and pass by the ruins of a gunpowder factory, built in 1808. Parallel runs the Rio dos Macacos, a stream that supplies most of the Jardim's irrigation needs. Arriving at Aléia Frei Velloso, you'll see the **Bromelário ❼**. Inside are more than 1,700 species of bromeliads, a strange but beautiful parasitic family of plants. Farther along, at the end of the alley, is the even more impressive **Orquidário ❽**, most of whose splendid orchid specimens are native to Brazil.

Turn onto Aléia Guilherme Guinle and then take a right on Aléia John Wills, which leads to the **Casa dos Pilões ❾**. Most of the explosives used to defend Brazil from invaders during the early 1800s were fabricated in this factory. A small museum interprets the site.

Back on Aléia John Wills, turn right onto

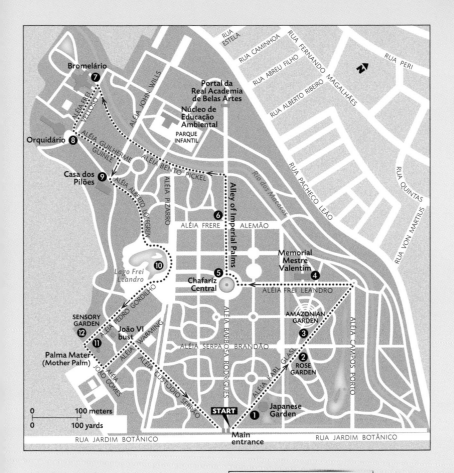

Aléia Alberto Löefgren, which winds its way
to the **Lago Frei Leandro ⑩**. This lake's star
attraction are the gigantic Amazonian *Victoria
amazonica* water lilies, whose glistening pads
can measure up to 7 feet (2 m) in diameter.
Flaunting 100 petals, their flowers bloom in the
afternoon and stay open all night, only to wither
the following morning.

Walk around the lake and turn onto Aléia
Pedro Gordilho. You'll soon arrive at a small
square sheltering a bust of João VI, a rare brazilwood specimen, and an imperial palm. Known
as the **Palma Mater ⑪** (Mother Palm), the
tree that originally stood here (and was replaced
by the present one after being hit by lightning
in 1972) was the progenitor of not only all the

> 🄼 See also area map p. 171
> ► Main entrance (Rua Jardim
>    Botânico 1008)
> ↔ 1.5 miles (2.4 km)
> 🕐 1.5 hours
> ► Main entrance

imperial palms in the Jardim but in Brazil as well.

At the end of Aléia Pedro Gordilho, the
**Sensory Garden ⑫** was designed for the
visually impaired; the fragrances and textures of
these medicinal and edible plants are a feast for
the senses (names are also given in braille).

From Aléia João Gomes, turn left onto Aléia
Warming, then right onto Aléia Custódio
Serrão, which leads back to the park's entrance.

# Parque Nacional da Tijuca

Created in 1961, Parque Nacional da Tijuca (Tijuca National Park) embraces the lush mountains of the Tijuca massif, a vast chunk of gneiss rock that can lay claim to being one of the oldest geologic formations on the planet.

Easily reached by car, Tijuca National Park's Vista Chinesa overlook offers glorious views of Rio.

During colonial times, the original Atlantic rain forest that comprised the Tijuca Forest captivated explorers, naturalists, and artists, who imagined they had stumbled upon an earthly Garden of Eden.

By the mid-19th century, however, the entire ecosystem had almost been destroyed. As a result of Brazil's coffee boom, vast swaths of virgin rain forest were decimated for the planting of the country's newest cash crop. Fortunately, an ecocatastrophe was averted by Pedro II. In a fit of greenness, the enlightened emperor—who often hiked through the forest—ordered

the hills to be reforested with a mixture of native and exotic species. In undertaking this pioneering project, Pedro II succeeded in preserving local flora and fauna and guaranteeing Rio's water supply (the Tijuca Forest guards the sources of most rivers that provided—and continue to furnish—water to the city).

Under the leadership of the Baron of Bom Retiro and Maj. Manoel Gomes Archer, six slaves planted close to 100,000 saplings over the span of 13 years. As a result of their superhuman efforts, by the end of the 19th century, the Tijuca Forest had become the largest reforested urban jungle on

Earth, home to a rich variety of wildlife ranging from anteaters, monkeys, and sloths to birds, butterflies, and reptiles.

**Lay of the Land:** The park is divided into four sectors: Floresta da Tijuca, Serra da Carioca, Pedras da Gávea e Bonita, and Pretos Forros/Covanca. While Pretos Forros/Covanca contains the largest quantity of virgin rain forest, it's relatively difficult to explore. The most visited sector is Serra da Carioca, which possesses the best infrastructure. The more interesting sectors for those intent on walking, hiking, and climbing are Pedras da Gávea e Bonita and Floresta da Tijuca. The latter houses the park's headquarters and main visitor center, where you can buy maps and get guide recommendations and security updates (a second visitor center is located within Parque Lage, in the Serra da Carioca sector).

More than 100 trails, of various lengths and difficulties, weave through the park. In most cases, it's highly recommended that you contract a guide—not only for security reasons but also due to the high incidence of people getting lost in the dense forest (despite the fact that many trails are well marked). An alternative solution is to go with an organized group; many great customized tours are available in English. Contact **Rio Hiking** *(tel 21/2552-9204, www.riohiking .com.br)* and **Jungle Me** *(tel 21/4105-7533, www.jungleme.com.br).*

## Serra da Carioca

The Serra da Carioca famously embraces Corcovado and the statue of Cristo Redentor along with the Dona Marta and Vista Chinesa lookouts. Reached by car, via Estrada Dona Castorina in Jardim Botânico, the **Vista Chinesa** owes its name to a pagoda constructed out of cement (imitating bamboo) in 1903. The unlikely structure honors the early Chinese immigrants who built roads through the forest in the early 1800s (and supposedly introduced tea cultivation to Brazil). Higher up

**Parque Nacional da Tijuca**

🅐 171 B3

**Floresta da Tijuca Sector**

✉ Main visitor center: Praça Afonso Viseu (Estrada da Cascatinha 850)

☎ 21/2492-2252

🚌 Bus: 301, 308, 309, 333, 345

**Serra da Carioca Sector**

✉ Visitor center: Parque Lage (Rua Jardim Botânico 414)

☎ 21/2492-2253

🚌 Metrô Na Superfície: Jardim Botânico. Bus: 161, 162, 570, 584

---

## The "One Dollar Man"

One of the founders of Rio's Museu de Arte Moderna (MAM), wealthy Carioca industrialist Raymundo Ottoni de Castro Maya (1894–1968) boasted one of the finest private art collections in Brazil—the exquisite bulk of which can be ogled at two of his former residences turned museums, the Museu da Chácara do Céu (see p. 113) and Museu do Açude (see p. 183). Yet, Castro Maya was as fond of nature as he was of culture. An avid outdoorsman, in 1943, he was "hired" by Rio's mayor to revitalize and restore the Parque Nacional da Tijuca, which had been neglected for decades. Apart from advancing the city funds for the project, during his stint as park administrator, Castro Maya famously accepted a token annual payment of one cruzeiro, thus earning the nickname "One Dollar Man" from grateful Cariocas who began flocking to the revamped park en masse—and never stopped.

along the same road (though with less impressive views), the **Mesa do Imperador** lookout marks the spot where Pedro II often stopped to relax when tramping through the forest. The enormous mesa is not the original table upon which he spread his picnic provisions.

## Floresta da Tijuca

The Floresta da Tijuca sector shelters many of the park's attractions, including those most easily accessed on foot, without a guide. The main entrance at Estrada da Cascatinha 850 is marked by a large gate just off the Praça Afonso Vizeu. Located in the Zona Norte neighbor-hood of Alto da Boa Vista, it's easily reached by bus.

Before arriving at the visi-tor center, the Estrada da Cascatinha passes by the **Cascatinha do Taunay,** a 100-foot-high (30 m) waterfall named for French painter Nicolas-Antoine Taunay (1755–1830). A member of the French Artistic Mission that arrived in Rio in 1816, Taunay was enchanted by this spot. Not only was he moved to paint the cascades in a celebrated canvas, "Cascatinha," but he also built a house right next

A 19th-century Portuguese ceramic vase, from the collection of colonial furnishings at the Museu do Açude

to them where he lived with his family (today it's occupied by a small restaurant).

Continuing ahead, take a detour by turning right along the Largo Mayrink to the **Capela Mayrink.** Originally built in 1850, this fetching pink chapel belonged to the Fazenda Boa Vista, a 19th-century estate where coffee, sugar, and fruit were cultivated. The interior houses reproductions of ceramic tile panels by artist Cândido Portinari (the originals are now at the Museu Nacional de Belas Artes, in Centro).

## INSIDER TIP:

**Trek up the Pedra da Gávea to get the best views of Rio, laid out below.**

—CAROLINA FREITAS
*National Geographic grantee*

The visitor center is the departure point for countless trails that wind through the forest. One of the most popular—and one of the few that can be done without a guide (although for safety, you should go in a group)—leads up to the **Pico da Tijuca,** which at 3,353 feet (1,022 m) is the park's highest peak. The 1.5-mile (2.4 km) trail begins at the Largo do Bom Retiro. It takes almost two hours to reach the top, but the views on a clear day are magnificent. It's also possible to reach the summit via various climbing routes (best undertaken in the morning to avoid the scald-ing afternoon sun).

**Museu do Açude:** Also within the Floresta da Tijuca is the Museu do Açude (accessible on foot or by car). This museum was formerly the summer house of wealthy art collector Raymundo Castro Maya, who purchased it in the early 20th century. Inside the neocolonial mansion—whose sophisticated European elegance provides a striking contrast to the surrounding tropical exuberance—are some exquisite 18th- and 19th-century European azulejo frescoes and antique colonial furnishings, in addition to Castro Maya's prized collection of Asian art, which includes some rare Chinese porcelain. However, the museum's true highlight, aside from the view, is the **outdoor permanent installation space.**

Created in 1999, this art space includes sculptures and interventions by some of Brazil's most daring contemporary artists, among them Iole de Freitas and Nuno Ramos, as well as Hélio Oiticica and Lygia Pape. Oiticica's "Penetrável Magic Square No. 5" and Pape's "New House" were among the last works they created prior to their respective deaths in 1980 and 2004. While the works are noteworthy in themselves, their simultaneous interaction with Castro Maya's formal mansion and the lush chaos of the jungle creates an indelible experience.

## Rocky Sentinels

Farthest west and closest to the sea lie the rocky massifs of Pedra da Gávea and Pedra Bonita, both of which are accessible from the upscale beach neighborhood of São Conrado (via the Estrada da Canoa). A trio of steep and demanding trails (the ascent alone takes two to four hours)—as well as some spectacular, and equally challenging, climbing routes—lead through dense forest to **Pedra da Gávea.**

**Museu do Açude**

✉ Estrada do Açude 764
☎ 21/3433-4990
🕐 Closed Tues.
🚌 Bus: 221, 225, 233, 234

## EXPERIENCE:
## Birds of a Feather

If you love birds, you'll find Rio full of feathered treasures. Rio's vast range of altitudes and ecosystems explains why this mega-metropolis is also a serious bird sanctuary. While Rio state contains 730 of the estimated 1,800 avian species in Brazil, the city itself is home to 511, making it one of the most richly birded cities on the planet. Among the top spots for birding are the Jardim Botânico (see pp. 176–179) and the Parque Nacional da Tijuca. To see what birds you can check off your life list, hook up with **Birding Rio** (www.birdingrio.com), operated by ornithologist Ricardo Parrini. Daylong—or multiday—tours focus on spotting such endemic rarities as star-throated antwrens and eye-ringed tody-tyrants in addition to the more common, but no less impressive, toucans and tanagers.

The views from its 2,762-foot (842 m) summit are stupendous.

**Pedra Bonita**'s fame stems from the fact that the 2,283-foot (696 m) mountaintop shelters the ramp from which hang gliders hurl themselves into the sky before wafting down to Praia do Pepino. It, too, can be reached via climbing or hiking; the well-marked, 30-minute trail that ascends from the hang-gliding ramp is steep but easy. ∎

# Gávea

Gávea takes its name from the Pedra da Gávea, a gigantic rock formation that towers above this affluent *bairro*. Although largely residential, this pleasant neighborhood is enlivened by the presence of some interesting cultural and culinary offerings.

Gávea's Joquei Clube hosts the Grand Prix do Brasil, the nation's most prestigious horse race.

**Gávea**
🅐 171 A1

**Joquei Clube**
🅐 171 B1–B2
✉ Praça Santos Dumont 31
☎ 21/3534-9000
🕐 Closed Tues.–Thurs.
🚇 Metrô Na Superfície: Gávea

## Praça Santos Dumont

Gávea's main square and nerve center is Praça Santos Dumont. From here, the main thoroughfare of Rua Marquês de São Vicente winds its way up past lofty, upscale dwellings toward the favela of Rocinha. In the middle of the *praça* sits a small, pretty park beneath whose trees an antiques fair is held every Sunday. Sundays—along with Mondays and Thursdays—are also the nights when the area surrounding Praça Santos Dumont, known as Baixo Gávea, really sizzles. Packs of students from the nearby

Pontifícia Universidade Católica (PUC) and well-heeled 20- and 30-somethings ritualistically cram the traditional *botecos* lining the square and spill into the surrounding streets, where vendors hawk roasted peanuts and icy beer.

Overlooking the praça is Rio's **Joquei Clube,** inaugurated in 1926 as the Hipódromo da Gávea. This racetrack "starred" in Hitchcock's classic 1946 film *Notorious* as a meeting place for Cary Grant's and Ingrid Bergman's spy characters—but the races were actually filmed at Los Angeles's racetrack. Visitors can place bets

## INSIDER TIP:

The best place to hang out in the Baixo Gávea is in and around Praça Santos Dumont, where the bars teem with people—especially young people, as the PUC university is right there.

—LUIZ RENATO MALCHER
*Manager, Rio de Janeiro
Urban Adventures*

on horses—in general, races are held Friday through Monday—but even those not interested in wagering might enjoy an inexpensive caipirinha or beer with a view at one of the track's several atmospheric bars.

People who prefer shopping to betting should check out the

**Babilônia Feira Hype,** an open-air market, staged a few times a year in the Joquei Clube, where young Carioca artists and up-and-coming designers display their often alluringly funky creations.

## Planetário

Rio's 1970s-era Planetarium is a classic kid-friendly outing that will appeal to astronomy buffs of all ages. In addition to a pair of **domes** on which visitors may gaze at thousands of projected stars *(open to the public weekends only),* those eager to cast their eyes upon nonvirtual galaxies can peer at the night sky's blanket of celestial objects through a quartet of **telescopes** *(open to the public Wed. p.m. only).* The exhibition at the **Museu do Universo** is somewhat didactic, but cool photos of Venus's phases and Saturn's rings impress, as do interactive exhibits such as

### Planetário

- 🅰 171 A1
- ✉ Rua Vice Governador Rubens Berardo 100
- ☎ 21/2274-0046
- 🕐 Museum: closed Mon. Domes: closed Mon.–Fri.
- 💲 Museum: $. Domes: $$$
- 🚌 Bus: 157, 432, 435

---

# EXPERIENCE: Watch & Learn the Art of Capoeira

Part dance, part martial art, capoeira is a popular sport practiced throughout Brazil in venues ranging from indoor academies to outdoor parks and squares. In Rio, it's not uncommon to come across two men or women lunging and kicking at each other within a *roda* (circle) of other *capoeiristas* who clap and chant. They are often accompanied by percussion instruments, particularly the *berimbau,* a long piece of wood whose sole metal string produces a hypnotic twang.

Capoeira's origins date back to colonial Bahia. To avoid being harshly punished by plantation owners for tribal fighting, African slaves camouflaged their fierce swings and kicks by adding

graceful moves and music that resembled an inoffensive dance.

Indeed, lithe capoeiristas never touch their opponents—and only their hands, feet, and heads ever touch the ground. The goal is to develop flexibility and strength and demonstrate agility. Rio has many capoeira academies where you can watch capoeiristas in action or even take classes yourself. Located in front of Gávea's Planetário, the **Galpão das Artes Hélio G. Pellegrino** *(Av. Padre Leonel França, tel 21/2249-2286)* offers capoeira classes at all levels, taught by some of Rio's top masters. Although rates are monthly, fees can be negotiated for shorter durations.

**Instituto Moreira Salles (IMS)**

🅰 171 A1

✉ Rua Marquês de São Vicente 476

☎ 21/3284-7400

🕐 Closed Mon.

🚌 Bus: 150, 178

the one that allows visitors to determine their weight on various planets.

After dark, the nightclub **00** (Zero Zero; *Av. Padre Leonel França 240, tel 21/2540-8041*), located on the premises, is a perennially stylish hot spot for late-night drinking, dancing, and lounging on the outdoor deck.

## Instituto Moreira Salles (IMS)

In 1948, Walter Moreira Salles (1912–2001), a cultured businessman, diplomat, and banker (his father, João, founded Unibanco, one of Brazil's largest private banks) hired local architect Olavo Redig de Campos to design a family residence on a 33,000-square-foot (3,000 sq m) patch of hillside carpeted in native Atlantic Forest. Completed in 1951, the house was considered Campos's masterpiece

due to the manner in which it "Brazilian-ified" international modernism through the addition of sensuous curves and traditional architectural elements such as inner courtyards and ceramic tiles (azulejos). In 1992, the Salles family (which includes Walter Salles, Jr., acclaimed film director of *Central Station* and *The Motorcycle Diaries*) decided to convert their home into a private cultural center. Apart from a rich archive of books, photos, and musical

Light-suffused interior and lush gardens of the Instituto Moreira Salles, a cultural center

recordings—the majority devoted to Rio's history and culture—the IMS hosts concerts, special events, and engaging art exhibits. A small cinema screens art films.

Regardless of the center's program of events, the residence itself is highly worth visiting. Elegantly streamlined and suffused with light, it blends with its natural surroundings in ways that are both harmonious and shocking. Designed by artist/landscaper Roberto Burle Marx, the extensive gardens—which merge with the surrounding Tijuca Forest—make use of homegrown species such as heliconias, anthuriums, and slender *pau mulato* (mulatto wood) trees, whose bronze bark peels away to reveal a bright green underbelly. Enjoy this oasis by nabbing a table at the café, where you can admire the fish pond tiled in blue-and-white azulejos, also the work of Burle Marx. Don't miss the bookstore, which sells fine editions of Brazilian fiction, poetry, and art books published under the IMS imprint.

## Parque da Cidade

If you're visiting the Instituto Moreira Salles, allot some extra time to explore the oft-overlooked Parque da Cidade, located just up the hill from the IMS on a continuation of Rua Marquês de São Vicente. In fact, this bucolic property was once owned by the Marquês de São Vicente (1803–1878) himself, who transformed the hilly estate into a coffee plantation while preserving considerable swaths of native Atlantic Forest. The

mingling of landscaped lawns with exuberant tropical vegetation—not to mention the views—make for some idyllic wandering along the well-marked trails (although it's advisable not to do so alone).

Originally constructed in 1809, the elegant main house—known as the Solar de Santa Marinha—has been occupied since 1948 by a

**Parque da Cidade**

 171 A1

✉ Estrada de Santa Marinha 505

☎ 21/2294-5990

🕐 Closed Mon.

🚍 Bus: 150, 178

---

## Pop Iconography

**Adjacent to the Museu Histórico da Cidade sits a small chapel devoted to São João Batista. Built in the 1920s, its interior is infamous for its mural depicting the life of St. John the Baptist. Painted in 1972 by Bahian artist Carlos Bastos (1925–2004), it caused a scandal due to the fact that the religious personages depicted bore extraordinary likenesses to public figures of the day—for example, John the Baptist possessed the face of singer-songwriter Caetano Veloso, and his decapitated head was held by a Salomé who bore an uncanny resemblance to the *mulata* model and actress Marina Montini (1948–2006). Meanwhile, an angel with blue wings was a dead ringer for soccer star Pelé. Because of these artistic liberties, the "blasphemous" work was never completed. ∎**

---

museum dedicated to the history of the city of Rio, the **Museu Histórico da Cidade.** Among the more compelling objects on display are paintings, dishware, and furniture rescued from the Paço Imperial (including a throne belonging to João VI), sculptures by Mestre Valentim, and engravings of 19th-century Rio by Jean-Baptiste Debret. Undergoing renovation, the museum is scheduled to reopen in 2013. ∎

Upscale suburban neighborhoods squeezed between towering mountains and wild beaches that attract hang gliders and surfers

# Zona Oeste Beaches

Kitesurfing on Praia da Barra da Tijuca

# Zona Oeste Beaches

From Leblon, the coastal road of Avenida Niemeyer shimmies past the Morro Dois Irmãos before reaching the small and tony beach *bairro* (neighborhood) of São Conrado. This marks the beginning of the Zona Oeste, whose long, wild beaches are bordered by highways, upscale condo complexes, and massive shopping malls favored by Rio's middle class and *novos ricos* (nouveaux riches).

Largely bereft of cultural and historical attractions—in terms of aesthetics, one could easily mistake these sprawling, car-friendly neighborhoods for suburban Miami or Houston in the United States—the Zona Oeste neighborhoods do have their draws: mountains and beaches that lure surfers and other radical sports aficionados (the rough waves make swimming dangerous).

## São Conrado

Although officially still the Zona Sul, São Conrado is most often considered to be part of the newer, more verticalized, and ultimately less interesting Zona Oeste beach neighborhoods. An upscale residential enclave, its high-priced, towering condos inhabit a dense band between Rio's largest and most notorious hilltop favela, Rocinha, and the stunning 2-mile (3 km) open Atlantic beach of Praia de São Conrado, which comprise the neighborhood's two main

attractions. Since undergoing pacification in 2011, Rocinha has become an essential stop on increasingly popular favela tours. Meanwhile, thrill-seeking hang gliders and paragliders who take flight from Pedra Bonita can be seen whirling through the sky until they land on the western tip of Praia de São Conrado, known as Praia do Pepino.

## Barra

Prior to the late 1960s, Barra da Tijuca consisted of little more than sand dunes, lagoons, and a marshy but rich ecosystem known as *restinga*. Then in the 1970s, with the Zona Sul already bursting at the seams, renowned urban planner Lúcio Costa was hired to create a new, modern bairro. Ideally, his planned constructions, modeled after U.S. suburbs, were to integrate

with the natural surroundings. Sadly, it didn't quite work out that way. Today, Barra is filled with endless strip malls, closed condominium complexes, and an endless parade of vehicles that whip up and down its two main freeway-like thoroughfares. Barra's saving grace is its beach—stretching 10 miles (16 km), it is Rio's longest strand. Quiet during the week, it's packed on weekends by sun worshippers, not to mention sea and sand enthusiasts who indulge in every sport under the sun, notably windsurfing, kitesurfing, and diving (for the aquatically inclined) and beach soccer, volleyball, and frescoball (for those unafraid to kick up a sandstorm).

## Recreio & Around

Barra segues into Recreio dos Bandeirantes, which is less urbanized (at least for now—construction is rampant) and whose beach, similar to Barra's, is generally emptier. Surfers, however, are enamored with it—and with the more wild and secluded, if less easily accessible (at least by public transit), beaches of Grumari and Prainha,

> **NOT TO BE MISSED:**
>
> **Hang gliding down to Praia do Pepino from Pedra Bonita  193**
>
> **A tour of Rocinha, Rio's largest favela  196**
>
> **Surfing (or watching others indulge) at the wild beaches of Prainha and Grumari  200–201**
>
> **The Casa do Pontal's collection of Brazilian folk art, the largest in the country  201–202**
>
> **Admiring the art—both painted and planted—at the Sítio Roberto Burle Marx  202–203**

whose preserved coves are backed by jungle-clad mountains. Inland, amid lush landscapes, lie hidden treasures such as the former home and atelier of artist and landscaper Roberto Burle Marx and the Casa do Pontal, a bucolic residence that houses one of Brazil's finest collections of folk art. ∎

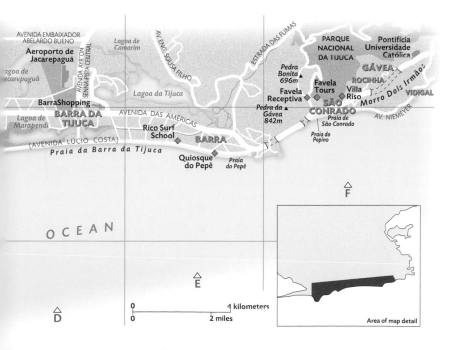

# São Conrado

Upscale, compact, and residential, São Conrado can be quickly zoomed through en route southwest from the Zona Sul to Barra. More interesting than the neighborhood itself are the surrounding mountains, from which the dense patchwork of Rocinha and Pedras da Gávea and Bonita gaze down.

Beachside vendors sell everything from grilled corn on the cob to icy cold drinks on Praia do Pepino.

**São Conrado**
191 F2–F3

Originally occupied by sugar and coffee plantations—including one owned by a certain Conrado Niemeyer, who lent his name to both the neighborhood and the avenue that connected it to the rest of the city in 1916—São Conrado is a neighborhood of stark visual and socioeconomic extremes. On one hand, there are swanky, modern, high-rise apartments that gaze out onto the tony grounds of the Gávea Golf and Country Club, a beach punctuated by five-star luxury hotels, and Rio's chicest shopping area of all, the São Conrado Fashion Mall. On the other hand, many residents of these very same buildings also gaze up at—and are gazed down upon in return by—the residents of Rocinha, a favela whose cubist cluster of houses stretches all the way up the hillside of Morro Dois Irmãos.

## Praia de São Conrado

In the shadow of Pedra da Gávea, stretching from the end of Avenida Niemeyer to the beginning of the São Conrado tunnel that leads to Barra, São Conrado's beach attracts a mélange of well-to-do residents from neighboring condos, along with kids from adjacent Rocinha and surfers lured by the enormous waves. The far end of the beach, known as **Praia do Pepino** (Cucumber Beach), is the landing spot for the hang-gliding daredevils who leap from Pedra Bonita (see sidebar this page).

## Villa Riso

In the 18th-century, the Fazenda da Alagoinha da Gávea sugarcane plantation covered a vast expanse of São Conrado. All that remains now is the main plantation house, which dates from 1750. In 1880, it was purchased by Antônio Ferreira Viana (1833–1903), justice minister and imperial adviser to Pedro II,

INSIDER TIP:

**If you're adventurous, go hang gliding off Pedra Bonita, which towers above São Conrado, to see all of Rio's main attractions from above.**

—ROBERT PHILLIPS
*Intelligent Leisure Solutions Group*

who was one of the authors of the Lei Áurea abolishing slavery.

In 1932, the property was purchased by Italian-born banker and art lover Osvaldo Riso, who with his Amazonian wife, Camélia, hosted glittering soirees as well as illustrious guests such as Russian composer Igor Stravinsky and American sculptor Alexander Calder. In the early 1980s, Riso's eldest daughter, pianist Cesarina Riso, transformed the house into a cultural and events center, which is open to visitors. ∎

**Praia de São Conrado**
191 F3

**Villa Riso**
191 F3
Estrada da Gávea 728
21/3322-1444
Free, but reservations req.
Bus: 360, 2333
**www.villariso.com.br**

## EXPERIENCE: A Flying Leap

Blessed by favorable winds, warm air currents, and stunning scenery (not to mention a soft landing spot in Praia do Pepino), hang gliding and paragliding off the 1,722-foot (525 m) ramp at Pedra Bonita is one of Rio's most famous radical sports rites of passage—one that you can do, if you dare. Flights, either solo or in tandem, last between 10 and 25 minutes, during which time you descend in spirals—the better to allow you to admire the scenery all around, which includes the rugged stone of the Pedra da Gávea, the green splash of the Tijuca Forest, and the dazzling blue of the Zona Sul beaches.

Before taking flight, you'll go through a brief training session with an instructor. Make sure your pilot has credentials with Associação de Vôo Livre do Rio de Janeiro, whose headquarters are located on Praia do Pepino. Reserve (but don't pay) in advance, and be prepared for last-minute cancellations due to sudden changes in weather and/or visibility. **Fly Tour** *(tel 21/9984-5643, www.flytourbrazil.com, $$$$$)* and **Just Fly** *(tel 21/2268-0565, www.justflyinrio.blogspot.com, $$$$$)* are two recommended outfits. Don't be shy to ask instructors to film or photograph you during your historic descent.

# Favelas Rising

*Favela* is most commonly translated as "slum" or "shantytown." Yet neither term gets close to encompassing the complexity of such an integral and widespread aspect of Carioca—and Brazilian—society.

**Young mother and child, Rocinha**

Most foreigners picture favelas as poor and squalid places where entire families live in precariously built shacks without electricity, running water, or sewage systems. Although true in some cases, over the years, an increasing number of favelas have developed into well-organized communities. Not only do many have plumbing and electricity, but some also have free Wi-Fi coverage, not to mention day care centers, schools, medical clinics, banks, sports clubs, cultural associations, and— of course—samba schools.

Covering the steep slopes of Morro Dois Irmãos, Rocinha is Rio's largest favela—and the largest in Latin America with an estimated population of more than 200,000 people. In 1993, in part due to an extremely organized residents association, it achieved neighborhood status. A veritable city within a city, Rocinha is a densely byzantine place with only one main thoroughfare (Estrada da Gávea, which connects Gávea and São Conrado) and four roads. The rest of the *bairro* is connected by a labyrinth of narrow alleyways (many unnamed) that would confound even Perseus.

Pacified since 2011, these days Rocinha hums with commercial and cultural activity. It boasts its own TV station (TV Roc), a music school, and the Coopa Roca, a clothing co-op that supplies creations to top local designers and sells fashions under its own label at chic Carioca shopping malls. Facing the favela is the home of Ivo Pitanguy, the most famous plastic surgeon in the world, who treats Rocinha residents pro bono. Also nearby is PUC, one of Rio's top universities, which attracts numerous foreign students. Unable to pay outrageous Gávea rents, many of them are renting in the favela—and loving it.

## Favela Revitalization

Among Brazilian favelas, Rio's have always been notorious. One reason is their visibility. Favelas such as Rocinha are literally right on top of the city's richest neighborhoods. While this guarantees favela residents views that are far more fabulous than those of their wealthy counterparts below, it also dramatically underscores Brazil's flagrant social and economic inequalities. It also meant that, until recently, not even residents of Ipanema and Leblon were safe from stray bullets. Indeed, much of favelas' notoriety stemmed from the fact that they were controlled by drug cartels. Ruling like feudal seigneurs, drug lords provided order and security in exchange for residents' allegiance (and looking the other way). The price paid for protection was living in perpetual danger due to the omnipresence of drugs and frequent shoot-outs between *traficantes* (traffickers), police, and rival gang members.

While civil warfare was taking place on the *morros*, elsewhere public authorities and private citizens alike persistently turned a blind eye to the existence of favelas (despite the fact that

**Only five roads cut through Rocinha's dense urban patchwork.**

many Cariocas employed favela residents as housekeepers, doormen, and nannies). Favelas were so invisible that, until recently, they didn't even appear on official municipal maps.

Over the last decade, there has been a shift in attitudes, and efforts have been made to integrate once marginalized communities into the rest of the city. A major breakthrough has been the government's expulsion of drug dealers from many of the most centrally located favelas. In their place, permanent Police Pacification Units (UPPs) have been installed.

Increased safety has brought newfound security to favelas, which are now increasingly referred to as *comunidades* (communities). It has also brought tourists (mostly foreigners, since many Brazilians continue to be stigmatized by their presence), who are eager to get a sense of a vital part of Carioca life that, for a long time, they were discouraged from experiencing.

# EXPERIENCE: Favela Tourism

Since 2010, the ousting of drug lords and the implantation of permanent Police Pacification Units (UPP) in most of the central and Zona Sul favelas has encouraged a small explosion of "favela tourism."

*Moto-taxis* are a popular means of getting around Rocinha.

outsiders to become familiar with an intimate slice of community life. Visitors accompany English-speaking local guides as they drop by the homes of friends, neighbors, and *figuras* (neighborhood characters), in addition to bars, restaurants, capoeira classes, and samba *festas*.

## More Than a Tour

If you're looking to explore with a twist, **Be a Local** *(tel 21/9643-0366, www.bealocal .com)* is an alternative for travelers with a fondness for two-wheel transportation. Apart from day trips into Rocinha, local English-speaking *moto-boys* (motorcycle-riding delivery boys) will also whisk tourists to funk *bailes* (parties) at night.

Meanwhile, "favela dining" is a suddenly sizzling culinary niche, as are favela accommodations, which range from backpacker-friendly bed-and-breakfasts to the five-star boutique hotel slated to open at the summit of Vidigal. For those who want an authentic homestay experience, **Favela Receptiva** *(tel 21/9848-6737, www.favelareceptiva .com)* organizes lodgings with residents of Vila Canoas and Vila da Pedra Bonita, two communities that hover above the glitzy *bairro* of São Conrado.

## Walking Tours

While the phenomenon is mushrooming, it's certainly not new. In existence for two decades is the pioneering **Favela Tours** *(tel 71/3322-2727, www.favelatour.com .br)*, operated by Carioca Marcelo Armstrong. Led by Armstrong and a team of sensitive and knowledgeable multilingual guides, the three-hour tour ferries small groups to Rocinha and Vila Canoas, where you can wander around and check out community schools, drink killer caipirinhas at a local bar, and purchase cool, locally made art and accessories. While some may have qualms about the exploitative or voyeuristic aspect of touring a favela, Armstrong

and his guides are well known within the communities. They emphasize that residents appreciate foreigners' openness to discovering that there's far more to favela life than the clichés of poverty, drugs, and violence. Moreover, tourism gives a boost to the local economy (in addition, Favela Tours donates a portion of its fee to community projects).

A more personalized option is to take a **Favela Adventure** *(tel 21/8221-5572, www.favelatour.org)* with a Rocinha native. Operated by DJ Zezinho, born and bred in Rocinha and the founder of a local media school, these "adventures"—lasting four to six hours, they can be customized—allow

# Barra da Tijuca

**An increasingly vertical and traffic-choked symbol of the New Rio, Barra da Tijuca may lack soul, but it certainly doesn't want for sand, sun, surf—or shopping centers. Its long, straight, never-ending beach—and the fascinating cross section of Cariocas it attracts—is the prime reason to make a trip here.**

There's no getting around the fact that Barra is an alienating place. It is cluttered with endless megamalls (the most mega of them all, BarraShopping, was once the largest mall in South America, with some 700 boutiques in addition to restaurants, cinemas, a bowling alley, and a small amusement park known as the HotZone), private condominium complexes, and hordes of vehicles that, when not mired in traffic, whiz up and down the main artery of Avenida das Américas and the seaside Avenida Sernambetiba (also known as Avenida Lúcio Costa). Although cars rule, the beach is well served by buses from the Zona Sul.

Helping to transcend its reputation as a glorified strip mall, in recent years several of Rio's top restaurants and trendiest bars have opened locations in Barra (often in shopping malls). There have also been attempts to infuse some cultural life into the area, most notably with the 2013 opening of the **Cidade das Artes,** a performing arts complex designed by celebrated French architect Christian de Portzamparc. Meanwhile, it is fitting that the majority of the sports venues for the 2016 Olympics will be located here; Barra—particularly its beach—concentrates an amazing number of lithe and supine Cariocas who keep their enviable shape by jogging, cycling,

**Barra da Tijuca**
🅰 191 D2

Kitesurfers flock to Praia do Pepê, a stretch of Barra's beach.

## EXPERIENCE: Surf's Up

Barra's beach is sprinkled with numerous surfing academies, and one of the oldest and most popular is **Rico Surf School** (Av. Lucio Costa 3300, tel 21/8777-7775, www.escoladesurfrico.blogspot.ca), located near Posto 4. Extremely affordable two-hour courses are held twice daily for all levels, including absolute beginners (one-hour private lessons are also available). Know in advance that the school's philosophy is that students should throw themselves into it (literally). Fortunately, Barra's waves are conducive to learning: regular, long, and without any walls to knock you out.

**Praia da Barra da Tijuca**
⚑ 191 D2–E2

surfing, and running after balls of all kinds: soccer balls, volleyballs, and frescoballs among them.

### Praia da Barra da Tijuca

Barra's wide and sweeping beach—the longest in the city—is cleaner than the Zona Sul beaches and, even on the steamiest summer weekends, never as elbow-to-elbow packed with bronzed bodies. The first 4 miles (6 km) are the most heavily urbanized, with tons of kiosks for eating, drinking, and checking out the natives (a mixed bunch that includes affluent residents as well as those from poorer and working-class Zona Oeste and Zona Norte neighborhoods).

The very beginning—a perennially hip 1-mile (1.5 km) stretch of sand known as **Praia do Pepê**—is a magnet for impeccably buff and bikinied surfers, soccer players, and minor soap opera stars who cluster around the **Quiosque do Pepê** (Av. do Pepê, Quiosque 11,

tel 21/2433-1400, www.pepe.com.br), sipping fresh fruit juice and chomping on sanduíches naturais (hearty sandwiches made with nutritious fillings). Pepê—in whose honor both the beach and kiosk are named—was the nickname of world-champion surfer and hang glider Pedro Paulo Guise Carneiro Lopes, an avid frequenter of these sands before his tragic 1991 death in a hang-gliding accident.

The entire length of Barra is beloved by surfers, windsurfers, and kitesurfers, but apart from Praia do Pepê, a particularly coveted spot is a 0.5-mile-long (1 km) stretch in the middle

**INSIDER TIP:**

**For pristine water, excellent bodysurfing, and people-watching, spend the day at Praia do Pepê. Be sure to have a sanduíche natural at the Barraca do Pepê.**

—PRISCILLA GOSLIN
*Author of* How to Be a Carioca

(around Avenida Sernambetiba 3100) where waves reach heights of 7 feet (2 m) and surfing championships often take place. At the very end, between Barra and Recreio, the relatively secluded **Praia da Reserva** is haunted by Globo TV actors and other celebs who want to dodge the paparazzi (easy access is hampered by the presence of a nature reserve and lack of public transportation). ∎

# Recreio & Around

Recreio and Recreio dos Bandeirantes are somewhat less developed and calmer than neighboring Barra. Instead of being completely hemmed in by condos, portions are still fringed by the odd patch of native *restinga* vegetation. Zoning laws keep developers from building higher than three stories, which ensures late afternoon sun for beachgoers.

Praia da Macumba with Pedra do Pontal in the background

## Recreio's Beaches

Essentially a continuation of Praia da Barra da Tijuca, **Praia do Recreio** is also extremely popular with surfers, and easily reached via buses running along the beachfront Avenida Sernambetiba. Its waves are particularly enticing near the Posto 10 lifeguard station as well as at the far end, known as Canto do Recreio, where the gigantic **Pedra do Pontal** divides Recreio from the soft sands of **Praia da Macumba,** home to some surfing academies. An attractive and relatively secluded beach *(bus No. 360 takes you the closest),* Macumba's rough waters yield small but long waves that are beloved by fans of longboarding.

**Praia do Recreio**
🅜 190 B2–C2

**Praia da Macumba**
🅜 190 B2

**Praia da Prainha**

▲ 190 B2

**Praia da Grumari**

▲ 190 A1

**Praia do Abricó**

▲ 190 A1

**Bira**

✉ Estrada da Vendinha 68A, Barra de Guaratiba

☎ 21/2410-8304

🕓 Closed Mon.– Wed.

**Wild & Scenic:** Prainha and Grumari are Rio's wildest and most primitive beaches. Their unspoiled aspect is guaranteed by not only their relative remoteness (only Prainha can be reached by bus) but also the fact that they are situated within an environmentally protected area. The landscape of mountains covered in lush, orchid-studded native restinga can be easily explored via walking trails. To reach these beaches from Recreio, follow Avenida Estado da Guanabara, a terrifically scenic

## The Surf Bus

Those with no wheels of their own, but in possession of a surfboard (not a requirement), can easily access all of Rio's beaches for a fistful of reais by jumping aboard the **Surf Bus** *(tel 21/8515-2189)*. With four daily departures from Largo do Machado, this orange-and-green bus—with room for 20 boards—hits all the best surf spots in town, from Arpoador all the way down to São Conrado, Barra, Recreio, Macumba, and Prainha (the last one otherwise inaccessible by bus). In the event you get bored watching all those beaches whip by, awesome surfing DVDs are constantly being screened.

road that gives appetite-whetting glimpses of both beaches prior to your arrival.

Prainha means "little beach," and what this snug strip of granular sand lacks in terms of size it more than makes up for in terms of substance. Sandwiched between a green sea and even greener hills, decorated with rugged boulders (and a few rustic kiosks), **Praia da**

**INSIDER TIP:**

It's worth making a trip to Guaratiba, a small town close to the beaches of Prainha and Grumari, to eat at Bira. This rustic seafood restaurant offers great food and stunning views across a nature reserve.

—DOUG GRAY
*National Geographic contributor*

**Prainha** is beloved by surfers due to its strong winds and rollers that last forever before breaking.

If anything, **Praia da Grumari** is more dramatic, with its 1.5-mile-long (2.5 km) expanse of pinkish sand and jade waters that oscillate between placid and rough. Arriving early, surfers haunt the portion closest to Prainha, which is also where those who want to let it all hang out can do so. Known as **Praia do Abricó,** this cozy stretch of sand separated from Grumari by protective rocks is Rio's only official nude beach. Aside from the young and the naked, it's also a refuge for those seeking to mellow out with a joint.

Despite the remoteness of these beaches—roughly 12 miles (20 km) from the center of Barra da Tijuca—on weekends and in the summertime all bets are off, as a diverse mix of locals, tourists, hippies, hipsters, and Zona Sul families fleeing the even more crowded Zona Sul beaches descends upon them. Between Prainha and

**The Museu Casa do Pontal displays a wealth of folk art from all over Brazil.**

Grumari, in particular, traffic can come to a standstill. To guarantee your place in the sun, consider arriving before 11 a.m.

## Casa do Pontal

In the late 1940s, a French art collector named Jacques Van de Beuque spent several years criss-crossing Brazil and was amazed to encounter a singularly rich folk art tradition that seemingly nobody—not even Brazilians—knew existed. With the aim of preserving and promoting these neglected treasures, Van de Beuque constructed a sprawling country house behind Praia do Recreio where, over the next four decades, his collection grew. Today, the 8,000-plus

works created by more than 200 artists (many from the culturally rich Northeast) constitute the largest ensemble of Brazilian *arte popular* in the country.

Distributed among 12 thematic galleries, the works range from the lavishly embroidered *boi* **(bull) costumes** worn during the traditional *bumba-meu-boi* festivities of Maranhão to hundreds of *figurinhas de barro,* highly expressive clay figures depicting North-eastern characters ranging from bandits and barflies to devils and dentists, many of which were produced by the supremely talented Mestre Vitalino (1909–1963) of Pernambuco. A particular highlight is the brilliantly rendered **mechanical diorama** featuring

**Casa do Pontal**
- 190 B2
- Estrada do Pontal 3295
- 21/2490-3278
- Closed Mon.
- $$
- Bus: 703, S-20

**www.museucasado pontal.com.br**

## Sítio Roberto Burle Marx

- 🅰 190 A2
- ✉ Estrada Roberto Burle Marx 2019
- ☎ 21/2410-1412
- 🕐 Closed Sun.–Mon. Guided visits (1.5 hours long, at 9:30 a.m. & 1:30 p.m.) must be reserved in advance.
- 💲 $$
- 🚌 Bus: 387

**www.sitioburle marx.blogspot.com**

an entire samba school parading through the Sambódromo during Rio's Carnaval.

Despite the somewhat remote location, it's worth visiting the Casa do Pontal to grasp the wealth, breadth, and clever improvisational nature of Brazil's artistic traditions, in which materials as diverse and unexpected as tin cans, palm fibers, sand, and bread crumbs possess limitless creative potential. The museum features descriptive text in English and also offers tours with bilingual guides on Saturdays.

## Sítio Roberto Burle Marx

One of Rio's greatest artists and bon vivants—and one of the world's most influential landscapers—was Roberto Burle Marx (1909–1994). His lush legacy lives on in this bucolic country estate an hour's drive from the Zona Sul. Situated in the largely rural district

The grounds at the Sítio Roberto Burle Marx reflect the landscaper's ethic.

## Redeemer of Plants

Although he's best known for having designed the black-and-white mosaic "wave" *calçadão* (promenade) lining Copacabana Beach, in green circles Roberto Burle Marx is often considered to be the inventor of the "modern garden." Burle Marx was born in São Paulo and raised in Rio, but ironically it was in Germany that he acquired an interest in Brazilian flora. At 19, while studying painting in Berlin, he was introduced to the exotic plants of his homeland at the Dahlem Botanical Garden.

At the time, Brazilian public parks—with their geometrical arrangements, imported rosebushes, and Roman statuary—were in thrall to the rigor of European gardens. Upon his return to Rio, Burle Marx took a job as director of parks and gardens for the city of Recife. Immediately, he set to work overturning these Eurocentric precepts by creating parks composed entirely of scorned native species, including palm trees, cacti, and bromeliads.

Burle Marx's gardens shocked—and then seduced—due to their form as well as their content. Plants were arranged in broad, organic swaths in which shapes, textures, and hues played off each other, often to surprising effect.

Throughout his life, Burle Marx corresponded with botanists and naturalists from around the world. He also journeyed all over Brazil on a constant quest to "redeem" ignored and unknown plants by inserting them into new contexts. One of his most successful rescue victims was the heliconia. Burle Marx's use of these scarlet blossoms transformed the lowly heliconia, traditionally disparaged as the flower of a wild banana tree, into a botanical star. Fittingly, one of the several new species of heliconia he discovered bears the scientific name of *Heliconia burle-marxii*.

of Barra de Guaratiba, the property lies inland from Praia da Grumari. Burle Marx purchased this 148-acre (60 ha) former banana plantation in 1949 and lived here from 1973 until his death.

The main colonial house functions as a **living museum** where it's easy to imagine many of the leading (and most bohemian) of Rio's *artistas* gathered for hours around the long dining-room table or in the music room. In his bedroom, Burle Marx's reading spectacles remain carefully poised on a dresser while his polished shoes are under an armoire. Meanwhile, up the hillside, his former **atelier**—the stone-by-stone re-creation of a building that had impressed

him in Centro's Praça Mauá—has been converted into a gallery showcasing his drawings, murals, and engravings in addition to an impressive collection of Brazilian folk art that Burle Marx referred to as "objects of poetic emotion."

Even more impressive, however, are the intricately laid-out gardens, in which multiple textures and gradations of green combine to create living, growing tapestries comprised of more than 3,500 tropical and semitropical species from all over Brazil and the world. It was often said that Burle Marx—an accomplished painter—used plants as other artists used paint; wandering amid his living compositions, it's easy to understand the comparison. ■

Paradisiacal beaches, deserted islands, and spectacular mountains cloaked in exuberant Atlantic Forest—all within four hours of Rio

# Excursions

Oscar Niemeyer's Museu de Arte Contemporânea, in Niterói, offers stunning views of Guanabara Bay and Rio de Janeiro.

# Excursions

The Cidade Maravilhosa is certainly marvelous, but it can also be noisy, crowded, chaotic, and even exhausting. When you need a break, do as Cariocas do and flee for the greener or bluer, but definitely calmer, pastures of surrounding Rio de Janeiro state.

## Niterói & Petrópolis

Niterói, Rio's sister city, possesses stunning views of Rio de Janeiro from the other side of Guanabara Bay, as well as a handful of interesting attractions. Aside from the largest collection of Oscar Niemeyer–designed buildings outside of Brasília (the most fantastic of which is the Museu de Arte Contemporânea) and one of Brazil's oldest ensemble of colonial fortifications, Niterói has some alluring beaches, particularly Itacoatiara, on the open Atlantic.

Back in the mid-1800s, when things got too hot (literally) for Brazil's imperial family, Pedro II hightailed it up to the fresher climes of the Serra do Mar mountain range, where he built a lavish pink summer palace (today the must-see Museu Imperial) and founded the town of Petrópolis. This pretty historic

town, with its bohemian airs and architecture, remains a favorite weekend refuge for Cariocas in search of sophisticated food and lodgings amid majestic scenery. Although Petrópolis's sights can be seen in a day, nature lovers should factor in extra time to hike, trek, or merely take a waterfall plunge in the nearby Parque Nacional daSerra dos Órgãos.

## Búzios

An idyllic 5-mile-long (8 km) peninsula of beckoning coves, Búzios's limpid waters are sprinkled with both yachts and fishing vessels, and its cobblestoned streets are lined with fashionable restaurants, boutique hotels, and plain old boutiques (selling international designer labels). Búzios attracts a lot of pretty people and partiers (especially in the summer). In the off-season, its two

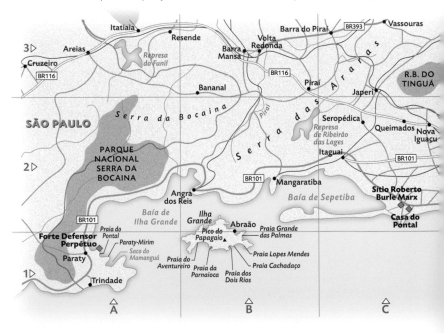

dozen beaches and quasi-Mediterranean charms continue to cast a seductive spell.

## Costa Verde

The Costa Verde (Green Coast), south of Rio, lives up to its name with its profusion of beautiful beaches backed by lush mountains. Accessible only by boat across the Baía de Ilha Grande, Ilha Grande is the quintessential island getaway. There are no vehicles and, for the most part, accommodations are deliciously rustic. Apart from the charming village of Abraão, the island is all about virgin Atlantic rain forest threaded with hiking trails and waterfalls, crystalline waters littered with sunken pirate ships, and more than 100 drop-dead gorgeous beaches, including the stunning Praia Lopes Mendes.

Farther south along the Costa Verde, Paraty is one of the most enchanting historic towns in the Americas, recognized as a national heritage site and a UNESCO World Heritage site. Tourists in the know also recognize it as an idyllic yet cosmopolitan place awash with atmospheric artists' galleries, cafés, restaurants, and bars where you can sample the local cachaça. Urban

allures aside, Paraty's scenic bay is strewn with deserted islands and unspoiled beaches. The surrounding Serra da Bocaina mountains are crisscrossed with hiking trails, including the historic Caminho de Ouro (Gold Route). ∎

---

**NOT TO BE MISSED:**

The emperor's crown at the Museu Imperial in Petrópolis **216**

Mountain trekking in the Parque Nacional da Serra dos Órgãos **216**

Combining chilling out and charm in Búzios **218–221**

A day lounging on Praia Lopes Mendes, one of many paradisiacal beaches on Ilha Grande **224**

Wandering colonial Paraty's cobblestoned streets **226–229**

Exploring Saco da Mamanguá, Brazil's only fjord **233**

Following the Caminho de Ouro into the Serra da Bocaina mountains **233**

---

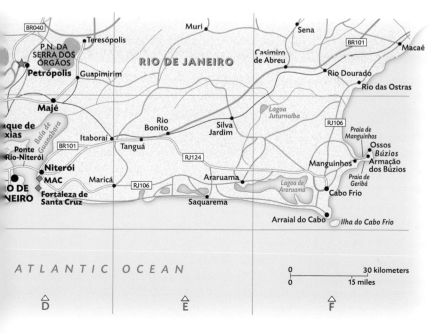

# Niterói

Only the beautiful Guanabara Bay separates Rio from Niterói, its slower-paced metropolitan neighbor of half a million. Those with a full or half day to spare should venture over and get a view of life on the Other Side.

The Portuguese built the Fortaleza de Santa Cruz in 1557 to guard the entrance to Guanabara Bay.

**Niterói**

🏔 207 D2

**Visitor Information**

✉ Neltur Municipal Tourist Office information kiosks at the Estação das Barcas (Praça Araribóia) & MAC (Boa Viagem)

☎ 0800/282-7755

www.niteroiturismo.com.br

Only 8 miles (13 km) from Rio de Janeiro, Niterói is easily reached by bus or boat. Buses regularly cross the Ponte Rio-Niterói, one of the longest bridges in the world, while boats depart from Rio's **Estação das Barcas** (*Praça XV, tel 0800/721-1012, Metrô: Carioca or Uruguaiana*) at 15- to 30-minute intervals throughout the day, docking at either the Estação das Barcas at Praça Araribóia

in the center of town or at the Estação Hidroviária at Charitas.

## Oscar Niemeyer Works

Niterói's most compelling attraction is the **Museu de Arte Contemporânea (MAC),** a futuristic construction perched on a cliff overlooking Guanabara Bay that was dreamed up by Oscar Niemeyer. Although the architect envisioned it as a gigantic white flower, the building is

**INSIDER TIP:**

Instead of driving to Niterói, on the opposite side of Guanabara Bay, take a ferry from Centro's Praça XV.

—LUIZ RENATO MALCHER
*Manager, Rio de Janeiro
Urban Adventures*

more commonly referred to as the "flying saucer." Balancing delicately on a slim, cylindrical base whose diameter measures 30 feet (9 m), the museum itself has minimal space to showcase temporary and permanent exhibitions of contemporary Brazilian art. Indeed, the exhibits often take a backseat to the spectacular panoramic views of the city across the bay, which can also be savored from the restaurant housed in the belly of the building.

**Caminho Niemeyer:**
Completed in 1996, the MAC was the first of many constructions that were to comprise the waterfront Caminho Niemeyer (Niemeyer Route), which extends from the center of Niterói to Boa Viagem, where the museum is located. Due to lack of financing, however, the original project remains incomplete, with some buildings in a state of suspension. Among the more interesting structures are the **Teatro Popular** and **Praça JK** as well as the

**Museu de Arte Contemporânea (MAC)**
 207 D2
✉ Mirante da Boa Viagem
☎ 21/2620-2481
🕐 Closed Mon.
💲 $. Free Wed.
🚌 Bus 47B (from Estação das Barcas, Praça Arariboia)

## Niemeyer's Curvaceous Vision

Oscar Niemeyer (1907–2012) had many occasions to be both adulated and dismissed. One of the first non-European modern architects to gain international acclaim, the passionate and political Rio-born Niemeyer turned modernism on its head, rejecting its rational lines, rigidity, and functionality in favor of organic curves, sensuality, and beauty. His flair for achieving lightness and fluidity using concrete and steel was pioneering. It was also utterly Brazilian.

As a prodigal young architect, Niemeyer was invited to build a new utopian capital in the middle of Brazilian nowhere. Brasília became a symbol of Brazil's leap into modernity, yet shortly after its 1960 inauguration, its communist creator was forced into exile by the military regime. Although Niemeyer returned to Rio in the early 1980s, for many years his oeuvre was disparaged and he was criticized for designing buildings lacking in comfort and functionality.

It wasn't until the 1990s that a young generation of architects began to celebrate the consistency of his vision. During all this time, Niemeyer just kept working. As he approached his 105th birthday, he had just completed the Centro Niemeyer in Spain as well as an exclusive line of Niemeyer sneakers for Converse.

A particularly famous quote sums up the architect's life as well as his work: "I deliberately disregarded the right angle and rationalist architecture designed with a ruler and square to boldly enter the world of curves . . . This deliberate protest arose from the environment in which I lived, with its white beaches, its huge mountains, its old baroque churches, and the beautiful suntanned women."

## EXPERIENCE: Buy Your Fish ... & Eat It, Too

In Niterói, you can have your fresh fish and eat it, too, at the traditional **Mercado São Pedro** *(Rua Visconde do Rio Branco 55, tel 21/2719-2600, closed Mon.)*, located just a few blocks north from the Estação das Barcas at Praça Araribóia. From gleaming tiled stalls, fishmongers sing the praises (and prices) of fresh squid, lobster, shark, and sardines. The quality is so unbeatable that many Rio restaurateurs cross the bay to buy their daily provisions here. However, you need only make your purchase and head upstairs—passing the statue of São Pedro, patron saint of fishermen—to the second-floor *botecos* where, for a small fee, you can have your catch fried or grilled while you refresh yourself with an icy beer.

### Fortaleza de Santa Cruz

207 D2

✉ Estrada General Eurico Gaspar Dutra, Jurujuba

☎ 21/3611-1209

🕐 Closed Mon.

💲 $

**Fundação Oscar Niemeyer** and (completed, but yet to be inaugurated) **Centro Petrobras de Cinema.** The former features a permanent exhibition of the architect's works in addition to an architecture school. Niemeyer also designed one of Niterói's ferry terminals, the Estação Hidroviária at Charitas. For die-hard Niemeyer fans, Neltur, the municipal tourist agency (see p. 208), offers 40-minute tours of Caminho Niemeyer led by bilingual guides.

### Fortaleza de Santa Cruz

In 1555, when Rio's colonial destiny was still up for grabs, the French sent a convoy led by Nicholas Durand de Villegaignon to stake a claim to what they hoped would become a strategic outpost for a future French Antarctica. With the goal of defending the entrance to Guanabara Bay, Villegaignon improvised a makeshift fortification. Only two years later, it was captured by the Portuguese, who then erected the Fortaleza de Santa Cruz da Barra. Originally a military fort, it was turned into a prison in 1831, complete with gallows and torture chambers.

Guided tours *(in Portuguese only; 45 min.)* of the fort depart from the 17th-century chapel devoted to St. Barbara, taking visitors past rows of cannon, prison cells (where political dissidents were jailed during Brazil's military dictatorship), and a firing wall pockmarked with bullet holes. The views of Rio and Guanabara Bay are incomparable.

The easiest way to get to the fort is to take a 15-minute taxi ride to the beach neighborhood of Jurujuba. Along the way, the road passes snug coves decorated with fishing boats; when you near Jurujuba, ask to detour to see en route three other fortifications: **Forte Barão do Rio Branco, Forte Imbuí,** and, perched atop the Morro do Pico, the ruins of **Forte São Luíz.**

### Beaches

The urban beaches in and around the center of Niterói tend to be crowded and too polluted for swimming. Vaunting its own mosaic walkway replete with walkers and joggers, lively **Icaraí** is Niterói's version of Ipanema and its prettiest beach on the bay. Lined with countless restaurants and bars serving fish and seafood, it's an ideal spot to watch the sun set, the silhouette of Rio backed by bands of yellow, gold, and rosy pink.

The beaches along the open Atlantic—known as *praias oceânicas*—are more appealing. One of the most popular, and increasingly developed but still stunning, is **Camboinhas,** located some 10 miles (16 km) from the center of town. This long beach boasts powdery white sands and calm green waters. From the waterfront kiosks serving seafood, you can see the glimmer of Copacabana. Several miles farther along and even more captivating is **Itacoatiara,** set amid the Serra da Tiririca nature reserve. Its rugged swells make it a surfer's delight.

Access to all beaches is easy; from the ferry terminal, take any bus bound for Itacoatiara and hop on and off at whim. For sustenance, there is no shortage of *barracas* (rustic beach bars) serving cool drinks and freshly grilled fish. ∎

**Fishing is a favorite pastime along the open Atlantic beaches of Niterói.**

# Petrópolis

When Cariocas can't take the heat, they take a page out of the history books and beat a quick retreat to Petrópolis. Located only 44 miles (71 km) from Rio, the imperial family's summer refuge offers temperatures that are always deliciously cooler, in addition to plenty of fine food, fresh air, and mountain scenery.

A pink neoclassical confection, Pedro II's former summer palace houses the Museu Imperial.

**Petrópolis**

🏔 207 D3

**Visitor Information**

✉ Petrotur tourist information kiosks: Terminal Rodoviário Leonel Brizola & Praça da Liberdade

☎ 0800/024-1516

**http://destino petropolis.com.br**

It was enchantment at first sight for Pedro I, who stopped at this idyllic spot nestled amid the Serra do Mar mountains during an 1822 trip to Minas Gerais. The emperor was so taken with the site that he later returned and purchased a farm with plans to build a rural estate. However, it was his nature-loving son who ended up following through with those intentions. Pedro II not only constructed a full-blown summer palace, he also founded (in 1843) the town that blossomed up around it and which bears his name: Petrópolis.

Trailing in Pedro's footsteps came counts, barons, and marquises, all intent on building palatial summer homes of their own. They were followed by an influx of immigrants from Germany, Austria, and Switzerland. Lured by the alpine topography and climate, these newcomers made themselves at home by building alpine-style chalets and opening breweries, bars, and delicatessens, some of which still exist.

Even after the fall of the empire in 1889, Petrópolis continued to prosper—and to lure hot and harried Cariocas regardless of the time of year. Indeed, the region is popular in the winter due to the combination of clear and sunny days followed by nights whose cool temperatures are alleviated by a profusion of roaring fireplaces. Independent of the season, keep in mind that weekends can be very crowded, and many sights are closed on Mondays.

## How to Visit

You can easily visit most of the sights in and around the compact historical center on foot. An alternative for the romantic, or downright imperial, is to hire one of the 19th-century-style horse-drawn carriages parked in front of the Museu Imperial. A car can be useful if you want to spend time exploring the surrounding Serra do Mar; many of the region's gourmet restaurants and mountain lodges are tucked away in bucolic rural locales.

If you're driving from Rio (a 1.5-hour trip), follow the scenic, if sometimes harrowing, BR-040 (but avoid the weekend crush and wet weather). From Rio's Rodoviária Novo, **Única Fácil** *(tel 21/2263-8792)* provides frequent daily bus service to Petrópolis's Terminal Rodoviário Leonel Brizola. From the bus station, take a cab or local bus to Centro.

## Museu Imperial

Built in neoclassical style, the Palácio Imperial was the summer residence constructed by Pedro II for family getaways with Empress Teresa Cristina and their two daughters, Isabel and Leopoldina. In 1943, it was transformed into a museum that conjures up the life and times of the imperial family during Pedro II's impressively long reign (1840–1889).

The fun begins when you first set foot in the marble entrance hall and exchange your shoes for soft-soled slippers. You can understand why when you catch sight of the lustrous parquet floors made of precious tropical hardwoods.

**INSIDER TIP:**

**Just an hour from Rio, Petrópolis is a historic mountain town. Colder than the city, it used to be a refuge from the heat for the Empire Aristocracy.**

—ROBERT PHILLIPS
*Intelligent Leisure Solutions Group*

Touring the palace, one has the impression that the royals just slipped out for a quick carriage ride. Faint plinks seem to come from the gold harp in the **music room,** and it's easy to imagine Teresa Cristina embroidering in front of her guests in the **empress's visiting salon,** where all the diminutive furniture was custom-made so as not to overwhelm the empress's tiny frame. Pedro II was particularly fond of his **office,** in which he spent
*(continued on p. 216)*

**Museu Imperial**

- ✉ Rua da Imperatriz 220
- ☎ 24/2245-5550
- 🕐 Closed Mon.
- 💲 $$

# A Walk Past the Palaces of Petrópolis

The first thing anyone who comes to Petrópolis must see is the Museu Imperial. Once you've absorbed all the imperial artifacts you can handle, take a leisurely stroll around the rest of the historic center to see how the town's loyal imperialists lived.

Palácio de Cristal, an 1884 gift to Princesa Isabel

Exit the grounds of the **Museu Imperial ❶** (see p. 213) and turn right on Rua da Imperatriz. On the corner, in front of Praça Visconde de Mauá, is the grand, canary yellow **Palácio Amarelo ❷**. Built in 1850, this opulent palace was home to the Barão de Guaraciaba before being converted into the city council in 1897.

Take a left and follow Avenida Tiradentes. At the three-way intersection with Rua Treze de Maio and Avenida Koeler stands the imposing silhouette of the **Catedral de São Pedro de Alcântara ❸** (see p. 216). Turn onto Avenida Koeler.

## NOT TO BE MISSED:

Museu Imperial • Palácio Amarelo • Palácio Rio Negro • Palácio de Cristal

## Avenida Koeler

This thoroughfare parallels a tree-shaded canal and is lined with the town's most splendid mansions. It's named for Julius Friedrich Koeler (1804–1847), a German engineer who became an officer in the imperial army. Pedro II hired him to design and construct not only the Imperial Palace but also the surrounding town. To achieve this goal, Koeler summoned numerous German immigrants; they transformed this wilderness into a city with an Arcadian edge.

Facing the cathedral, the **Casa da Princesa Isabel ❹** (Av. Koeler 42) is a pretty pink neoclassical confection that resembles a miniature version of the Imperial Palace. Built in 1853, it was home to Princesa Isabel and her husband, Gaston d'Orléans, grandson of France's last king, Louis Philippe I, who was also known

## Cervejaria Bohemia

A German immigrant to Petrópolis, Henrique Kremer began crafting Brazil's first beer in 1853, using water from mountain sources. Considered one of the country's finer brews (Pedro II was an ardent fan), Bohemia was, until recently, made in the **Cervejaria Bohemia** (Rua Alfredo Pachá 166, tel 24/3064-9127, closed Mon.–Tues., $$). In 2012, however, the

historic brewery was transformed into a beer research center in which a bedazzling barrage of touchscreen panels, videos, and 3-D holograms trace ale's 6,000-year history. After focusing on ingredients and the production process, visitors arrive in the Bohemia Boteco for sampling. (Note: The explanations on this two-hour experience are only in Portuguese.)

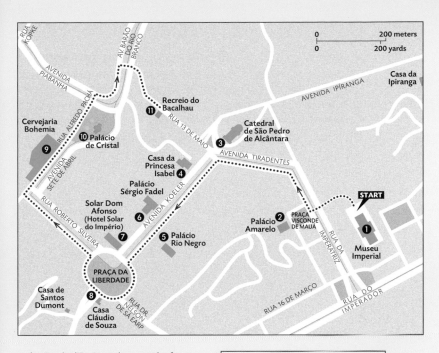

as the Conde d'Eu. It was here, on the front porch, that the famous "Final Photograph of the Imperial Family in Brazil"—Pedro II, Teresa Cristina, and Isabel with her husband and three children—was taken before they went into exile.

Continue down the avenue to No. 255, the **Palácio Rio Negro** ⑤ *(tel 24/2246-2423, closed Sun.–Mon., $)*, the most impressive manse on the block. Built in 1890 by the Barão do Rio Negro, a rich coffee planter, it was acquired by the federal government as the official summer residence of Brazil's presidents, each of whom left his own personal mark. Getúlio Vargas, for instance, transformed the original wine cellar into Roman baths. Also of note are the **Palácio Sérgio Fadel** ⑥ *(Av. Koeler 260)*, which now houses the seat of municipal government, and, overlooking the Praça da Liberdade, the **Solar Dom Afonso** ⑦ *(Av. Koeler 376)*, occupied by the luxurious Hotel Solar do Império.

## Praça da Liberdade & Beyond

Traveling clockwise around the Praça da Liberdade, you'll pass the **Casa Cláudio**

---

> ▲ See also area map pp. 206–207
> ▶ Museu Imperial
> ↔ 1.4 miles (2.2 km)
> ⏱ 1.5 hours
> ▶ Recreio do Bacalhau (Rua Treze de Maio 195)

---

**de Souza** ⑧ *(Praça da Liberdade 247, tel 24/2245-3418, closed Sat.–Mon.)*. Aside from personal objects and period furnishings belonging to renowned author Cláudio de Souza (1876–1954), it is home to Petrópolis's Historical Institute. Follow Rua Roberto Silveira to the end and turn right on Rua Alfredo Pachá. At No. 166, you'll pass the **Cervejaria Bohemia** ⑨ brewery (see sidebar opposite) before arriving at the **Palácio de Cristal** ⑩ (see pp. 216–217). As a reward for your efforts, treat yourself to an icy beer at nearby **Recreio do Bacalhau** ⑪ *(Rua Treze de Maio 195, tel 24/2231-1180, closed Sun.)*, a decades-old local haunt where the cigar-shaped *bolinhos de bacalhau* (deep-fried cod balls) are rumored to be the best in town.

## Catedral de São Pedro de Alcântara

⊠ Rua São Pedro de Alcântara 60

☎ 24/2242-4300

## Palácio de Cristal

⊠ Rua Alfredo Pacha

☎ 24/2247-3721

🕐 Closed Mon.

## Parque Nacional da Serra dos Órgãos

🏔 207 E3

long hours corresponding with scientists and intellectuals. The telephone on his desk was given to him in person by Alexander Graham Bell in 1876.

The treasures on display in the **throne room** never fail to impress. Particularly dazzling are Pedro I's golden scepter and Pedro II's majestic crown encrusted with 639 diamonds and 77 pearls, which he wore upon his coronation at the tender age of 15. Complete your visit with a stroll through the **gardens,** designed by renowned French botanist Jean-Baptiste Binot. Don't forget to peek in at the **royal stables,** where a fairy-tale golden carriage—imported from London in 1837—is housed.

## Catedral de São Pedro de Alcântara

Constructed between 1884 and 1925, this imposing cathedral mingles French and German Gothic influences. Inside, an

atmosphere of sobriety reigns, alleviated on sunny days by jewel-hued stained-glass windows, whose scenes are taken from poems composed by the multitalented Pedro II. Wrought out of marble, bronze, and onyx, the Imperial Mausoleum houses the remains of Pedro II, Teresa Cristina, Princesa Isabel, and the Conde d'Eu, in tombstones upon which life-size likenesses of their occupants have been carved. For a fee—if it is open—one can ascend the 169 steps that lead to the top of the 230-foot (70 m) church tower.

## Palácio de Cristal

Inspired by London's Crystal Palace, this delicate glass palace, with its supportive vertebrae of iron, was a gift from the Conde d'Eu to Princesa Isabel. Custom-built in the count's native France, it was transported across the Atlantic in pieces before being assembled on site in 1884. While the princess

---

## EXPERIENCE: Trekking in the Serra dos Órgãos

Between Petrópolis and its sister city of Teresópolis, a 45-minute drive to the east, lies the **Parque Nacional da Serra dos Órgãos.** Within this national park are 30,000 acres (12,000 ha) of Atlantic Forest threaded with trails that lead through a bizarrely shaped mountain range that, as early Portuguese explorers noted, bears a resemblance to a church pipe organ (hence the name Serra dos Órgãos). Rising 5,550 feet (1,692 m) above sea level, the equally aptly named Dedo de Deus (Finger of God) is the park's most well-known peak. Yet there are plenty of other summits you can gape at, and even scale.

The park's numerous hiking trails range from easy 30-minute strolls to the challenging but spectacular three-day, 22-mile (35 km) journey from Petrópolis to Teresópolis that links two of the park's entrances. A guide is necessary to navigate the more arduous trails. **Trekking Petrópolis** *(tel 24/2235-7607)* organizes long hikes as well as rappelling and canyoneering excursions. Although the park's main entrance and headquarters is near Teresópolis *(Av. Rotariana, tel 21/2152-1100),* there is also an entrance 10 miles (16 km) from Petrópolis's center on the Estrada União-Indústria.

hosted balls and parties in the palace, she also permitted her husband to use it as a hothouse for his beloved orchids. In present times, musical performances often take place here.

## Casa de Santos Dumont

According to Brazilians, the first person to take to the firmament in an airplane wasn't a Wright brother, but Alberto Santos Dumont (1873–1932). Santos Dumont became a national hero in 1906 upon completing the first nonassisted flight in a fixed-wing aircraft of his own design and construction. Apart from being an aviation pioneer, this eccentric character was a passionate inventor, whose many brainchildren clutter an alpine-style chalet that he built on the slopes of Morro da Encantada.

Uninterested in creature comforts, the diminutive (5 ft/1.5 m) aviator slept in a desk that converted into a bed, and bucking the trend for luxurious bathtubs, he created a shower whose hot water was heated by alcohol. Although he didn't have a kitchen (he ordered in meals from a nearby grand hotel), he took care to install stairs leading to the rooftop, where he could hoist the Brazilian flag. Among the intriguing personal effects on display is a balloon-shape lamp that was a gift from his great friend Princesa Isabel; a little-known fact is that Santos Dumont invented the modern hangar so he could store the balloons he often flew without letting the air out of them.

The Gothic spire of the Catedral de São Pedro de Alcântara towers above Petrópolis.

## Casa da Ipiranga

Also known as the Casa de Petrópolis and, among those critical of its asymetrical facade, as the Casa de Sete Erros (House of Seven Errors), the Victorian-style Casa da Ipiranga was the home of José Tavares Guerra, a nephew of the illustrious Barão de Mauá, a banker, industrialist, and abolitionist who created Brazil's first railroad (from Petrópolis to Rio). Guided tours of the opulent interior reveal walls hung in brocade, crystal chandeliers, and burnished jacaranda furniture. Designed by leading French landscaper Auguste Glaziou, the gardens were one of Pedro II's favorite refuges. The coach house has been converted into an atmospheric bistro called **Bordeaux** *(tel 24/2242-5111),* where live music is often played. ■

### Casa de Santos Dumont
- ✉ Rua do Encanto 22
- ☎ 24/2247-5222
- 🕐 Closed Mon.
- 💲 $

### Casa da Ipiranga
- ✉ Av. Ipiranga 716
- ☎ 24/2231-8718
- 🕐 Closed Tues.
- 💲 $$

# Búzios

Poised upon the Costa do Sol, 105 miles (170 km) east of Rio, Búzios is one of Brazil's most internationally renowned beach resorts—and with good reason. It carries off the feat of being both utterly sophisticated and disarmingly casual with great flair. To experience both extremes, and enjoy relaxing horizontal time, an overnight stay is essential.

Praia da Ferradurinha's placid waters prove perfect for swimming and kayaking.

**Búzios**

🏛 207 F2

**Visitor Information**

✉ Búzios Tourist Office, Praça Santos Dumont, Armação

☎ 22/2623-2099

www.buziosonline
.com.br

A great deal of buzz is generated by Búzios's lush life: the luxurious spa hotels, fashionable restaurants, and Ibiza-worthy nightclubs that throb all night long, all summer long. Fortunately, it's possible to drown out the pulsing electronica and escape the hordes of upscale Cariocas and sun-deprived Argentines and Chileans. Despite the onslaught

of development and tourism, if your timing is right, you can (re-)discover the charming old fishing settlement of decades past, with its cobblestones and colonial cottages, not to mention its two dozen alluring beaches, many of them surrounded by surprisingly wild, yet softly hued, landscapes.

If you're not a hard-core party or (10,000) people person, avoid visiting Búzios on a long holiday weekend or during the summer. Since many of the nicest beaches are on the small side, you'll have a better chance at securing a place in the sand. There's also the question of budget. Befitting its moneyed clientele, Búzios is an expensive destination (although budget options do exist). While high-season prices are astronomical, discounts can be obtained at other times of the year.

Getting to Búzios from Rio is easy. **Viação 1001** (tel 21/4004-5001, www.autoviacao1001.com.br) operates daily buses from Rio's Rodoviária Novo. Departing every one to two hours, they arrive at Búzios's bus terminal in Armação. If driving, take the Ponte Rio-Niterói across Guanabara Bay and head east along the BR-101 leading to Rio Bonito before turning onto the RJ-124, the RJ-106, and finally the RJ-102, following the last straight into Búzios.

### Three Populated Areas

The peninsula of Búzios contains three main settlements. Nearest to the mainland, **Manguinhos** is the most urbanized and commercial. Well served by municipal buses, its main road, Avenida José Bento Ribeiro Dantas, cuts straight through the peninsula, turning into the Estrada Usina Nova as it arrives in the main village of Armação dos Búzios.

**Armação dos Búzios** is the historic, touristic, and hedonistic center of Búzios. Most of the most thronged and fashionable boutiques, galleries, restaurants, hotels, and nightspots are located here, clustered in and around the main cobblestoned drag of Rua das Pedras. Its picturesque seaside extension, baptized the Orla Bardot (see sidebar p. 221), winds along the waterfront, a 20-minute walk to the fishing village of Ossos.

Búzios's oldest settlement, **Ossos** dates back to the peninsula's early whaling days, a past evoked by its very name; *ossos* (Portuguese for "bones") is a reference to the gigantic carcasses that lay strewn along the beach following the extrication of whales' oil and flesh.

**INSIDER TIP:**

**From Búzios, day-trip to nearby Arraial do Cabo, a town with beautiful beaches and clear waters known for good diving.**

—CAROLINA FREITAS
*National Geographic grantee*

### Beaches

Independent of Búzios's sophisticated trappings, it's impossible to resist the lure of its beaches. Running the gamut from deserted bathtub-size coves surrounded by wild vegetation to expansive sweeps of sand lined with beach bars and condos, there's a patch of sand to suit every need, mood, and personality.

### North Coast Beaches:

Closest to the mainland, on the north coast, **Praia de**

**Manguinhos** and **Praia Rasa** beckon sailors, windsurfers, and families with their combination of high winds and small waves. Traveling toward Armação, you'll pass access points to **Praia dos Amores** and **Praia das Virgens,** secluded beaches framed by lush foliage. Particularly warm, the blue waters of **Praia da Tartaruga** are great for snorkeling.

While pretty to gaze at, Armação's beaches are too polluted for bathing, but its sands are wonderful for lounging. Watched over by the 18th-century Igreja de Sant'Ana, the sugary sands of **Praia dos Ossos** beckon those inclined to nap in the shade of almond trees, but its calm seas are littered with boats. A five-minute walk brings you to the small but bewitching twin beaches of **Azeda** and **Azedinha,** both framed by exuberant greenery; arrive early to enjoy them in their primitive state. From Ossos, a hilly road leads to **João Fernandes** and **João Fernandinho.** Long and wide, João Fernandes is a favorite of visiting Argentines—who not only fill the rental chairs but also own a number of the beach bars as well. Smaller and more tranquil João Fernandinho possesses natural pools that are ideal for leisurely soaking.

Strolling along Búzio's Orla Bardot, a promenade named after onetime visitor Brigitte Bardot

**Peninsula Tip Beaches:** The extreme eastern tip of the peninsula hides some of the most remote and wildly windswept of Búzios beaches. All of them can be reached by car or via scenic (sometimes hilly) roads leading off the Estrada Usina Velha. The most majestic, **Praia Brava,** is the most surprising, with rose-colored sand backed by cliffs that do a fine imitation of the Scottish Highlands. The rough waves are a natural lure for surfers. Smaller but equally enticing are **Praia Olho de Boi,** a tiny cove haunted by nudists, **Praia do Forno,** and **Praia da Foca,** whose pools of transparent blue are framed by rocks sprouting sculptural cacti.

**South Coast Beaches:** On the south side of the peninsula, **Praia da Ferradura** ("horseshoe beach") hews true to its name. The semicircular bay is surrounded by mansions, condos, *pousadas* (inns), and bars. Its wide beach and sheltered waters are ideal for families as well as for sailing, kayaking, and windsurfing aficionados. Bigger, more developed, and closer to the mainland, sweeping **Praia de Geribá** is extremely popular with serious *surfistas* (surfing academies dot the beach) and young party animals drawn by the electronic beat that emanates from the **Fishbone Café** *(tel 22/2623-7348).* From the left extreme of Geribá, a short trail leads to pretty **Praia da Ferradurinha,** whose crystalline waters are ideal for diving.

Continuing toward the mainland—and accessible from the road that leads from Búzios to Cabo Frio—are a trio of practically deserted beaches, **Praia dos Tucuns, Praia José Gonçalves,** and **Praia das Caravelas,** all of which compensate for their scant infrastructure with impressively rugged natural surroundings.

## The Bardot Factor

In 1964, at the height of her fame, French actress Brigitte Bardot accompanied her Brazilian boyfriend for a two-month getaway to Búzios. At the time, the bucolic little fishing village was unknown—that is, until the paparazzi got wind of Bardot's whereabouts and zoomed in with the hopes of capturing the sultry starlet in a bikini. Bardot's legacy survives in the stylish seaside walkway that bears her name—the Orla Bardot—where a bronze likeness of the actress (ca 1965) sits contemplating the colorful fishing boats bobbing on the sea.

**Getting to the Beaches:** Aside from walking, you can access most of Búzios's beaches by hopping a municipal bus, taking a taxi, or renting a buggy. You may also approach them by sea. Daily schooner, catamaran, and speedboat excursions depart from Armação pier to a dozen beaches and a few islands where passengers can snorkel. And with room for up to seven people, *taxis marítimos* shuttle to and from the sheltered northern peninsula beaches between Manguinhos and Azedinha; taxi stands are located at Armação and Praia dos Ossos. ∎

# Ilha Grande

Only 100 miles (160 km) south of Rio is the Baía de Ilha Grande, a shimmering green-blue bay whose aquatic kingdom embraces some 1,000 beaches and more than 300 islands. The largest of them all, Ilha Grande, also happens to be the most escape-worthy. Two days is a minimum stay before forcing yourself back to civilization.

The summit of Pico do Papagaio rewards great views to hikers who make the 6-mile (9 km) climb.

**Ilha Grande**

🏔 206 B1–B2

**Visitor Information**

✉ Ilha Grande Tourist Office, Ferry Dock

☎ 24/9922-9614

Ilha Grande's splendid isolation has determined much of its colorful history. During colonial times, French, Dutch, and English pirates often hid in the island's coves, waiting to ambush gold-laden Spanish ships. In the 19th century, even following abolition, Ilha Grande was a haunt for illegal traders selling slaves on the sly to sugar and coffee plantations. It also contained a leper colony, not to mention two prisons where some of Brazil's

most hardened criminals and political dissidents were jailed. Occasional breakouts terrified the island's population of fishermen. It wasn't until the second prison's 1994 demolition that Ilha Grande began to attract tourists. Its immaculately preserved forests and beaches, coupled with the blissful absence of all motorized vehicles, have made this tropical isle a favored getaway for nature lovers, hikers, and hippies (with a sprinkling of discreetly wealthy yacht owners tossed in for good measure).

Measuring 46 square miles (119 sq km), Ilha Grande is only an 80-minute boat ride from the mainland towns of Angra dos Reis and Mangaratiba, from which **CCR Barcas** (tel 0800/721-1012) offers daily ferry service. Another alternative is to take a high-speed catamaran from Angra. **Viação Costa Verde** (tel 21/3622-3123) offers hourly bus service between Rio and Angra. If you choose to drive from Rio, just follow the BR-101 south. The journey should take 2.5 to 3 hours. Note that there are no bank machines on Ilha Grande; although some upscale establishments on the island accept cards, stock up on cash beforehand.

## Abraão

Ferries from the mainland dock at the colonial fishing village of Abraao, the island's "capital" of 3,000. Its pastel-hued houses and cobblestoned streets are atmospheric, although easily overwhelmed by tourists, particularly in the summer when cruise ships anchor in the bay. Most of the island's rustic *pousadas* (inns), eateries, and excursion agencies are located in and around town, which serves as the main base for exploring the island on foot or by boat.

One of the easiest walks from town is the 20-minute route that leads to **Lazareto.** Here you can wander amid the haunting vestiges of the late 19th-century infectious disease hospital, where leprosy and cholera patients, as well as foreign sailors, were quarantined. The building was later transformed into a prison, which operated until 1964. Behind the ruins looms a striking 26-arch aqueduct. Built in 1833 from stone and whale oil, it was used to supply the hospital with water.

**Abraão**

🅰 206 B2

## This Boat for Hire

There are many means of aquatically exploring the bays, islands, and beaches of Rio de Janeiro state. Popular with large groups of extroverted Brazilians with a pre-dilection for all-you-can-drink caipirinhas and all-you-can-blast music are schooner excursions that often seat up to 60 people. More exclusive, but more expensive, are smaller catamaran and motorboat excursions. An ideal in-between solution is to take a taxi. *Taxis marítimos*—also known as taxi-boats—often operate along preestablished routes. On Ilha Grande, you can literally flag a passing cab down from the beach (there is usually room for eight passengers). However, in Abraão, you can also hire your own cabbie to take you wherever you want—and wait while you sun, snorkel, or build a sand castle.

Note the sofa-shaped stone at the beginning of the aqueduct; it was a favorite perch of Emperor Pedro II, who often sat to write poetry and make sketches of the landscape. Should you need refreshment, you can plunge into the nearby calm seawaters of **Praia Preta.** From the aqueduct, a 1.5-hour walk along a trail through the rain forest leads to the spectacularly Tarzanesque **Cachoeira da Feiticeira,** a 50-foot-high (15 m) waterfall that cascades into myriad natural pools. Due to the poor signage, it's best to go with a guide.

## Beaches

Ilha Grande's beaches—many of them preserved, primitive, and utterly paradisiacal—are its main attraction. There are more than 100 of them, and you could spend weeks exploring them

**With its crystal clear waters and numerous marine species, Ilha Grande is a paradise for snorkelers.**

all (serious beach junkies fall into this habit). If your days are limited, focus your attentions on the best of the best, most of which are open Atlantic beaches concentrated along the southern coast of the island.

An hour's walk south from Abraão brings you to **Praia Grande das Palmas,** a small fishing village whose palm-fringed beach is lined with rustic bars. Continue for another 45 minutes to **Praia dos Mangues,** where the beach is surrounded by mangroves. Don't linger too long here, though, since only another 20 minutes' walk separates you from the island's most worshipped beach: **Praia Lopes Mendes** consistently racks up accolades as the most blissfully beautiful beach not only on Ilha Grande but in all Brazil. It's hard not to agree when faced with 2 miles (3 km) of firm white sand (ideal for strolling) lapped by shimmery waves of jade and turquoise. The portion to the right is popular with surfers. Those without their own board can rent one (or take lessons). The pristine state of Lopes Mendes is guaranteed by the fact that boats are banned from anchoring offshore; instead the nearest disembarkation point is Praia dos Mangues (a 45-minute ride from Abraão).

**Remoter & Remoter Still:** Other more remote beaches are also worth the effort. Measuring only 50 feet (15 m), **Praia Cachadaço** is a small gem nestled amid giant rocks and jungle; its invisibility from the sea made it a favorite pirate hideout. From Abraão, it's more than three hours on foot, and two hours by boat. A two-hour trek south from town on an old prison road leads to **Praia dos Dois Rios,** whose sandy beach is bracketed by *dois rios* (two

## INSIDER TIP:

Go to Ilha Grande for a relaxing vacation that blends beautiful land- scapes of sea, forests, and mountains.

—CAROLINA FREITAS
*National Geographic grantee*

rivers), giving you the option of both fresh- and saltwater bath- ing. The rain forest behind the beach hides the remains of the Cândido Mendes penal colony. Among the illustrious prison- ers who did time here were acclaimed 20th-century novelist Graciliano Ramos (1892–1953), who wrote about his experi- ences in *Mémorias do Cárcere,* and legendary Lapa *malandro* Madame Sata, who did 16 years of time for killing a policeman (see pp. 106–107).

Still more remote (a serious six-hour hike from Abraão), but equally captivating, is **Praia da Parnaioca,** where the Rio Parnaioca forms a delicious lagoon with a small waterfall. Much farther west, enchanting **Praia do Aventureiro** is located within a biological reserve. Its waters are usually calm, but when southern winds blow, waves grow to heights of 13 feet (4 m), luring surfers. It,

too, can be reached on foot and by boat.

**Snorkeling & Diving:** With its calm, transparent jade waters, the Baía de Ilha Grande is one of the best places in Brazil for both snorkeling and deep- sea diving. Aside from more than 900 species of marine life—including dolphins, sea turtles, and Day-Glo-colored tropical fish—15 sunken ships are located off the coast. Top diving destinations include **Ilha de Jorge Grego** (for the fish) and **Enseada do Bananal** (for the shipwrecks). Elite Dive Center *(Abraão, tel 24/3361-5501)* offers lessons, equipment rental, and excursions.

## Pico do Papagaio

Numerous hiking trails cut through the lush Atlantic rain forest that covers Ilha Grande. Some short and well-signed paths can be navigated on your own. However, for longer hikes— such as the six-hour trek across the island to Praia da Parnaioca— it's best to contact a local guide (check with the tourism office; see p. 222). Among the most challenging but rewarding treks is the three-hour, 6-mile (9 km) climb to the summit of Pico do Papagaio (Parrot's Peak). Along the way, expect to encounter plenty of monkeys, squirrels, and brightly colored birds and butterflies. The 360-degree view from the top is mindblowing; on a clear day, you can make out the silhouette of Pedra da Gávea in Rio. ∎

**Pico do Papagaio**
⚠ 206 B1

# Paraty

Poised between majestic green mountains and a diaphanous blue sea, Paraty is one of the most charismatic colonial towns this side of paradise. Located 160 miles (256 km) southwest of Rio de Janeiro, it needs a minimum of two full days to soak up its charms and surrounding nature.

View of Paraty with the Igreja de Santa Rita dos Pardos Libertos in foreground

**Paraty**

🗺 206 A1

**Visitor Information**

✉ Centro de Informações Turísticas, Av. Roberto Silveira 1

☎ 24/3371-3064

Paraty's frequent comparison to a "colonial gem" is appropriate, given its origins. In the late 17th century, the Portuguese needed a safe port from which to transport the vast quantities of diamonds, emeralds, and gold from neighboring Minas Gerais state to Lisbon. Traders enlarged an ancient trail that native Guaianá had carved through the Serra do Mar mountain range. Where the route

encountered the sea, the founding stones of Paraty were laid.

During the early 1700s, Paraty blossomed into a modest port town, yet its remote location always made it difficult to defend from marauding pirates and bandits. When a new and improved gold route was built between Minas and the port of Rio de Janeiro, Paraty was abandoned—for centuries. Indeed, if the town appears to be trapped in time, it's because it wasn't until the early 1970s that Paraty was connected to the rest of the world via the BR-101 coastal highway linking Rio and Santos. Soon after that, intrepid hippies discovered Paraty's historic and bucolic charms. As word got out, artists, entrepreneurs, and expats began transforming the faded colonial mansions into ateliers, cafés, restaurants, and hotels, which in turn attracted weekenders from Rio and São Paulo as well as international tourists, including a vibrant gay and lesbian crowd.

## Visiting Paraty

During the summer, Paraty can get packed, yet it's kept the overblown tourism and trendiness of places such as Búzios at bay. At other times of the year, the town is languidly tranquil, and it's easier to wallow in its timeless atmosphere. The compact historical center, with streets laid out on a grid plan, lends itself marvelously to aimless wandering around. The

INSIDER TIP:

**Visit Paraty on one of the various June *festa* days that honor a saint to see performances of the *ciranda*, a clog dance with guitar accompaniment that you're unlikely to encounter in Rio.**

—LESLIE ALLEN
*National Geographic author*

streets themselves, however, are a challenge, possessing multiple names. In addition, they are paved with big, irregularly set stones—colorfully referred to as *pés de moleque* (street kids' feet). While this means that they are closed to vehicle traffic, it also makes for tricky walking for those with physical disabilities or without flat-soled shoes. When the tide is high, the ocean invades the streets nearest to the port, transforming them into canals—a beguiling sight.

## Festive Paraty

Paraty celebrates Carnaval with marching bands and a Bloco da Lama (in which revelers cover themselves in mud), but Carnaval is not the only time Paraty throws a big *festa*. Held 50 days after Easter, the **Festa do Divino** was imported by 17th-century Portuguese settlers and features ten days of processions and pageantry in the streets in honor of the third person of the Holy Trinity. Then, in late May, a roster of top performers lures jazz lovers to town during the three-day

**Bourbon Festival Paraty.** And in August, makers and imbibers of cachaça congregate for the **Festival da Pinga.** Paraty's most famous event, however, is the **Festa Literária Internacional Paraty** (*www.flip .org.br*), held in July. With such big names as Salman Rushdie, Margaret Atwood, and Ian McEwan as past headliners, this literary festival attracts more throngs to Paraty than even Carnaval. Note: During these festas, accommodations are booked far in advance.

Viação Costa Verde *(tel 21/2233-3809)* provides frequent daily bus service from Rio's Rodoviária Novo to Paraty. By car, simply follow the BR-101 south. Expect the journey to take between 3.5 and 4.5 hours.

---

## EXPERIENCE:
## Cooking With Yara

Although Paraty has no shortage of fine-dining opportunities, the **Academy of Cooking and Other Pleasures** *(Rua Dona Geralda 288, tel 24/3371-6025, www.chef brasil.com, $$$$$)* offers intrepid foodies the only fine-cooking opportunity in town. Several nights a week, chef Yara Costa Roberts—whose impeccable English comes from years of cooking Brazilian food in the United States—opens her kitchen to small groups of willing sous-chefs, eager to prepare typical dishes from Bahia, the Amazon, the Cerrado (central-west), and Roberts's home state of Minas Gerais. Lesson over, participants get to savor the fruits of their labor.

---

**Casa da Cultura**
- ✉ Rua Dona Geralda 177
- ☎ 24/3371-2325
- 🕐 Closed Tues.
- 💲 $$

**Igreja de Nossa Senhora das Dores**
- ✉ Rua Fresca
- 🕐 Closed Mon.
- 💲 $

**Igreja de Nossa Senhora dos Remédios**
- ✉ Praça da Matriz
- 🕐 Closed Mon.
- 💲 $

## Centro Histórico

In 1966, Paraty's Centro Histórico was declared a national historic site. Although most of its bleached-white 18th- and 19th-century houses and *sobrados* (mansions) are quite modest, one of the most striking is the **Casa da Cultura,** built in 1758. Aside from playing host to diverse cultural events, this cultural center houses a permanent exhibition devoted to Paraty's history, which dates back to its indigenous origins. Also on site is a small shop selling locally produced *artesanato* and a café, whose tables

beneath a 100-year-old pitanga tree offer shady respite.

Paraty boasts a quartet of fetching churches, each of which reflects the needs (and means) of the communities that built them. From the Casa da Cultura, walk two blocks north to Rua da Capela. Turn right and walk to the edge of the sea, where you'll see the single tower belonging to **Igreja de Nossa Senhora das Dores.** Built in 1800 on behalf of Paraty's wealthy doyennes, the church's strategic location assured local aristocrats access to refreshing breezes during long services.

Retracing your steps back up Rua da Capela brings you to Paraty's principal and most lavish church, **Igreja de Nossa Senhora dos Remédios,** better known as Igreja da Matriz. Constructed on the site of a 17th-century chapel devoted to Paraty's patron saint (Our Lady of Remedies), this neoclassical church where the city's bourgeoisie worshipped was completed in 1873. The surrounding **Praça da Matriz** is a picturesque square where a daily crafts market takes place.

Following Rua da Matriz for two blocks, then turning right on Rua Dr. Samuel Costa and taking it until Rua do Comércio, will bring you to the **Igreja de Nossa Senhora do Rosário e São Benedito,** a simple church built in 1725 by and for Paraty's slave population. Interestingly, it's the only church in town whose altars are doused with gold (added in the 20th century). Continue following Rua do Comércio to

Rua Aurora, then turn and walk toward the bay until you reach Paraty's oldest surviving church, the **Igreja de Santa Rita dos Pardos Libertos.** Its gleaming white baroque facade contrasts strikingly with the surrounding emerald lawn. Built by freed slaves, its lovely interior contains a small sacred art museum.

## Forte Defensor Perpétuo

Beyond the Centro Histórico, a pleasant 15-minute stroll past the main urban beach of Praia do Pontal leads to the Forte Defensor Perpétuo. Perched atop the Morro da Velha, this defensive fortress was built in 1703 in an attempt to dissuade pirates from trying to get their hands on gold shipments. Restored in 1822, it shelters a modest museum of regional folk art.

*(continued on p. 232)*

**Igreja de Nossa Senhora do Rosário e São Benedito**
- ✉ Rua do Comércio
- 🕐 Closed Mon.

**Igreja de Santa Rita dos Pardos Libertos**
- ✉ Largo de Santa Rita
- 🕐 Closed Mon.–Tues.

**Forte Defensor Perpétuo**
- 🗺 206 A1
- ☎ 24/3371-1038
- 🕐 Closed Mon. (museum)
- 💲 $

Paraty's Centro Histórico presents a snapshot of colonial Brazil.

# Cachaça

Just as Mexicans have their tequila and Cubans swear by their rum, Brazilians can't do without their cachaça. Indeed, according to the Brazilian Cachaça Institute (IBRAC), the average Brazilian annually tipples around 2.5 gallons (11 L) of this powerful spirit (whose alcohol content ranges from 38 to 80 percent).

Cachaça serves as the base of numerous (and potent) Brazilian cocktails.

Distilled from unrefined sugarcane juice (rum is distilled from sugarcane molasses), cachaça dates back to early colonial days, when African slaves in Brazil's Northeast discovered that the by-products of sugarcane, boiled and fermented, rendered a potent brew that helped ease the crushing physical labor of sugar plantations. Harsh tasting and nasty smelling, yet very cheap to produce, for centuries cachaça was looked down upon as *aguardente* (firewater) of the (colored) masses by Brazil's wine- and Port-swilling white aristocrats.

Beginning in the 1990s, however, influenced by the global trend toward appreciating

traditional, local products and artisanal production methods, cachaça began to receive some well-deserved respect from Brazil's upper classes, not to mention the government, which, in 2001, trademarked the cachaça name with the aim of marketing it, both domestically and overseas, as a fine spirit. Indeed, in recent years, rising interest coupled with innovative new techniques have resulted in some extremely fine artisanal, and even organic, cachaças. Fragrant, heady, and ranging in color from honey to bronze, like premium whiskeys, this new generation of cachaças is intended to be savored pure. They are very different from the

**INSIDER TIP:**

Served in the world's most sophisticated watering holes, the caipirinha, Brazil's national cocktail, is a heady mix of cachaça, sugar, and limes; ironically, its name derives from *caipira,* bumpkin.

—LESLIE ALLEN
*National Geographic author*

inexpensive, clear cachaças created by Pitú, Ypióca, 51, and Sagabita, which are the brands most often used in combination with ample quantities of sugar, crushed lime, and ice to make Brazil's national cocktail, the caipirinha.

Various Brazilian regions are famed for making excellent cachaças. Foremost among them is Minas Gerais, where there is proliferation of small mills, and Paraty, whose production of *pinga* (a popular euphemism for cachaça that means "drop") dates back to the late 18th century. At the time, the area surrounding Paraty was home to hundreds of sugarcane plantations and distilleries. Not only did sugar and cachaça fuel the local economy, but the superior quality of the local product resulted in the name Paraty becoming synonymous with top-notch cachaça.

## Paraty's Cachaça Tradition

Today, seven traditional distilleries keep Paraty's cachaça tradition alive and thriving. You can purchase their wares in *cachaçarias* and emporiums in the historical center—particularly well stocked are **Armazém da Cachaça** *(Rua do Comércio 279, tel 24/3371-7519)* and **Empório da Cachaça** *(Rua Dr. Samuel Costa 22, tel 24/3371-6329),* which has a cachaça museum featuring more than 5,000 labels. It's also possible to visit the *alambiques* themselves. Located a short distance from town, many have been in existence for generations, including **Maria Izabel** *(access at km 568*

*of BR-101, tel 24/9999-9908).* The most artisanal of the bunch, it is also the only distillery owned and operated by a woman, Maria Izabel Gibrail Costa, who incorporates tricks of the trade passed down by her great-great-grandfather. Also worth dropping by are **Engenho D'Ouro** *(Estrada Paraty-Cunha, km 8, tel 24/9832-7339),* where a lovely restaurant serves regional home-cooked fare, and **Pedra Branca** *(Estrada da Pedra Branca, km 1, tel 24/7835-4065),* which possesses a small shop selling typical *doces* (sweets).

And if you are not already a cachaça convert, you will be if you hit town during the annual **Festival da Pinga.** Held the third week of August, local pingas are celebrated and sampled during four days and four nights of tastings and related events at Praça da Matriz.

Barrels of fine cachaça, aging for flavor

Untamed beach landscape at Trindade

**Trindade**
 206 A1

## Beaches

The beaches closest to Paraty are hardly indicative of the paradisiacal crème de la crème available if you make a little effort. Only a ten-minute walk from the historical center, **Praia do Pontal** boasts a vibrant beach bar scene, but is too polluted for bathing. Happily, every day, fleets of sailboats, schooners, launches, and fishermen's boats depart from the Cais de Porto, in front of the Igreja de Santa Rita, offering tourists a small but indelible sampling of the 65 islands (many of them private) and 200 beaches located around the Bay of Paraty. **Paraty Tours** (*Av. Roberto Silveira 11, tel 24/3371-1327, www.paratytours.com.br*) offers popular five-hour schooner trips around the bay, which include stops at such islands as **Ilha Comprida** (ideal for diving) and otherwise hard-to-get-to beaches such as **Praia Vermelha** (known for its rusty-red sands). Because many of these group trips include caipirinhas and loud Brazilian pop, those who prefer a little peace and quiet should consider chartering their own boat from the *barqueiros* at the Cais; you can negotiate an hourly rate (based on group size) and customize your voyage.

**Around Trindade:** Some of the region's most alluring and easily accessible beaches can be found at Trindade, a fishing village and former hippie haven. Only 16 miles (25 km) south of

Paraty on the main Rio–Santos highway, it is easily reached by regular local buses departing from Paraty's terminal. Trindade's main urban beach is the long, white-sand **Praia de Fora.**

To the east lie the wild and windswept **Praia de Cepilho** and **Praia Brava,** whose rough waves are sought out by surfers. To the west, **Praia do Meio** and **Praia Cachadaço** beckon those in search of natural pools in which you can snorkel or float. Cachadaço can be reached by hiking for 20 minutes through lush forest (or a 5-minute boat ride) from Praia do Meio. From Praia do Meio, you can also grab a boat to two of Trindade's farthest and most deliciously unspoiled beaches: **Praia do Sono** and **Praia dos Antigos,** 20 and 30 minutes away, respectively.

**Paraty-Mirim & Around:**
Another easily accessible beach is **Paraty-Mirim.** Only 11 miles (18 km) southwest of Paraty, it can be reached by municipal bus or driving along the BR-101 Although one can easily divide

**INSIDER TIP:**

**Paraty is my favorite place outside Rio. It is a wild place, full of incredible beaches, outdoor activities, and affordable accommodations. It's best to go during the workweek.**

—LUIZ RENATO MALCHER
*Manager, Rio de Janeiro Urban Adventures*

**Paraty-Mirim**
⚓ 206 A1

the day between kicking back at a *barraca* (rustic beach bar) and floating in the tranquil waters of the bay, it's only a quick 30-minute boat ride away from **Saco do Mamanguá—** Brazil's only fjord. Hemmed in by dramatic mountains and surrounded by a protected mixture of Atlantic Forest and mangroves, this narrow 5-mile (8 km) bay shelters no fewer than 30 pristine beaches. Paraty Tours offers canoeing and hiking excursions to the fjord. ∎

---

## EXPERIENCE: Going for the Gold

In the event you should tire of the life horizontal on Paraty's beaches, there is no shortage of hiking trails that weave up and down the jungly coastline and into the mountains of the Serra da Bocaina.

One of the quickest, easiest, and most fascinating walks you can do is a 1.5-mile (2.5 km) stretch of the historic 746-mile (1,200 km) **Caminho do Ouro.** A feat of engineering—not to mention back-breaking labor by the slaves who paved the mountainous route with irregular

stones—this trail was the route by which gold from Minas Gerais was transported down to Paraty. The 1.5-hour trek can be undertaken with a guide from the **Centro de Informações Turísticas Caminho do Ouro** (*Estrada Paraty-Cunha, tel 24/3371-1222, closed Mon.–Tues., $$$*). **Paraty Tours** (see p. 232) also leads a trek up the mountain. During the ascent into the heights, you are treated to some stupendous views of Paraty and its bay as well as refreshing dips into waterfalls.

# TRAVELWISE

Bike Rio is the city's public bicycle rental system.

## PLANNING YOUR TRIP

### When to Visit

Because of its tropical climate, Rio can be visited throughout the year; however, certain times are preferable to others.

While things begin heating up (and not just climatically) as early as November, Rio's summer starts with a bang on New Year's Eve when Réveillon festivities lure scores of tourists to the city. From January 1 until Carnaval, the Rio summer blazes away. Temperatures can reach 104°F (40°C), and beaches are packed with vacationers (Christmas through mid-February is school summer vacation). Samba schools and *blocos* across the city go into rehearsal overdrive. During this time, a laid-back yet hedonistic atmosphere reigns, culminating in the eruption that marks the five days of Carnaval festivities (usually sometime in February). Those who love parties, animation, music, and heat (literally and figuratively) will enjoy Rio during the summer.

There are also several downsides to summer in Rio, though. Not only is the city hot, it's extremely humid. Brief but often torrential rains are frequent and can cause flooding, and even landslides, in the city and surrounding mountains. The city is more crowded—and chaotic—during the summer months, too. Tourism (both national and international) is at its peak, which means lines and crowds at the more popular sites and other destinations in the mountains or along the coast. Summer also sees the highest prices in Rio. Recently it's been said that high season in Rio is year-round, but rates for everything from hotels to beach chairs and beer spike around New Year's and Carnaval, when accommodations across the board are hiked up astronomically (most places only sell fixed-price packages for a minimum number of days).

Winter in Rio—which lasts from June through September—can be a nice time to visit, especially if you like cool weather. There are many bright, clear days with temperatures hovering comfortably in the 70s°F (mid to high 20s°C). However, also expect cold fronts from Antarctica that bring brisker winds and temperatures, along with rain that can sometimes last for two or three days—which puts a damper on beach excursions, for sure. While the milder temperatures can be invigorating for those who like hiking and climbing in the mountains, bathing in waterfalls (and even the ocean) can be a challenge for those wary of cold water. Since the month of July coincides with winter vacations for schools and universities throughout Brazil, tourism (and prices) usually escalate during that month.

Fall and spring are not very pronounced seasons in Rio, but both bring with them the city's most moderate temperatures and the least rainfall. They are also the closest thing Rio has to a low season, which means greater availability and lower prices for accommodations and far fewer fellow tourists. Visting during these seasons enables you to explore Rio much more at your ease, which can be very rewarding.

Regardless of the time of year, Brazilians have a great many public and religious holidays. When they fall on a Friday or Monday (or even Thursday or Tuesday), Cariocas are fond of taking long weekends during which they escape to nearby beaches, mountains, or even other Brazilian states. It's worth doing some advance research to make sure you avoid these times. If not, you may find it difficult to find accommodations or flights and bus tickets, while having to contend with traffic, crowds, and higher prices (particularly if you're planning a getaway in Rio state).

## What to Take

While Cariocas are a notoriously relaxed and casual bunch, they place considerable emphasis on grooming and appearance. You don't want to draw too much attention to yourself (leave the jewels, watches, and obvious designer duds at home). However, you also mustn't confuse summery with slovenly—oversized T-shirts and baggy cargo shorts qualify as the latter. Go with lighter colors (dark shades will absorb heat, though black is popular for evening wear). Opt for natural fabrics that breathe and don't require ironing. A lightweight waterproof jacket and a portable umbrella are useful for sudden rainstorms. Comfortable walking shoes are necessary for navigating the streets and forest trails (hardcore hikers will want to bring light boots). Even during the summer, a sweater or jacket is a must on account of frigid air-conditioning in many interiors. Remember that the mountains are always cooler, especially in the winter months. Hats and dark glasses provide essential protection from the powerful sun year-round.

For security purposes, a money belt is useful for transporting cash, credit cards, and documents. Bring multiple credit cards in case one gets lost, is cloned, or is temporarily frozen by your bank (as many a chagrined traveler knows, this sometimes occurs even if you've conscientiously informed your bank that you'll be traveling). A cheap, unlocked cell or smartphone and a tablet or laptop can come in very handy. If you insist on bringing more expensive gadgets, be careful not to flash them in public; transport them (and all other valuables) in nondescript bags that don't announce the contents.

Bring copies of all prescriptions; in a pinch, a pharmacist can find the Brazilian equivalent for you. Although you can easily find common OTC remedies such as acetaminophen and antidiarrheals, you might want to bring your customary brands from home.

Definitely bring potent mosquito repellent (with citronella), which is hard to find in Brazil, as well as tons of high-SPF sunblock. In Brazil, sunscreen is marketed as a high-ticket beauty product and is priced accordingly (it's little wonder the country has the highest incidence of skin cancer on the planet).

## ENTRY FORMALITIES
### Passports & Visas

Brazil has a policy of diplomatic reciprocity, which means that if your country requires Brazilians to acquire a tourist visa, they will require you to get one at the nearest Brazilian consulate prior to your trip. Presently, citizens of the United States, Canada, and Australia require visas. Visa application forms can be filled out online (http://scedv.serpro.gov.br). You can make the necessary appointment for an interview online as well. Appointments are required for each visa applicant. Try to do this in advance, since slots can get booked up. Some travel agents specializing in Brazil can process your visa for you for an extra fee. Citizens of European Union countries and New Zealand don't require visas, but must have a passport, valid for six months, in addition to a return ticket. Upon arrival, you'll be issued a 90-day tourist visa.

It generally takes about a week to process a tourist visa. Requirements include a color passport photo, proof of a return ticket (or e-ticket confirmation), and payment of a fee (usually in the form of a money order). Tourist visas are valid for multiple entries within the period shown on the visa stamp.

Should you want to stay longer in Brazil, visas can be renewed for another 90 days at the visa section of the Polícia Federal headquarters in any major Brazilian city (a list of offices can be found online at www.dpf.gov.br). This should be done 15 days prior to your visa's expiration. Online, you can schedule an appointment for your extension and fill out the necessary form, the Guia de Recolhimento da União (GRU), which you should bring, along with your passport, airline ticket, credit card (as proof of financial means), and the entry/exit form that all foreigners receive upon entering Brazil. The GRU includes the fee for an extension, which can be paid at any Banco do Brasil branch. Upon payment, you'll receive a receipt, which you must also bring to the Polícia Federal. If you overstay your 180-day limit, you'll be charged a fine.

## Brazilian Embassies

### United States
3006 Massachusetts Avenue NW
Washington, D.C. 20008
(202) 238-2823
http://washington.itamaraty
.gov.br

### Canada
450 Wilbrod Street
Ottawa, ON K1N 8J2
(613) 237-1090
http://ottawa.itamaraty.gov.br

### United Kingdom
14–16 Cockspur Street
London SW1Y 5BL
(020) 7747-4500
www.brazil.org.uk

## Immigration & Customs

Upon entering Brazil, foreign travelers will receive a customs form and an entry/exit card (cartão de entrada/saída) to fill out. Immigrations officials will stamp the card and give you a copy. Keep it with your passport, since it will be collected upon your departure (losing it can result in bureau-cratic wrestling with the Federal Police and a possible fine). Due to Brazil's reciprocity policy, U.S. citizens entering the country will be

photographed and fingerprinted, just as Brazilians are upon their arrival in the United States.

All passengers can be arbitrarily pulled over for baggage inspection when going through customs, although officials are more concerned with Brazilians who return loaded down with clothing and gadgets after going on foreign shopping sprees. The current duty-free limit is US$500. Cash in excess of R$10,000 must be declared. Prior to going through customs, passengers can opt to shop at the airport duty-free shops (a perk available to arriving as well as departing international travelers) where they can make up to US$500 in duty-free purchases.

## GETTING TO RIO
### Airports & Airlines

Rio has two airports. International flights and most domestic flights arrive at **Aeroporto Internacional Antônio Carlos Jobim** (tel 21/3398-4527, www.aeroporto galeao.net). Also known as Galeão, it is located on the Ilha de Governador, in the Zona Norte, some 12 miles (20 km) from Centro. The smaller, older, and more scenic **Aeroporto Santos Dumont** (tel 21/3814-7070, www.aeroportosantosdumont.net) is reserved for certain domestic flights, particularly the air shuttle that links Rio with São Paulo. Perched on Guanabara Bay, it is located in Centro.

Most leading international air carriers have flights to "Tom" Jobim Airport, although some entail stopovers or connections in São Paulo's Guarulhos International Airport, a principal international point of entry into Brazil. Flight time from São Paulo to Rio is approximately 40 minutes.

Many hotels and guesthouses can organize airport transfers. After a long overnight flight, this is the easiest, but often most expensive,

means of getting to your final destination. In terms of taxis, you can prepay a fare based on distance at the private airport taxi kiosks located in the arrivals terminal. You can also grab one of the white radio taxis at the outdoor stand, for which you'll be charged a (less expensive) metered fare. Make sure you use a registered taxi company. Unofficial "pirate" taxis are not uncommon, and there are cases of unsuspecting tourists being taken for a ride and robbed. If a driver approaches you and offers to take you into town, always refuse.

The least expensive way to get into town is to hop aboard the regular shuttle buses operated by **Premium Auto Ônibus** (tel 21/3194-3030, www.premiumauto onibus.com.br, R$12). Departing at 30-minute intervals between 5:30 a.m. and 11:30 p.m. from the arrivals terminal, buses head to Centro before continuing along all the main oceanfront avenidas of Flamengo, Botafogo, Copacabana, Ipanema, Leblon, and Barra. Aside from making stops along the way (you'll need to request one), the buses pull into the main bus terminal (Rodoviária Novo) and Santos Dumont Airport. Depending on traffic, expect a 30-minute journey to Centro and 60 minutes to Copacabana and Ipanema.

### By Boat

Rio is Brazil's biggest port of call for the escalating number of international cruise ships to South America. Currently undergoing a major expansion and renovation process, the **Porto do Rio de Janeiro** (tel 21/2223-3004, www .portosrio.gov.br) is located in Centro's Praça Mauá. While cruises can be expensive, portions can often be purchased at a considerable discount.

## By Bus & Car

Located in the Zona Norte neighborhood of São Cristovão (midway between Galeão and Centro), Rio's constantly expanding, increasingly modern, main long-distance bus terminal is the **Rodoviária Novo Rio** *(tel 21/3213-1800, www.novorio.com .br)*. Buses arrive from all over Rio de Janeiro state and Brazil, as well as from some neighboring South American countries. Long-distance bus travel within Rio state is quite efficient and comfortable. Numerous companies operate vehicles equipped with plush, fold-back seats, bathrooms, and air-conditioning.

From Rio, well-paved highways lead up and down the coast (east toward Búzios and west toward Paraty) and north into the mountainous interior. Highways are well maintained (some are privately owned and charge tolls). Beware of traffic, however, particularly at the beginnings and ends of weekends and holidays. Also beware of driving at night or in the rain, particularly on curving mountain roads.

## GETTING AROUND
### Public Transport

Rio has an extensive and fairly inexpensive public transportation system, which consists of an efficient but limited—albeit slowly expanding—Metrô system and a wide-reaching, if sometimes tricky-to-navigate, bus system.

### Metrô

Rio's Metrô is safe, efficient, clean, and air-conditioned. Unfortunately, it's extent is limited. While plans are underway to extend Linha 1 to Barra (this new line will be Linha 4), presently one can get only as far south as the beginning of Ipanema. (Until the end of 2013, Ipanema/ General Osório station is closed

while the line is being extended; in the meantime, the last stop is Cantagalo in Copacabana.) However, the Metrô is handy for gliding around between Copacabana, Botafogo, Flamengo, Catete, Glória, and parts of the Zona Norte (such as Maracanã), as well as Centro, which has many stations. While rush hour can be a crush, the Metrô can be a time-saving alternative to surface gridlock, even if it seems perverse to miss the scenery.

In recent years, **MetrôRio** *(tel 0800/595-1111, www.metrorio.com .br)* has expanded coverage by adding "surface" Metrôs. These are special connecting express buses that depart from certain hub Metrô stations such as Botafogo and, until Ipanema/General Osório station is reopened, Siqueira Campos (Copacabana) and provide express service to neighborhoods such as Urca, Jardim Botânico, Gávea, and Barra via São Conrado. Simple Metrô and combined Metrô/surface Metrô and Metrô/bus tickets can be purchased in all stations, as can prepaid R$10 cards to which credit can be added. This option can help you avoid long lines. The Metrô operates from 5 a.m. to midnight Monday to Saturday, and 7 a.m.– 11 p.m. on Sunday. On weekends and holidays, bicycles and surfboards can be taken on trains.

### Bus

You can get virtually everywhere you want to go in Rio by bus; there are more than 400 lines. When not slowed by traffic, Carioca bus drivers have a tendency to go very fast. In general, Rio's buses are fairly safe; however, tales of pickpockets and even armed holdups are not uncommon. That said, during the day, careening around between points in Centro, the Zona Sul, and the Zona Oeste beaches of Barra and Recreio is fairly safe. After dark,

it's best to limit your bus-riding to the busier, better policed neighborhoods of the Zona Sul. Regardless of the hour, don't carry around a lot of valuables, and make sure nobody can slip a hand into your pocket or bag (remove your backpack from your back). Have change ready to avoid sorting through wads of bills.

Bus line numbers and final destinations are displayed on the front of the bus. On the side, the route's first, last, and major stops will be indicated. It's important to clarify the route, since there are often several that lead to the same destination. For instance, some buses whose final destination is Leblon will travel along a coastal route, via Copacabana and Ipanema; others go inland, via the Lagoa Rodrigo de Freitas, making stops in Botafogo, Jardim Botânico, and Gávea. Passengers enter the bus at the front and pay the *cobrador* (collector) before going through a turnstile. Keep in mind that cobradores won't have change for large bills. If the bus is crowded, make your way to the middle or back-door exit well in advance of your stop.

### Driving in Rio

Driving in Rio is not for the faint of heart. Cariocas have a natural tendency to drive as if they're competing in a Formula One event. Add factors such as steep, potholed, one-way streets, poor signage, difficulties with parking, and security issues—which range from parked car break-ins to holdups when drivers are stalled in traffic or at stoplights—and you'll see the wisdom of relying on public transit and taxis.

The only instance in which renting a car truly makes sense is for getting out of town and exploring the mountains and coastline of surrounding Rio de Janeiro state. If you're traveling with children or have mobility problems, you also may want to consider renting a car. Major companies include **Avis** *(tel 0800/725-2847, www.avis.com .br)* in Copacabana; **Hertz** *(tel 0800/701-7300, www.hertz.com.br)* with agencies at the airports and in Copacabana; and **Localiza** *(tel 0800/979-2000, www.localiza.com .br)* with agencies at both airports and in Leme and Barra.

Those who do choose to drive should know that Brazil has a "zero tolerance" law. As a result, you'll encounter impromptu police "blitzes" in which drivers are arbitrarily pulled over and required to take breathalyzer tests. Even the slightest trace of alcohol can result in a hefty fine and a driving suspension.

There are few parking lots and no parking meters in Rio. Instead, when you find a spot on the street, you'll immediately be approached by an informal attendant known as a *flanelinha*. Aside from helping you navigate in and out of (often tight) spaces, the flanelinha will promise to watch over your car. Unless you're just stopping for a short while, you're pretty much obliged to pay him for his services (failure to do so can result in reactions that range from surliness to a mysterious scratch on your fender). Regardless, don't leave any valuables in the car, even in the trunk.

## Taxis

Taxis—plentiful, comfortable, and relatively inexpensive—are a great option for getting around Rio. There are two types. The most common are the yellow vehicles with blue stripes, which can be hailed in the streets and are generally cheaper. Larger white, air-conditioned radio cabs can be ordered by phone and are a little more expensive. **Central de Taxis** *(tel 21/2593-2598)* and **Coopacarioca** *(tel 21/2518-1818)* are two reliable companies.

Unless a fixed rate is agreed upon, all fares are metered (before starting a journey, make sure the meter is reset to R$4.30). Throughout the day, until 8 p.m., a standard rate—known as Bandeira 1—is used. At night, on Sunday, and during holidays and the entire month of December, a more expensive Bandeira 2 rate is applied.

Rio cab drivers are generally friendly, knowledgeable, and honest. Very few speak English, although this is changing due to a municipal program that aspires to teach hundreds of cabbies English in time for the 2014 FIFA World Cup. For longer trips as well as half-, full-, or multiple-day outings to points around the city and Rio de Janeiro state, you can usually bargain an attractive fixed rate. If you hit it off with a specific driver, you can even end up using him or her as your own personal driver (many smaller hotels and guesthouses do this).

## Cycling in Rio

Rio's natural setting combined with its climate makes it idyllic for cycling. The city possesses 80 miles (130 km) of bicycle paths. The flattest, and least strenuous, stretch along the ocean from Flamengo to Leblon and then along to Barra, or circle around the Lagoa Rodrigo de Freitas. More challenging are the steep trails leading into the Parque da Tijuca.

Off the bike routes, however, cycling in Rio becomes a dangerous undertaking. In addition to less-than-ideal road conditions, contending with heavy and erratic vehicle and pedestrian traffic is problematic; most Cariocas view biking as a recreational activity, not as a viable means of transportation, and they haven't been trained to share road space with cyclists.

However, like other major cities, Rio has implemented a bike

rental system, SAMBA. Constantly expanding, it currently boasts close to 60 terminals. To rent one involves registering at *www.mobilici dade.com.br*. There are rental options for a day or a month. Rides of up to 60 minutes are free, after which you'll be charged R$5 an hour. Registration and subsequent payments can be made with a credit card. The only catch is that to register and activate bikes, a cell phone number is necessary. Because of this, it's often easier to rent a bike at many of the reasonably priced rental services and kiosks in the Zona Sul and around the Lagoa, among them **Bike & Lazer** *(www.bikel azer.com.br)*.

## PRACTICAL ADVICE
### Addresses

In Brazil, street numbers always follow the name of the street itself. People usually include the name of their building—*edifício* (abbreviation: "Ed.")—since building names are often easier to spot (and better known) than the numbers. When giving directions, Brazilians actually rely a lot on visual reference points (for instance, a language school on the corner or a bar next door) as much as street names and numbers (it helps to have such information available for taxi drivers). In terms of commercial addresses, particularly those in shopping malls, addresses will include the number of the *loja* ("Lj"), or store. Addresses in residential and commercial buildings will also often include the *andar*, or floor. In Brazil, zip codes, known as CEPs, are 8 digits long.

### Communications
#### Cell Phones

Cell phones are extraordinarily widespread in Brazil, far more so than landlines. Unless you have a local calling plan, however, calls between cell phones are more expensive than those between fixed lines. North American cell phones should work in Brazil, provided they're unlocked (meaning you can remove and insert a Brazilian SIM card) and are compatible with international triband GSM 1800 standards. Traditionally, international roaming charges have been astronomically priced, but an increasing number of U.S. companies are offering special international packages. Another alternative is to purchase a Brazilian SIM card from cell phone provider TIM. TIM boutiques and kiosks can be found in Rio's shopping malls. You can also reach them by dialing #144. All you need to activate a SIM card is a copy of your passport.

### Internet

Internet access is rarely a problem in Rio. These days, in both the capital and the surrounding state, every type of accommodation, from the humblest hostel to the swankiest five-star hotel, will have Wi-Fi access. In most cases, this will be free, although some large chain hotels have taken to charging sometimes rather exaggerated rates. While it's best if you have your own smartphone, tablet, or laptop, a number of hotels and *pousadas* often have a computer (or media room with several) that you can use. Most shopping malls and an increasing number of cafés have free Wi-Fi zones, as well. Due to the high price of international roaming charges, it makes more sense to access local Wi-Fi. However, if you want to be constantly connected, **TIM** (*www.tim.com.br*), one of Brazil's largest cell phone providers, sells unlocked 3G mini-modems along with chips that allow you to browse on laptops and tablets for only R$2 per day.

Internet cafés were once legion throughout Brazil, but their numbers have dwindled with the expansion of laptops and smartphones. However, you'll still find plenty of "LAN houses" (LAN stands for Local Area Network). They tend to be more prominent in poorer neighborhoods or small towns where people have less access to expensive electronic gadgets or where telecommunications companies have expressed little interest in investing in high-speed fiber-optic systems. Rates are extremely affordable.

### Phone Numbers

All phone numbers in Rio de Janeiro (as throughout Brazil) have eight digits. It's necessary to dial the capital's area code of 21 only when dialing from outside the municipality. Other regions throughout Rio state also have two-digit area codes that begin with 2 (for example, 24 for Paraty). When calling long distance within Brazil, you need to precede the area code with 0 followed by a two-digit code, known as a DDD, belonging to one of several long-distance operators. The most universally used DDD—21—belongs to telecommunications giant Embratel. To call a pousada in Paraty from Rio, for example, you would dial 0-21-24 followed by the eight-digit number. You can also call Embratel if you want to make a collect call overseas. Just dial 0800/703-2111 and provide the operator with your number. Calling overseas directly from Brazil is expensive, but should you need to do so, dial 00-21 before the country code, area code, and number.

### Electricity

Depending on where you are in Brazil, you'll find the electric current varies from 110 to 220 volts, but in Rio and southeast Brazil, it is almost uniformly 110. This means that you can easily use all North American electronic devices and gadgets. The only problem is that, while most older outlets have the same two-pin flat-pronged outlets found in North America, increasingly the newer ones have the two-pin round-pronged outlets and three-pin outlets that are standard in Europe. While you can find inexpensive adaptors in most hardware stores, it's a good idea to pick one up at home prior to traveling.

### Etiquette & Local Customs

Brazilians, and Cariocas in particular, are famously relaxed and casual. This reigning attitude extends from notions of time (very fluid) and adherence to rules and regulations (sometimes surprisingly elastic) to dress (stylish, but laid back) and formalities (often viewed as hopelessly Anglo-Saxon). Cariocas' warmth is legendary, and rightfully so. They tend to embrace strangers—and foreigners, often quite literally. Kisses (one on each cheek) comprise the standard form of greeting between two women and a woman and a man. While men usually shake hands, an additional shoulder squeeze, slap on the back, or semi-hug is not uncommon.

Because Cariocas as a rule are more sensual and sexually open—not to mention less hung up about exposing their bodies—than many nations of the Northern Hemisphere, some foreigners confuse certain cultural codes—frank gazes, body proximity, affectionate touching—with sexual advances. Usually, however, such behavior merely reflects a playfulness and uninhibited manner of displaying affection characteristic of Brazilians.

At the same time, Brazil is a land of paradoxes. So, it's important to remember that beneath all the freewheeling, anything-goes ethos that Rio exudes, it's also a culture shaped by bureaucracy, machismo, and conservative religious beliefs. As such, when entering a place of worship—Christian or otherwise—take care to dress and behave with a degree of modesty. In government buildings, including archives, libraries, and municipal theaters, certain standards of decorum apply. Women should eschew miniskirts and skimpy tops, while men should opt for long pants. Flip-flops are a definite no-no.

## Liquor Laws

The official drinking age in Brazil is 18, but this is rarely enforced. Beer, wine, cachaça, and all other types of alcohol can be purchased easily and all the time at bars, grocery stores, and supermarkets, not to mention on the beach and from street vendors. Alcohol can also be consumed just about anywhere (with the exception, increasingly, of soccer stadiums). Indeed, North Americans will be thrilled by the ease with which they can stroll along a Carioca beach with a caipirinha in one hand. Although it's not a crime to drink in a car, it's a serious crime for a driver to have any alcohol in his or her system.

## Media

It's easy to get ahold of print versions of leading English-language international media (the *International New York Times*, *Time*, the *Economist*, and other major magazines) at airports as well as bookstores and large *bancas de revistas* (magazine stands) in the Zona Sul neighborhoods of Copacabana, Ipanema, and Leblon. Don't expect the latest editions, though, and count on paying inflated prices.

Rio has two daily papers: *Jornal do Brasil* (published only online) and *O Globo*, the latter published by the Globo media conglomerate. Both have arts and entertainment listings and are good sources for what's going on, even for non-Portuguese speakers. *O Globo* has an excellent entertainment supplement, "Rio Show," on Fridays. *Veja Rio*, a weekly guide to what's happening in the city, comes free with the purchase of *Veja*, one of Brazil's leading weekly news magazines. The *Rio Times* is a weekly English-language paper written by English-speaking expats living in the city. Apart from news, it covers events and activities in the city. The paper is distributed in hotels, hostels, restaurants, bars, boutiques, and cultural venues frequented by expats and travelers (primarily in the Zona Sul). You can also check it out online at *www.riotimesonline.com*. Also available online is *Time Out's* comprehensive guide to the city (*www.timeout.com/rio/en*) along with reviews of bars, restaurants, clubs, and cultural happenings, in both English and Portuguese versions.

In terms of television, most mid- and upscale hotels have cable packages that include all the leading English-language news, sports, and entertainment channels.

## Money Matters

### Brazilian Currency

Brazil's currency is the *real* (pronounced "ray-ALL"; the plural, *reais*, is pronounced "ray-EYES"). One real (R$1) is further divided into 100 *centavos*. Highly colorful, easily distinguishable real bills come in denominations of 2, 5, 10, 20, 50, and 100. Coins—of which there are sometimes multiple versions—come in 5, 10, 25, and 50 centavos as well as 1 real. Several years ago, 1 centavo coins were discontinued due to their relative worthlessness. As such, when making purchases, the total will be rounded up or down to the nearest multiple of 5 (so if you pay R$10 for something that costs R$9.98, you won't receive change; if it costs R$9.97, you'll receive 5 centavos).

### Banks

Banks are generally open Monday to Friday, from 10 a.m. to 4 p.m. ATMs (known as *caixas automáticas*) are open every day, but—for security reasons—usually only from 6 a.m. until 10 p.m. It's always a good idea to withdraw money during the day at a bank, street, or shopping center where there's a lot of activity. Most branches of Banco do Brasil and Bradesco have at least one ATM that accepts international Visa cards, while Bradesco, HSBC, and Citibank accept international Mastercard/Cirrus cards. Red Banco 24 Horas ATMs accept all cards, 24/7. In all cases, you'll need to have a four-digit PIN number. Most ATMs have an option for English users. The maximum daily withdrawal limit is usually R$1,000, and many machines have a withdrawal limit of R$300 after 10 p.m. for security reasons. If you're going somewhere off the beaten track in Rio state, it's wise to stock up on cash beforehand, although credit cards will be accepted by most hotels and larger restaurants.

### Credit & Debit Cards

In recent years, there has been a credit and debit card revolution in Brazil, to the extent that it's rare to see middle- and upper-class Brazilians using cash for even minor purchases. In Rio, you'll find few places that don't accept either Visa or Mastercard (if you can, it's a good idea to bring both). American Express and Diner's Club are less widely used. However, in more popular neighborhoods and at simple stores, kiosks, restaurants, bars, and markets (and at the beach), cash is often the only option. Cards offer more security than carrying around a lot of cash (although, due to credit card fraud, avoid letting your card out of your sight). However, one advantage of cash is that you can often negotiate discounts in terms of accommodations or purchases "em dinheiro."

## Opening Hours

Opening hours in Rio tend to vary slightly depending on the type of business and its location. Most stores, however, are open from 9 or 10 a.m. to 6 or 7 p.m. during the week and on Saturday. Some businesses close at noon or in the early afternoon on Saturday. An increasing number of stores are open on Sunday (usually opening later and closing earlier). Supermarkets and delicatessens are open daily, often until 10 p.m., but close earlier on Sunday. Shopping malls (and the boutiques, restaurants, and other services they shelter) are open every day from 10 a.m. to 10 p.m. and usually have reduced hours (such as 3–9 p.m.) on Sundays. Many Zona Sul bookstores—which often host literary and musical events—also have late-night hours. Most bars and the majority of restaurants are open until at least 11 p.m. early in the week, with extended hours on Friday and Saturday nights. Depending on the neighborhood, some bars (including juice bars) remain open until the small hours of the morning or until the last patron leaves. On Sundays and Mondays, some restaurants and bars close early or entirely.

## Public Holidays

Rio has a fair number of public holidays, most of which are national, others commemorated only within the capital or the state of Rio de Janeiro. While banks and other public services close on most of these occasions, many businesses—particularly those in tourist areas—stay open. The majority of museums and other tourist sites are usually open on these holidays (and often quite crowded as a result). Be forewarned that whenever these dates fall close to a weekend, Cariocas will transform them into a long holiday and hightail it out of town to popular getaways throughout Rio state.

January 1—New Year's Day
January 20—São Sebastião Day (birthday of Saint Sebastian, Rio's patron saint)
February or March—Carnaval (the Monday and Tuesday prior to Ash Wednesday are public holidays)
March or April—Good Friday
April 21—Tiradentes Day
April 23—São Jorge (Saint George) Day
May 1—Labor Day
September 7—Brazilian Independence Day
October 12—Nossa Senhora de Aparecida Day (Our Lady of Aparecida is Brazil's patron saint)
November 2—All Soul's Day
November 15—Proclamation of the Republic Day
November 20—Black Consciousness Day
December 25—Christmas Day

## Religion

Brazil is a secular nation that also happens to possess the world's largest concentration of Catholics. In recent years, the number of Catholics has dropped, from 81 percent of the population in 1991 to 65 percent in 2010, while Protestantism (mainly Pentecostal and evangelical churches, which have spiked in poor urban neighborhoods and rural areas) has soared—today close to 25 percent of Brazilians are adherents. An astonishing diversity of other religions, cults, and sects exist, as well, albeit in much smaller numbers. Due to its important African legacy, Afro-Brazilian religions such as Candomblé—whose followers worship divinities known as orixás—have a particularly strong influence in Rio, culturally as well as spiritually. You'll find proof in the number of flowers washed ashore on any given day along the city's beaches, offerings to the orixá Iemanjá, Queen of the Seas.

For those seeking services in English, the **Christ Church Anglican Church** (www.christchurchrio.org.br) and **Our Lady of Mercy Catholic School** (www.olmrio.com), both in Botafogo, offer Mass on Sunday mornings. Also in Botafogo is **ARI** (Associação Religiosa Israelita, www.arirj.com.br), a reform synagogue that offers services open to an international congregation.

## Restrooms

Public restrooms in Rio are pretty much nonexistent, the biggest exception being those located at some of the lifeguard postos along the beaches of Copacabana, Ipanema, and Leblon. Copacabana's new beachfront kiosks also have public restrooms that, like the postos, charge R$2. Legions of chemical port-a-potties fill the streets during major street festas, most notably Carnaval. However, free and clean facilities can be found in all museums and cultural centers (entrance to most of which is also free), as well as tourist attractions, shopping centers, bookstores, and bus and ferry terminals (for a small fee).

The newer Metrô stations have public toilets too.

## Smoking

In Rio, smoking is prohibited in most indoor spaces, including public buildings, restaurants, and bars (you can smoke outside on terraces or sidewalks). It's also prohibited on domestic flights and long-distance buses. In general, Brazilians are quite considerate about smoking and usually ask those around them if the smoke bothers them before lighting up.

## Time Differences

Rio is in the BRT (Brasilia Official Time) zone. Depending on the time of year—and whether the clocks have been advanced (for daylight saving time) or turned back (standard time)—the time difference between Rio and North American cities in the Eastern time zone can range from 1 to 3 hours. For instance, from March to September, when Rio is on standard time and North America is on daylight time, when it's 8 p.m. in Rio, it's 7 p.m. in New York City. In the summer months of October–February, however, Rio goes on daylight saving time, meaning the clocks go forward (and it stays light an hour later). During this period (which overlaps with the clocks being turned back in North America), when it's 8 p.m. in Rio, it's 5 p.m. in New York City.

## Tipping

Rio doesn't have a tipping culture. Restaurants and bars add a 10 percent service charge to all bills, which—at least, in theory—is to be shared among the staff. Should you find the service to be particularly outstanding, you can add a small and separate gratuity to your server (and let him or her

know). Most hotels also have a service charge (including on room service bills), but you can tip staff, particularly bellboys, a few reais. Instead of tipping taxi drivers, passengers usually round up the fare. It's customary to tip staff in spas and beauty salons 10 percent.

## Travelers With Disabilities

Despite ongoing improvements, Rio continues to be a major challenge for travelers with disabilities. An increasing number of (mostly larger and upscale) hotels and restaurants feature wheelchair facilities. So do a growing number of public buildings and tourist sites, among them Sugarloaf, the statue of Christ the Redeemer, and the Museu de Arte Moderna. Even Ipanema beach has a sidewalk for wheelchairs that cuts through the sand toward the sea. Riotur publishes a "Guide to Accessible Tourist Attractions," which lists more than 30 attractions equipped with elevators, ramps, level surfaces, and trained staff; it's available at information kiosks and at some hotels and tourist sites. The problem is less the venues themselves, than the chaotic traffic and poorly maintained or irregular streets and sidewalks. To date, a dozen Metrô stations have elevators (including those in Copacabana and Ipanema). An increasing number of buses have hydraulic lifts and reserved spaces for wheelchair users. It's also possible to hire a taxi equipped with boarding platforms. With the 2016 Olympics approaching, the city is investing more in accessibility; plans include sidewalk renovations and the installation of accessible public restrooms.

## Unit Conversions

Brazil uses the metric system. Weight is calculated in grams and kilograms (1 kg = 2.2 pounds), while liquids are measured in liters (1 L = 0.2 gallons). Distances are given in meters (1 m = 3.3 feet) and kilometers (1 km = 0.62 miles). Temperatures are in degrees Celsius (0°C = 32°F); to make a quick approximate conversion, double the Celsius temperature and add 30 (e.g., for 30°C, 30 x 2 + 30 = 90°F).

## Visitor Information

Riotur is the tourism agency for the city of Rio. It operates various information kiosks around town, including at the international arrivals sections of both terminals at Jobim International Airport, in the arrival hall of Novo Rio bus terminal, in Centro's Port Zone (Rua Barão de Tefé 5), on the first floor of Shopping da Gávea in Gávea, and in Copacabana—both at Av. Princesa Isabel 183 (bordering Leme) and on the beach (Av. Atlântica facing Rua Hilário de Gouveia). With varying hours, all are open seven days a week. Attendants usually speak passable and sometimes very good English. They can provide free maps and a useful bilingual Rio Guide, published monthly, which offers quite extensive (although not completely updated) listings along with a few timely feature articles. Many hotels also have copies on hand. Additionally, Riotur operates a 24-hour tourist hotline (tel 1746), with information available in English and Portuguese, and a vibrant, easy-to-access online guide (www.rioguiaoficial.com .br) that is quite exhaustive and includes news, images, videos, itineraries, and customized mini-guides devoted to Carnaval or LGBT travelers, for example.

# EMERGENCIES
## Crime & Police

For years, Rio was synonymous with crime and violence. However, over the past decade, the city has made significant strides in becoming safer, particularly in the central and Zona Sul areas. Much of this is due to a combination of the UPPs (Police Pacification Units), whose ongoing presence in favelas has cut down on drug trafficking and other violent crime, and beefed-up police presence in key tourist areas. Crimes such as thefts, pickpocketing, and hold-ups are still common, though, and precautions should always be taken, particularly after dark.

Rio has a special Tourist Police unit, the Delegacia Especial de Atendimento ao Turista, which specializes in all crimes against tourists. Agents are helpful and speak English. Open 24 hours a day, its Leblon headquarters are at Av. Afrânio de Melo Franco 159 *(tel 21/2332-2924)*.

## Lost or Stolen Property

Thefts should be reported to the Tourist Police, if only for insurance purposes. In the event of a loss or stolen passport, get in touch with your local consulate.

## Foreign Consulates in Rio
**United States Consulate**
Av. Presidente Wilson 147, Centro
21/3823-2000
http://riodejaneiro.usconsulate.gov

**Canadian Consulate**
Av. Atlantica 1130, 5th Floor, Copacabana
21/2543-3004
› www.canadainternational.gc.ca

**British Consulate**
Praia do Flamengo 284, 2nd Floor, Flamengo

21/2555-9600
http://ukinbrazil.fco.gov.uk

## Medical Emergencies

One of the top hospitals in Rio, the **Hospital Copa D'Or** *(Rua Figueiredo de Magalhaes 875, tel 21/2545-3600, www.copador.com.br)* has a private emergency room and English-speaking staff. Operated by the internationally accredited Rede D'Or Group, it is located in Copacabana. Also in Copa is the **Clínica Galdino Campos** *(Av. Nossa Senhora de Copacabana 492, tel 21/2548-9966, www.galdinocampos.com.br)*, a 24-hour private clinic with a multilingual staff that specializes in the treatment of foreigners.

## Emergency Phone Numbers
Fire: 193
Police: 190
Ambulance: 192

# FURTHER READING
## Fiction
*City of God* by Paulo Lins (1997)
*The Hour of the Star* by Clarice Lispector (1977)
*Posthumous Memoirs of Bras Cubas* by Machado de Assis (1881)
*Spilt Milk* by Chico Buarque (2012)
*The Taker, and Other Stories* by Rubem Fonseca (2008)

## History & Society
*Brazil on the Rise: The Story of a Country Transformed* by Larry Rohter (2010)
*Brazilian Journal* by P. K. Page (1987)
*Favela: Four Decades of Living on the Edge* by Janice Perlman (2010)
*Futebol: The Brazilian Way of Life* by Alex Bellos (2002)
*A Parisian in Brazil: The Travel Account of a Frenchwoman in 19th-Century Rio de Janeiro* by Adele Toussaint-Samson (2001)
*To Be a Slave in Brazil* by Katia M. de Queiroz Mattoso (1986)

## Music & the Arts
*Bossa Nova: The Story of the Brazilian Music That Seduced the World* by Ruy Castro (2003)
*Brazil Body and Soul* edited by Edward J. Sullivan (2003)
*Elizabeth Bishop in Brazil and After: A Poetic Career Transformed* by George Monteiro (2012)
*Samba* by Alma Guillermoprieto (1990)
*Tropical Truth: A Story of Music and Revolution in Brazil* by Caetano Veloso (2003)

## Food & Drink
*The Brazilian Table* by Yara Roberts (2009)
*Eat Smart in Brazil: How to Decipher the Menu, Know the Market Foods and Embark on a Tasting Adventure* by Joan and David Peterson (2006)

# Hotels & Restaurants

As the biggest tourist destination in the Southern Hemisphere, Rio is sometimes dismaying with its underwhelming, overpriced hotel accommodations. A handful of top luxury hotels are truly worth the splurge, but many conventional high-rise options can disappoint—which is why the birth of a new generation of small boutique hotels and guesthouses is so welcome. Meanwhile, Rio's restaurant scene is as hybrid and innovative, yet steeped in tradition, as the city itself—with the bonus that many spots take full advantage of its incomparable natural setting.

## Hotels

In recent years—much to the shock of many foreign visitors—Rio has become an expensive city in which to stay. Many of its traditional, chain-owned beach hotels are seriously overpriced, not to mention sadly out of date. Fortunately, spurred on by the upcoming World Cup and Olympics, much-needed renovations are taking place. Meanwhile, the city has witnessed a major blossoming of independently run boutique hotels, intimate *pousadas* (inns), and B&Bs offering personalized decor and service. While many of these are in the lovely hilltop neighborhood of Santa Teresa—where many foreigners have invested in old mansions rich in ambience and views—this trend is happily spreading to other parts of the city.

Most visitors to Rio understandably yearn to stay on the beach—particularly the Zona Sul beaches of Copacabana, Ipanema, and Leblon. Be aware, however, that beachfront hotels are extremely expensive—particularly if you want a room with a sea view. Rooms without views are more affordable, as are hotels situated back from the beach. If budget or charm is an issue, consider other residential, less touristy, but interesting neighborhoods—Flamengo, Botafogo, Laranjeiras, Gávea, and Santa Teresa—where smaller, more atmospheric choices abound.

Although Brazilian hotels adhere to a five-star rating system, what passes for three stars in Rio won't necessarily meet with North American or European three-star expectations. In Brazilian hotels, breakfast is generally included in the rate. Depending on your digs, this can range from a couple of rolls, ham slices, and fruit juice to lavish tropical banquets that will keep you sated until midafternoon. Most accommodations have air-conditioning; if not, you can count on a ceiling fan (*ventilador*), which can also be effective.

## Restaurants

Rio has no shortage of restaurants, ranging from chic purveyors of haute and international cuisine to modest hole-in-the-walls where R$10–$15 will get you a homecooked "PF" *(prato feito)* consisting of just rustled-up beef, chicken, or fish, a small salad, and the ubiquitous *arroz* (rice) and *feijão* (beans) that are the traditional base of a popular Brazilian meal. It's worth splurging at some of the city's pricey temples of haute gastronomy, particularly those in which a dynamic new generation of chefs is busy creating a contemporary Brazilian cuisine that draws on local recipes and ingredients. However, keep in mind that many upscale, international-style restaurants haunted by Rio's upper classes are more expensive than equivalents you might encounter back home. Meanwhile, some of Rio's freshest and tastiest—not to mention most affordable—food can be found at its juice bars, self-service *quilo* restaurants (where you pay for your food by weight), and cafés, many of which are conveniently located in museums, cultural centers, and bookstores. One of the best sources of affordable and authentic Carioca food is the city's traditional neighborhood *botecos*, a considerable number of whose home-cooked specialties are renowned enough to have earned them the designation *baixa gastronomia*.

In Brazil, there is no tipping in restaurants or bars; instead, a service charge of 10 percent is added to the bill. In the rare event you encounter terrible (as opposed to merely lethargic) service, know that this is optional. That said, should service be really stellar, it's not uncommon to generously round up the bill.

## Organization & Notes

Hotels and restaurants are listed by chapter, then by price, and finally by alphabetical order. Hotels are listed before restaurants within each section. The no-smoking symbol can mean that the hotel either has nonsmoking rooms or floors or is entirely nonsmoking. Smoking in restaurants and bars is prohibited.

## ■ CENTRO

### HOTELS

🏨 **OK**
**$$–$$$**
RUA SENADOR DANTAS 24
CENTRO
TEL 21/3479-4500
www.hotelok.com.br
Wedged onto a noisy little

## PRICES

### HOTELS

An indication of the cost of a double room in the high season is given by **$** signs.

| | |
|---|---|
| **$$$$$** | Over R$1,000 |
| **$$$$** | R$600–R$1,000 |
| **$$$** | R$400–R$600 |
| **$$** | R$200–R$400 |
| **$** | Under R$200 |

### RESTAURANTS

The average cost of a two-course meal for one person, excluding drinks, is given by $ signs.

| | |
|---|---|
| **$$$$$** | Over R$150 |
| **$$$$** | R$100–R$150 |
| **$$$** | R$60–R$100 |
| **$$** | R$30–R$60 |
| **$** | Under R$30 |

street behind Cinelândia, within spitting distance of Lapa, this is one of Centro's most convenient and best value options. Unprepossessing modern rooms vary in size, but boast big bathrooms and parquet floors. There's also a grand art deco lobby. Staff are notoriously friendly.
🛈 155 🍴 ❄ 🏊 💪 🏊 🪪

### 🏨 HOTEL BELAS ARTES
**$**
AV. VISCONDE DO RIO
BRANCO 52
CENTRO
TEL 21/2252-6336
www.hotelbelasartes.com.br
Tucked away in the heart of Centro, the rooms within this gracious historic building are very basic, but spotless. High ceilings and wooden floors add some personality. The price is unbeatable, but expect some street noise.
🛈 65 🅿 ❄ 🪪

## RESTAURANTS

### 🍴 RIO MINHO
**$$$$**
RUA DO OUVIDOR 10
CENTRO
TEL 21/2509-2338
Brazil was still an empire when Rio's oldest extant restaurant opened in 1884. Little about this traditional eatery has changed since then—including the recipe for its famous *sopa Leão Veloso*, a bouillabaisse-like stew that's become a Carioca institution. The Anexo next door serves smaller and less expensive versions of the same fish and seafood dishes.
🪑 60 🕐 Closed Sat. & Sun. ❄ 🪪

### 🍴 BAR LUIZ
**$$$**
RUA DA CARIOCA 39
CENTRO
TEL 21/2262-6900
This old-school German bar dates back to 1887 (during World War II, anti-Nazi protestors caused it to undergo a name change from Bar Adolph). Aside from schnitzels, sausages, and a famed potato salad, the bar is renowned for serving one of the best *chopps* (draft beers) in Rio.
🕐 Closed Sun. ❄ 🪪

### 🍴 ACONCHEGO CARIOCA
**$$**
RUA BARÃO DE IGUATEMI 379
SÃO CRISTOVÃO
TEL 21/2273-1035
Since being "discovered" by French superchef Claude Troisgros, this refreshingly unfashionable boteco in the refreshingly unfashionable Zona Norte (a stone's throw from Maracanã) has become a mecca for lovers of cold beer and lip-smacking *petiscos* (tapas). Full-fledged dishes are available, but don't dig in without indulging in *bolinhos de feijoada*, crispy black bean balls

served with orange slices and pork rinds. Be prepared to wait for a table.
🪑 75 ❄ 🪪

### 🍴 BISTRÔ DO PAÇO
**$$**
PRAÇA XV 48
CENTRO
TEL 21/2262-3613
Overlooking the central courtyard of the Paço Imperial, this cool and cavernous Swiss-owned bistro provides a calm oasis amid the mayhem of Centro. Light and rapid lunch offerings include salads, hot daily specials, and delicious quiches. Once the work crowd clears out, you can linger over coffee and bittersweet chocolate Brazil nut torte.
🪑 60 ❄ 🪪

### 🍴 SÍRIO E LIBANÊS
**$$**
RUA SENHOR DOS PASSOS 217
CENTRO
TEL 21/2224-1629
Located in the souklike heart of Saara, this simple family-owned restaurant has been serving Lebanese delicacies since 1965. The all-you-can-eat lunch *rodízio* is ideal if you're famished. Otherwise munch on a crunchy *kibe* at the counter.
🪑 96 🕐 Closed Sun. ❄

## SOMETHING SPECIAL

### 🍴 CONFEITARIA COLOMBO
**$–$$**
RUA GONÇALVES DIAS 32
CENTRO
TEL 21/2505-1500
The sumptuous belle epoque decor of this landmark café is more of a draw than the meals. Do as Cariocas do and order Portuguese pastries (sweet or savory) along with strong shots of *cafezinho*. Then sit back and pretend you're a 19th-century Brazilian

aristocrat.
🛏 330 🕒 Closed Sun.
🚫 ♿ 🏊

---

### 🍴 PALADINO

**$**

RUA URUGUAIANA 224/226
CENTRO
TEL 21/2263-2094
This century-old boteco/
emporium, its ceiling-high
wooden shelves teetering with
glistening bottles, is beloved
by Centro's workers for its
inexpensive home-cooked
lunches. Standouts include the
omelets, filled with the likes of
shrimp and bacalhau.
🕒 Closed Sun. 🚫

## ■ LAPA & AROUND

## HOTELS

### 🏨 SANTA TERESA
### 🍴 $$$$$

AV. ALMIRANTE ALEXANDRINO
660
SANTA TERESA
TEL 21/3380-0200
www.santa-teresa-hotel.com
Rio's only member of the
Relais & Chateaux group, this
luxurious hotel occupies a
200-year-old coffee plantation.
The decor riffs beautifully on
its Brazilian heritage by making
elegant use of tropical woods,
natural fibers, and folk art
from the Northeast. A jungle-
like garden, spa, infinity pool,
the achingly hip Bar dos Descasados, and one of the city's
most innovative contemporary
Brazilian restaurants, Térèze,
round out the sophisticated
trappings.
🛏 41 🚫 ♿ 🏊 🛗

### 🏨 CASA COOL BEANS
### $$

RUA LAURINDA SANTOS
LOBO 136
SANTA TERESA
TEL 21/2262-0552

www.casacoolbeans.com
The bright, cheery chalets and
rooms—each decorated by a
local artist—at this welcoming
B&B are operated by an
American couple that is as
friendly as they are organized;
aside from creating customized itineraries (complete
with directions and maps) for
guests, they offer a welcoming
array of U.S. home comforts
ranging from super-fluffy tow-
els to morning waffles topped
with Aunt Jemima syrup.
🛏 10 🚫 ♿ 🏊

### 🏨 QUINTA AZUL
### $$

RUA ALMIRANTE
ALEXANDRE 256
SANTA TERESA
TEL 21/3253-1021
www.quintaazul.com
Perched on Santa Teresa's
main long-and-winding
road, this friendly pousada's
rustically designed rooms are
stacked precipitously on a
hillside looking over Centro.
The largest and most coveted
Deluxe Room has a veranda
with a Jacuzzi. The staff is
warm and obliging.
🛏 11 🛗 🚫 ♿ 🏊 🛗

### 🏨 CASA DA GENTE
### $

RUA GONÇALVES FONTES 33
SANTA TERESA
TEL 21/2232-2634
www.casadagente.com
Tucked away on a residential
dead-end street, this French-
owned, environmentally
conscious guesthouse feels
like crashing at your cool and
very homey Carioca aunt's
extremely vertical five-story
house. You're given a key
and can come and go at your
leisure. Lapa's bohemia is
only a 5-minute walk away,
which can result in some lively
background noise.
🛏 9 🚫 ♿

---

## PRICES

**HOTELS**
An indication of the cost of
a double room in the high
season is given by $ signs.

| | |
|---|---|
| **$$$$$** | Over R$1,000 |
| **$$$$** | R$600–R$1,000 |
| **$$$** | R$400–R$600 |
| **$$** | R$200–R$400 |
| **$** | Under R$200 |

**RESTAURANTS**
The average cost of a two-
course meal for one person,
excluding drinks, is given
by $ signs.

| | |
|---|---|
| **$$$$$** | Over R$150 |
| **$$$$** | R$100–R$150 |
| **$$$** | R$60–R$100 |
| **$$** | R$30–R$60 |
| **$** | Under R$30 |

## RESTAURANTS

### 🍴 TÉRÈZE
### $$$$$

RUA FELÍCIO DOS SANTOS
SANTA TERESA
TEL 21/3380-0220
This elegant contemporary
restaurant belongs to the
luxurious Santa Teresa Hotel,
so expect a fair number
of wealthy and worldly
cosmopolitan types to be scat-
tered around the exquisitely
minimalist dining room. The
daring culinary creations draw
heavily on tropical ingredients
such as the brazil-nut-rolled
goat cheese with cupuaçu
jelly and the popular lobster
*moqueca*.
🪑 80 🚫 ♿ 🛗

### 🍴 ESPÍRITO SANTA
### $$$

RUA ALMIRANTE
ALEXANDRINO 264
SANTA TERESA

---

TEL 21/2507-4840
Chef Natacha Fink draws on the exotic produce of her native Amazon in surprising and seductive ways. Creamy cheese from Ilha de Marajó buffalos, fragrant cupuaçu, *bacuri,* and *jambu* fruit, even the odd piranha, all make their way into innovative dishes. Located in a 1930s hilltop house with a small terrace; request the coveted al fresco tables when making reservations.
🍴 70 🕐 Closed Tues.
🚭 ❄ 🗝

### 🍴 NOVA CAPELA
**$$$**
AV. MEM DE SÁ 96
LAPA
TEL 21/2252-6228
Dating back to 1903, this atmospheric bar is a classic after-hours Lapa pit stop. After samba-ing the night away, the legendary *cabrito assado* (roasted kid) with broccoli rice is particularly replenishing.
🚭 🗝

### 🍴 BAR BRASIL
**$$**
AV. MEM DE SÁ 90
LAPA
TEL 21/2509-5943
Open since 1907, this traditional boteco is renowned for its German specialties, such as *eisbein* (pigs' cheeks) and sauerkraut, as well as tap beer reputed to be the best in the city. The art covering the walls is by Selarón, creator of Lapa's famous mosaic staircase.
🍴 50 🕐 Closed Sun.
🚭 ❄ 🗝

### 🍴 BAR DO MINEIRO
**$$**
RUA PASCHOAL CARLOS MAGNO 99
SANTA TERESA
TEL 21/2221-9227
This small boteco imitates the style of a typically rustic

Minas Gerais bar and draws on Minas's rich culinary and distillery legacy with a delicious array of snacks such as *pastéis* filled with black beans, and sun-dried beef with pumpkin, not to mention some potent artisanal cachaças. On weekends, it's packed with Santa's bohos who flock in droves for one of the city's best feijoadas.
🍴 60 🕐 Closed Mon. 🚭 🗝

### 🍴 COSMOPOLITA
**$$**
TRAVESSA DO MOSQUEIRO 4
LAPA
TEL 21/2224-7820
This retro 1920s restaurant-bar is the birthplace of one of Rio's most iconic dishes: the *filé Oswaldo Aranha,* named after the local senator whose carnivorous cravings inspired this juicy steak slathered in garlic and served with rice, potatoes, and toasted manioc flour. Other less famous but equally tasty options abound. Portions easily serve two or three.
🍴 90 🕐 Closed Sun.
🚭 ❄ 🗝

### ■ CORCOVADO & PÃO DE AÇÚCAR

## HOTELS

### 🏨 CASA 32
**$$$$**
LARGO DO BOTICÁRIO 32
COSME VELHO, 22241-120
www.casa32.com
Those captivated by the movie-set-like charm of Largo do Boticário, with its colonial villas surrounded by jungle, can take comfort in the fact that it's actually possible to move into No. 32. This mid-19th-century house has been converted into an exclusive B&B with three impeccably decorated apartments that mingle antiques with modern conveniences. Guests have

the run of the entire house as well as the exuberant gardens watched over by Christ the Redeemer.
🚪 3 🚭 🗝 🏊 🗝

### 🏨 O VELEIRO
**$$**
RUA MUNDO NOVO 1440
BOTAFOGO, 22251-020
TEL 21/2554-8980
www.oveleiro.com
One of Rio's pioneering B&Bs, this restive home sits perched on a residential street halfway up to Corcovado, which means that the Tijuca Forest—and its chattering inhabitants—share the garden with guests. The Canadian-Carioca hosts are warm and very knowledgable.
🚪 3 🅿 🚭 ❄ 🏊

### 🏨 REGINA
**$$**
RUA FERREIRA VIANA 29
FLAMENGO, 22210-085
TEL 21/3289-9999
www.hotelregina.com.br
Few vestiges remain of this hotel's former life as a grand 1920s-era haven that was popular with statesmen and ministers due to its proximity to the Palácio do Catete. However, the clean, neutral rooms are comfortable and nicely priced. The location, half a block from Parque do Flamengo, is convenient and quiet.
🚪 117 🅿 🚭 ❄ 🗝 🎽 🗝

### 🏨 RIAZOR
**$**
RUA DO CATETE 160
CATETE, 22220-000
TEL 21/2225-0121
www.hotelriazor.com.br
The impressive 1890 facade is deceptive; the rooms are clean but threadbare. How much you enjoy the atmosphere of retro down-and-outness will depend on your frame of mind. Its strongest selling points are the location (across

from the Parque do Catete and next to the Metrô) and the low price.

ⓘ 50 🅿 🔲 🟦 🔲

## RESTAURANTS

### 🍴 PORCÃO RIO'S
$$$$
AV. INFANTE DOM HENRIQUE,
PARQUE DO FLAMENGO
FLAMENGO
TEL 21/3389-8989
Porcão (literally "big pig") is not for the mildly famished. The main event at this popular chain of *churrascarias* (barbecue houses) is the *rodízio*, a system whereby, every two minutes, a waiter arrives at your table brandishing a succulent cut of meat, which could be anything from blood sausage to ostrich. The irresistible all-you-can-eat buffet, piled high with sea-food, sushi, and salads, makes belt-loosening inevitable. This original location has the bonus of an in-your-face view of Sugarloaf. Kid-friendly, the place fills up on weekends with Carioca families.

🔲 800 🅿 🔲 🟦 🔲

### 🍴 MIAM MIAM
$$$
RUA GENERAL GÓES
MONTEIRO 34
BOTAFOGO
TEL 21/2244-0125
*Miam miam* is the Brazilian equivalent of "yum yum," which succinctly sums up the innovative French-infused Bra-zilian comfort food served at this stylish yet cozy restaurant, a convenient stone's throw from Shopping Rio Sul.

🔲 55 🕐 Closed Sun. &
Mon. 🟦 🔲

### 🍴 TACACÁ DO NORTE
$$
RUA BARÃO DO FLAMENGO 35
FLAMENGO
TEL 21/2205-7545

The next best thing to visiting the Amazon (from a culinary standpoint) is to make a foray to this humble but authentic boteco that specializes in dishes (and juices made with ambrosial Amazonian fruits such as bacuri) from the northern Brazilian states of Pará and Amazonas. Aside from an abundance of freshwater fish, try the *tacacá*, a heady shrimp-packed broth flavored with *tucupi* (a yellow sauce made from wild manioc root) and verdant jambu leaves, which will literally leave your tongue tingling.

🟦 🔲 🔲

### 🍴 BAR URCA
$–$$
RUA CÂNDIDO GAFRÉE 205
URCA
TEL 21/2295-8744
Tucked away in a 1930s building in tranquil Urca, this simple *botequim* is one of the most scenic in Rio, which is why on weekends it's mobbed with beautiful young Cariocas. It's also why you'll forsake the upstairs seafood restaurant and copy the locals: Take an icy beer and an order of *empadas*, grilled sardines, or seafood chowder to the sea-wall overlooking Guanabara Bay. Particularly captivating at sunset.

🟦 🔲 🔲

## ■ ZONA SUL BEACHES

## HOTELS

## SOMETHING SPECIAL

### 🏨 COPACABANA PALACE
$$$$$
AV. ATLÂNTICA 1702
COPACABANA, 22021-001
TEL 21/2548-7070
www.copacabanapalace.com
A landmark and a legend, as

famous as the namesake beach it sits upon, the Copacabana Palace is Rio's only surviving grand hotel. Though far from stylish, the rooms are sizable, and those who can splurge won't be disappointed by the barrage of old-school luxury and elegance. It has the city's best hotel pool. Truly one of the world's great hotels.

ⓘ 243 🅿 🔲 🟦 🔲 🔲
🔲 🔲

### 🏨 FASANO
$$$$$
AV. VIEIRA SOUTO 80
IPANEMA, 20241-260
TEL 21/3202-4000
www.fasano.com.br
For their Rio debut, the Fasano family—owners of São Paulo's most refined restaurants and hotels since 1900—hired French designer Philippe Starck to inject a heavy shot of contemporary into Ipanema's lackluster luxury hotel offer-

ings. Warm tropical accents merge with the coolness of glass, steel, wood, marble, and lots of blue Atlantic. The rooftop pool and clubby Londra bar are perennial hipster hangouts.

ⓘ 89 🅿 🔁 ⊗ 🔳 ⛱ 🎾 🔷

### 🏨 MARINA ALL SUITES
**$$$$$**

AV. DELFIM MOREIRA 696
LEBLON, 22241-000
TEL 21/2172-1100
www.marinaallsuites.com.br
The suites in question range from large to immense and are injected with decorative touches that are as personalized as the service. Celebrities in search of a discreet yet luxurious home away from home can be found dipping manicured toes into the penthouse pool and slinging back exotic *caipiroskas* at the insanely romantic Bar d'Hotel.

ⓘ 39 🅿 🔁 ⊗ 🔳 ⛱ 🎾 🔷

### 🏨 SOFITEL RIO DE
### 🍴 JANEIRO
**$$$$$**

AV. ATLÂNTICA 4240
COPACABANA, 22070-000
TEL 21/2525-1232
www.sofitel.com.br
Conscious that it can't compete with the Copacabana Palace for pedigree, Copa's "other" luxury beachfront hotel goes all out in terms of comfort, pampering, and services. All the ultramodern rooms have balconies overlooking the entire glorious crescent of beach, as do the expertly angled rooftop pools. The Le Pre Catalan is considered both the best French and best hotel restaurant in town.

ⓘ 388 🅿 🔁 ⊗ 🔳 ⛱
🎾 🔷

### 🏨 CASA MOSQUITO
**$$$$**

B RUA SAINT ROMAN 222
IPANEMA, 22071-060

TEL 21/3586-5042
www.casamosquito.com
Tucked behind Praça General Osório, on a steep street that rises up Morro do Pavão and overlooks both the favela and the beach, this French-owned boutiquey B&B is an unexpected oasis. Decorated with Gallic flair and dripping with terraces, rooms are divided between a 1940s house and a newer annex. Daily market produce inspires the menu (breakfast isn't included in the rate).

ⓘ 10 ⊗ 🔳 🔷

### 🏨 PROMENADE
### PALLADIUM
**$$$–$$$$**

RUA GENERAL ARTIGAS 200
LEBLON, 22441-140
TEL 21/3171-7400
www.hotel-promenade-palladium.com
Although the decor is bland, the clean, comfortable rooms, decent prices, and a terrific location 5 minutes from the beach make this innocuous, business-oriented apartment-hotel a superior option for Leblon-a-holics.

ⓘ 71 🅿 🔁 ⊗ 🔳 ⛱ 🎾 🔷

### 🏨 ARENA COPACABANA
**$$$**

AV. ATLÂNTICA 2064
COPACABANA, 22040-010
TEL 21/3034-1501
www.arenahotel.com.br
One of Avenida Atlântica's newest arrivals and best values, the Arena is all about gloss and modernity—from the decor to the amenities (including high-priced Wi-Fi). Rooms are bright and spacious; superior ones come with outstanding beach views. Friendly, accommodating service is a standout.

ⓘ 135 🔁 ⊗ 🔳 ⛱ 🎾 🔷

### 🏨 ARPOADOR INN
**$$$**

RUA FRANCISCO OTAVIANO 177

ARPOADOR, 22080-040
TEL 21/2523-0060
www.arpoadorinn.com.br
Mere feet away from the *surfista* mecca of Praia do Arpoador, with an enviable location straddling Ipanema and Copacabana beaches, this is Rio's only hotel that's actually right on the beach. It's worth forking out the considerable difference for the oceanfront rooms.

ⓘ 50 🔁 ⊗ 🔳 🔷

### 🏨 IPANEMA INN
**$$$**

RUA MARIA QUITÉRIA 27
IPANEMA, 22410-040
TEL 21/2523-6092
www.ipanemainn.com.br
The half block that separates this hotel from Ipanema's famous sands makes for lackluster views, but it also means affordable prices for this neck of the beach. Rooms are smallish and ordinary, but clean and functional. Ask for a recently renovated one (the remodeling process is working its way down from the upper floors). The multilingual staff is friendly.

ⓘ 56 🔁 ⊗ 🔳 🎾 🔷

### 🏨 OLINDA RIO
**$$$**

AV. ATLÂNTICA 2230
COPACABANA, 22041-001
TEL 21/2159-9000
www.othon.com.br
One of the few relics of Copa's glamour days, this late-1940s hotel has preserved retro charm—from the streamlined art deco facade to the glossy lobby adorned with Italian marble and crystal chandeliers. The comfortable rooms are disappointingly modern, though, despite original moldings, window frames, and high ceilings.

ⓘ 101 🔁 ⊗ 🔳 ⛱ 🔷

---

🔷 Nonsmoking 🔁 Air-conditioning 🔳 Indoor Pool ⛱ Outdoor Pool 🎾 Health Club 🔷 Credit Cards

### 🏨 MARGARIDA'S POUSADA
**$$**

RUA BARÃO DA TORRE 600
IPANEMA, 20241-260
TEL 21/2238-1840
www.margaridaspousada.com
One of Ipanema's best budget deals is this spartan yet clean and well-run place presided over by the maternal, no-nonsense owner, Margarida. Living quarters in the three-story house are basic and a little cramped, but the big payoff is location: a 5-minute walk from both Ipanema beach and the Lagoa.

🛏 11 🚭 ♿

### 🏨 RIO GUESTHOUSE
**$$**

RUA FRANCISCO SÁ 5
COPACABANA, 22080-010
TEL 21/2521-8568
www.rioguesthouse.com
Charming Carioca hostess Marta presides over the comfy, color-coded rooms and vast salons of this sprawling deco penthouse. Windows and terrace overlook the entire sweep of Copacabana. The only beachside B&B in the city, this is a refreshingly homey antidote to Avenida Atlântica's generic and gigantic chain hotels.

🛏 6 🚭 ♿ 🏊

### 🏨 SANTA CLARA
**$$**

RUA DÉCIO VILLARES 316
COPACABANA, 22041-040
TEL 21/2256-2650
www.hotelsantaclara.com.br
Five blocks from the beach, and far from the madding Copa crowd (but close to the Metrô), this modest, cozy hotel occupies a whitewashed house with blue shutters in the traditional and tranquil Bairro Peixoto part of Copa. Front-facing rooms with balconies are the brightest and breeziest.

🛏 12 🚭 ♿

### 🏨 SESC COPACABANA
**$$**

RUA DOMINGOS FERREIRA 160
COPACABANA, 20050-010
TEL 21/2548-1088
www.sescrio.org.br
Bedding down in this SESC cultural center has more bonuses than just easy access to in-house films and musical performances. The modernist building was designed by Oscar Niemeyer—and it's only one block from the beach. The good-value rooms are airy and minimalist. Those above the tenth floor offer impressive views of Corcovado.

🛏 120 🚭 🚭 ♿

## RESTAURANTS

### 🍴 AZUMI
**$$$**

RUA MINISTRO VIVEIROS DE CASTRO 127
COPACABANA
TEL 21/2541-4294
Eschewing trendy tricks and decor (but not lofty prices), this modest Japanese restaurant, one of the city's best, focuses on the impeccable preparation and presentation of classic dishes. The sparse, split-level space includes private bamboo-screened rooms where you can take off your shoes and enjoy the Zen environment.

🪑 70 🚭 ♿

### 🍴 CASA DA FEIJOADA
**$$$**

RUA PRUDENTE DE MORAES 10
IPANEMA
TEL 21/2247-2776
While Saturday is the day Cariocas traditionally reserve for eating feijoada, this restaurant's succulent version of the national stew of beans and various sundry pork parts can be savored every day, along with traditional garnishes ranging from sauteed collard greens and crispy pork rinds to *farofa* (crunchy manioc flour). To accompany it, order a lime caipirinha or passion fruit *batida*.

🪑 65 🚭 ♿

### 🍴 CT BOUCHERIE
**$$$**

RUA DIAS FERREIRA 636
LEBLON
TEL 21/2529-2329
Pioneering French chef Claude Troisgros—who revolutionized Brazil's gastronomic scene by applying French haute cuisine to Brazilian ingredients—has numerous restaurants in Rio (including the celebrated and swank Olympe; see p. 252). This tight yet airy, pared-down bistro on Leblon's restaurant row serves the finest cuts of meat this side of Argentina. Ideal for a carnivore's splurge.

🪑 52 🚭 ♿

---

## PRICES

**HOTELS**
An indication of the cost of a double room in the high season is given by $ signs.

| | |
|---|---|
| $$$$$ | Over R$1,000 |
| $$$$ | R$600–R$1,000 |
| $$$ | R$400–R$600 |
| $$ | R$200–R$400 |
| $ | Under R$200 |

**RESTAURANTS**
The average cost of a two-course meal for one person, excluding drinks, is given by $ signs.

| | |
|---|---|
| $$$$$ | Over R$150 |
| $$$$ | R$100–R$150 |
| $$$ | R$60–R$100 |
| $$ | R$30–R$60 |
| $ | Under R$30 |

---

🏨 Hotel  🍴 Restaurant  🛏 No. of Guest Rooms  🪑 No. of Seats  🅿 Parking  🚇 Metrô  🕐 Closed  🛗 Elevator

## 🍴 ZAZÁ BISTRÔ TROPICAL
$$$
RUA JOANA ANGÉLICA 40
IPANEMA
TEL 21/2247-9101
This hippie-chic eatery fuses organic ingredients and influences from tropical locales in Africa, Asia, and the Americas, resulting in such dishes as Arabian ravioli with yogurt mint sauce and almonds. Romance abounds; choose between the upstairs room, with silk pillows strewn on the floor (shoes are optional) and red velvet flowers dangling from the ceiling, and the candlelit terrace.
🛏 90 🅢 🅢

## 🍴 BRASILEIRINHO
$$
RUA JANGEDEIROS 10, LOJA A
IPANEMA
TEL 21/2513-5184
Oozing a rusticity typical of rural Brazil, Brasileirinho serves up robust portions of country cooking with a predilection for the heady cuisine of Minas Gerais. Specialties such as *tutu à mineira* (a thick stew of pureed beans and pork) and *carne seca com abóbora* (sun-dried beef with pumpkin) can be savored à la carte or as part of an all-you-can-eat buffet.
🛏 54 🅢 🅢 🅢

## 🍴 FELLINI
$$
RUA GENERAL URQUIZA 104
LEBLON
TEL 21/2511-3600
One of Rio's highest quality per-kilo banquets, Fellini puts on a surprisingly eclectic spread. Apart from the refined likes of foie gras ravioli, lobster, and escargots, there are offerings for vegetarians and diabetics. On weekends, arrive early or late to avoid long lines.
🛏 140 🅢 🅢 🅢

## 🍴 MARKET IPANEMA
$$
RUA VISCONDE DE PIRAJÁ 499
IPANEMA
TEL 21/3283-1438
Down a narrow alley off Ipanema's main drag, Market is a relaxing oasis where both carnivores and herbivores can find fresh, flavorful sustenance. The food is as vibrant and colorful as the surroundings—which include a lovely outdoor courtyard—jewel-colored, vitamin-packed juices and the caipirinhas.
🛏 80 🅢 🅢

# SOMETHING SPECIAL

## 🍴 BAR DO DAVID
$-$$
LADEIRA ARY BARROSO 66,
LOJA 3
CHAPÉU MANGUEIRA, LEME
TEL 21/7808-2200
Although this simple bar attracts both Cariocas and foreigners who are curious to sample the acclaimed star of the "favela dining" phenomenon, the laid-back outdoor ambience, charm of owner David, and inventive take on Carioca classics speak for themselves. Aside from the generously portioned lunch specials, the petiscos—particularly the rapturous seafood croquettes—are sublime. On Saturday, arrive early for live *pagode* and seafood feijoada.
🅢 🅢

## 🍴 BRACARENSE
$-$$
RUA JOSÉ LINHARES 85-B
LEBLON
TEL 21/2294-3549
This deliciously unpretentious neighborhood boteco is a favorite haunt of Leblon's after-beach and happy-hour crowd, when the sidewalk tables threaten to overflow into the street. The *caldo de*

*feijão* (black bean soup) is thick and velvety, and the famous *bolinho de aipim com camarão* (manioc shrimp balls) are addictive.
🅢 🅢

## 🍴 DELÍRIO TROPICAL
$-$$
RUA GARCIA D'ÁVILA 48
IPANEMA
TEL 21/3624-8164
This mellow per-kilo joint offers an enticing range of fresh salads and other hot healthy specials. From the glassed-in upstairs tables, you can peer down on the bronzed beach bums going to and from nearby Ipanema beach.
🛏 100 🅢 🅢 🅢

## 🍴 PAVÃO AZUL
$-$$
RUA HILÁRIO GOUVEIA 71
COPACABANA
TEL 21/2236-2381
This unpretentious, neighborhood Copa bar is always filled with locals spilling onto the sidewalk (tables are hard to come by). Aside from the conviviality, the "Blue Peacock's" big attraction is the crunchy bolinhos de bacalhau, reputedly the best in the city.
🛏 100 🅢 🅢

## 🍴 BIBI SUCOS
$
AV. ATAULFO DE PAIVA 591-A
LEBLON
TEL 21/2259-0000
This hard-core juice bar is frequented by Leblon's body-conscious residents as well as the jujitsu crowd who pack on the protein with açaí fortified with honey and tapioca. Aside from more than 60 *sucos*—faves include watermelon/ginger and *água de coco*/fig—you can concoct your own healthy (and whopping) *sanduíche natural*.
🅢 🅢

---

## 🍴 MIL FRUTAS

**$**

RUA GARCIA D'ÁVILA 134
IPANEMA
TEL 21/2521-1384

The name, Mil Frutas ("one thousand fruits"), may be pure hyperbole—to date, there are only some 200 flavors—but each frozen ball of artisanally produced ice cream packs a wallop of pure taste. Aside from exotic native *frutas* such as bacuri, *jabuticaba,* and *pitanga,* there is an abundance of nonfruity flavors such as white chocolate with *pimenta* and absinthe. While there are several branches of this eatery around town, this Ipanema café also serves light meals.

🚭 ♿ 🗸

## ■ AROUND THE LAGOA

### HOTEL

## 🏨 LA MAISON

**$$$**

RUA SERGIO PORTO 58
GÁVEA, 22451-400
TEL 21/3205-3585
www.lamaisonario.com

Perched on a verdant hillside in residential Gávea, this villa owned by Frenchman Jacques Dussol offers stylish lodgings in thematically (and dramatically) decorated suites ranging from a 19th-century Parisian salon to a Bollywood fantasy, along with personalized service. A garden—with a tent for lounging and a pool for soaking—guarantees a space for respite. Although the villa is only about a 5-minute drive from Leblon, the seclusion is such that you'll need a car or a taxi to make your way to and from it.

🛏 5 🚭 ♿ 🏊 🍷 🗸

## RESTAURANTS

## 🍴 OLYMPE

**$$$$$**

RUA CUSTÓDIO SERRÃO 62
JARDIM BOTÂNICO
TEL 21/2537-8582

One of Brazil's most celebrated chefs, Claude Troisgros emigrated in 1980 from France to Rio, where he launched a culinary revolution by applying French techniques to Brazil's tropical abundance. The results—featured in various prix fixe tasting menus whose dishes are prepared by Claude's son, Thomas—can be savored at this refined, discreetly low-key dining room. Reservations are a must.

🪑 42 🕐 Closed Sun.
🚭 ♿ 🗸

## 🍴 ROBERTA SUDBRACK

**$$$$$**

AV. LINEU DE PAULA
MACHADO 916
JARDIM BOTÂNICO
TEL 21/3874-0139

One of Brazil's most innovative contemporary chefs, Roberta Sudbrack got her auspicious start as cook to then president Fernando Henrique Cardoso (1994–2002) before opening her own eponymous restaurant. Tasting menus are devised daily (lofty prices are reduced on Tuesday) according to the freshness of local ingredients at hand. Sudbrack has a penchant for rescuing "marginalized" Brazilian ingredients, and she appreciates music—the soundtrack that inspires her also wafts through this soothing villa. Recommended for foodies who want to splurge.

🪑 62 🕐 Closed Sun. &
Mon. 🚭 ♿ 🗸

## 🍴 PALAPHITA KITCH

**$$$**

AV. EPITÁCIO PESSOA,
QUIOSQUE 20

## PRICES

### HOTELS

An indication of the cost of a double room in the high season is given by **$** signs.

| | |
|---|---|
| **$$$$$** | Over R$1,000 |
| **$$$$** | R$600–R$1,000 |
| **$$$** | R$400–R$600 |
| **$$** | R$200–R$400 |
| **$** | Under R$200 |

### RESTAURANTS

The average cost of a two-course meal for one person, excluding drinks, is given by $ signs.

| | |
|---|---|
| **$$$$$** | Over R$150 |
| **$$$$** | R$100–R$150 |
| **$$$** | R$60–R$100 |
| **$$** | R$30–R$60 |
| **$** | Under R$30 |

LAGOA
TEL 21/2227-0837

Located in the Parque do Cantagalo, overlooking the Lagoa, this *quiosque* specializing in contemporary Amazonian fare has a decorative scheme best described as Tarzan nouveau, with rustic wooden sofas and lots of jungly foliage. The menu is equally creative, with snacks such as wild boar carpaccio and camembert stuffed with açaí chutney, paired with drinks concocted from exotic Amazonian fruits.

🪑 120 🅿 🗸

## 🍴 BRASEIRO DA GÁVEA

**$$**

PRAÇA SANTOS DUMONT 116
GÁVEA
TEL 21/2239-7494

The former "bar across from the racetrack" is a ritual gathering spot for Zona Sul young bloods, particularly on weekends and Monday evenings. To avoid the crowds, come during the week to feast on celebrated grilled *picanha* (rump steak) and *galeto* (rotisserie chicken).

🛏 120 ⓢ 🅶 🅰

## SOMETHING SPECIAL

### 🍴 DRI CAFÉ
$
RUA JARDIM BOTÂNICO 414, PARQUE LAGE
JARDIM BOTÂNICO
TEL 21/2226-8125
With tables sprinkled beneath the arcaded patio of a palatial home built by wealthy industrialist Henrique Lage (today home to Rio's School of Visual Arts), this café overlooks a turquoise swimming pool and, in turn, is overlooked by Christ the Redeemer. The striking setting is conducive for long Sunday brunches, late afternoon coffee, or a languorous weekday lunch of gourmet sandwiches accompanied by a glass or two of wine.

ⓢ 🅰

## ■ ZONA OESTE BEACHES

## HOTELS

## SOMETHING SPECIAL

### 🏨 TUAKAZA
$$$$$
ESTRADA DA CANOA 2600
SÃO CONRADO
TEL 21/3322-6715
www.tuakaza.com
It doesn't get more back to nature than Tuakaza, whose handsomely outfitted, tropically hued, rustic chalets on stilts are plunged into a lush Edenic junglescape and watched over by the Pedra da Gávea. Taking refuge here necessitates a car (or taxi)—São Conrado beach is 2.5 miles (4 km) away—but in compen-

sation, the beautiful pool is fed by a live waterfall.

ⓘ 6 🅿 ⓢ 🅶 🅰 🅰

### 🏨 LA SUITE
$$$$–$$$$$
RUA JACKSON DE FIGUEIROA 501
SÃO CONRADO
TEL 21/2484-1962
www.lasuiterio.com
It's no surprise that La Suite pops up regularly in fashion magazines. Owned by François-Xavier Dussol (brother of Jacques, who owns La Maison in Gávea; see p. 252), the three-story cliff-top mansion's candy-hued suites (with matching marble bathrooms) are glamorously furnished with a mix of antiques and contemporary art. Accents include an infinity pool and the only black crystal Philippe Starck chandelier in South America. The delightfully isolated locale can be reached by car, taxi, or helicopter.

ⓘ 7 🅿 🍴 ⓢ 🅶 🅰 🅰

## RESTAURANTS

### 🍴 GOURMET TROPICAL
$$–$$$
AV. DOM ROSALVO DA COSTA RÊGO 420
BARRA DA TIJUCA
TEL 21/2495-8068
Set amid a nursery of tropical plants, this surprising restaurant mingles a back-to-nature vibe—rustic furnishings are made from reclaimed wood while the roof is hung with plant fibers—with sophisticated international dishes ranging from risotto to yakisoba. There is also afternoon tea, weekend brunch (with waffles), and an impressive wine cellar for sipping the afternoon away. Aside from decorative shrubs, the Brazilian *artesanato* on display is also for sale.

🛏 70 🅿 ⓢ 🅰

## ■ EXCURSIONS

## BÚZIOS

## HOTELS

## SOMETHING SPECIAL

### 🏨 CACHOEIRA INN
$$$$–$$$$$
RUA E-1, LOTE 18
PRAIA DA FERRADURA
BÚZIOS
TEL 21/2623-2118
www.cachoeirainnbuzios .com
*Cachoeira* is Portuguese for waterfall, and this inspired, American-owned guesthouse boasts nine of them—built into an ingeniously landscaped cliffside overlooking Ferradura Bay. The luxurious lodgings are outfitted with Asian furnishings that harmonize with the tropical setting. The transplanted Californian hosts are as friendly as can be.

ⓘ 4 🅿 ⓢ 🅶 🅰 🎽 🅰

### 🏨 CASAS BRANCAS
$$$$–$$$$$
RUA MORRO DO HUMAITÁ 10, ORLA BARDOT,
ARMAÇÃO DE BÚZIOS
BÚZIOS
TEL 22/2623-1458
www.casasbrancas.com.br
This granddaddy of Búzios's posh hotels has been around since 1973, and it still surpasses newer boutique upstarts in terms of uncontrived charm and atmosphere. The maze-like ensemble of Mediterranean-style whitewashed *casas* overlooking the Orla Bardot shelter spacious, soothing rooms where light colors and natural woods harmonize with the surroundings.

ⓘ 32 🅿 🍴 ⓢ 🅶 🅰 🎽 🅰

---

### 🏨 POUSADA CASA BÚZIOS
**$$**

RUA MORRO DA HUMAITÁ,
CASA 1
ORLA BARDOT,
ARMAÇÃO DE BÚZIOS
BÚZIOS
TEL 22/2623-7002
www.pousadacasabuzios.com
This casual French-owned pousada possesses a wonderfully relaxed vibe. Thematically decorated rooms are warm and personalized enough to make you feel as if you're crashing at a friend's beachhouse (a friend with impeccable taste). Very good value.
ⓘ 6 🅿 🚫 🍴 🏊 ⛵

## RESTAURANTS

### 🍴 O BARCO
**$$**

AV. JOSÉ RIBEIRO DANTAS 1054
BÚZIOS
TEL 22/2629-8307
Amid the swank eateries along the Orla Bardot, O Barco serves up heaping portions of delicious home-cooked fresh fish and seafood at refreshingly affordable prices. At dinner, nab a terrace or sidewalk table so you can watch the sun set over the bay.
🪑 50 🕐 Closed Sun. 🚫 ⛵

### 🍴 BANANALAND
**$**

RUA MANUAL TURÍBIA DE FREITAS 50
BÚZIOS
TEL 22/2623-2666
This cheery per-kilo restaurant has an enticing banquet of healthy and tasty salads, appetizers, hot entrees, and desserts that will make you want to pile your plate high—and then indulge in seconds.
🪑 60 🚫 ⛵

## ILHA GRANDE

## HOTELS

### 🏨 POUSADA ASALEM
**$$$**

PRAIA DA CRENA
TEL 24/9673-5331 OR 3361-5602
www.asalem.com.br
Set into a jungly hillside overlooking the sea, the spacious guest rooms combine comfort with splendid seclusion—despite being only 25 minutes by foot (or 15 minutes by boat) from Vila Abraão. Bonuses include complimentary kayaks and canoes and a vast collection of art books (the place is managed by a professional photographer).
ⓘ 8 🚫 🍴 ⛵

### 🏨 POUSADA NATURÁLIA
**$$**

RUA DA PRAIA 149
TEL 24/3361-9583
www.pousadanaturalia.net
Squeezed between lush jungle and a diaphanous bay, the rustic yet lovingly finished double, triple, and quadruple suites—all with verandas and hammocks looking out to sea—make this extremely well-run pousada one of Ilha Grande's most enticing and best value options.
ⓘ 12 🚫 🍴

## RESTAURANTS

### 🍴 O PESCADOR
**$$–$$$**

RUA DA PRAIA 647
Located in the pousada of the same name, this romantic beachfront eatery serves innovative fish and seafood dishes such as fish cooked in banana leaves with shrimp and heart of palm farofa. Open for dinner only.
🪑 60 🕐 Closed Sun. 🚫 ⛵

## PARATY

## HOTELS

### 🏨 POUSADA DO OURO
**$$–$$$**

RUA DR. PEREIRA 145
TEL 24/3371-2033
www.pousadaouro.com.br
Authentic colonial charm reigns in the unpretentious rooms at this 18th-century mansion (nicer than those in the more modern annex). Myriad small flourishes—ranging from the fresh orchids planted by the bedside to the helpful gestures of the welcoming staff—are a big selling point.
ⓘ 27 🅿 🍴 🚫 🏊 ⛵

### 🏨 VIVENDA
**$$**

RUA BEIJA FLOR 9, CABORÉ
TEL 24/3371-4272
www.vivendaparaty.com

A far cry—but only a 10-minute walk—from Paraty's Centro Histórico, the tastefully appointed modern bungalows owned by Englishman John Hudson are unbeatable in terms of the level of comfort and pampering guests receive. Kitchen and dining areas, an alluring pool, and lovely gardens are some attractive accents of this home away from home.

🏠 3 🅿 🚬 🚭 🌊

### 🏨 SOLAR DOS GERÂNIOS
**$**
PRAÇA DA MATRIZ
TEL 24/3371-1550
www.paraty.com.br/geranio
One of the Centro Histórico's most affordable options, this rambling old mansion is a wonderfully atmospheric place presided over by the Swiss owner and her friendly felines. Room are small but homey. The nicest have balconies overlooking Praça Matriz.

🏠 12 🚭 🌊

## RESTAURANTS

### 🍴 BANANA DA TERRA
**$$$$**
RUA DR. SAMUEL COSTA 198
TEL 24/3371-1725
In her romantic restaurant, noted chef Ana Bueno performs refined riffs on local *caiçara* specialties, many of which feature the restaurant's namesake fruit in versions savory, sweet, and even liquid (in the form of banana caipirinhas).

🍴 70 🕐 Closed Tues.
🚬 🚭 🌊

### 🍴 CASA DO FOGO
**$$$**
RUA COMENDADOR JOSÉ LUIS 390
TEL 24/3371-3163
Casa do Fogo takes its name

("house of fire") quite seriously by setting many of its main dishes—ranging from locally sourced fresh palm hearts to shrimp and star fruit and even desserts and drinks—aflame with the fragrant aid of regionally produced cachaça. Aside from the glow of flames, the romantic (dinner only) ambience is heightened by live music performances.

🍴 47 🕐 Closed Wed.
🚬 🚭 🌊

### 🍴 SABOR DA TERRA
**$**
AV. ROBERTO SILVEIRA 180
TEL 24/3371-2384
Located a few steps beyond the Centro Histórico, this modest per-kilo restaurant compensates for the lack of decor with a wealth of freshly prepared salads, grilled fish and meats, and seafood dishes.

🍴 70 🚭

## PETRÓPOLIS

## HOTELS

### 🏨 SOLAR DO IMPÉRIO
**$$$**
AV. KOELER 376
TEL 24/2103-3000
www.solardoimperio.com.br
Located on the most historic and bucolic street in town, this 1875 mansion is only one of many lavish summer abodes built by vacationing counts and barons. Decorated with period furnishings, the elegant, high-ceilinged rooms offer all the modern conveniences. Afternoon tea—served Friday and Saturday at 5 p.m. in the exquisite Leopoldina restaurant—is included in the rate.

🏠 24 🅿 🚬 🏊 🚭 🌊

### 🏨 POUSADA 14 BIS
**$**
RUA BUENOS AIRES 192
TEL 24/2231-0946

www.pousada14bis.com.br
Nicely priced and centrally located, this rustic guesthouse pays homage to Petrópolis's resident aviation pioneer; aside from the pousada's name—which alludes to Santos Dumont's historic aircraft—the lounge is decorated with memorabilia. The modest rooms are warm and comfortable.

🏠 16 🅿 🚬 🚭 🏊 🌊

## RESTAURANTS

### 🍴 BORDEAUX
**$$**
RUA IPIRANGA 716
TEL 24/2242-5711
This atmospheric wine bar/emporium is located in the coach house of the historic Casa de Petrópolis. Aside from 1,200 wines, delicious gourmet sandwiches and appetizers are available to munch on.

🍴 40 🅿 🚭 🌊

---

🚭 Nonsmoking   🆒 Air-conditioning   🏊 Indoor Pool   🌊 Outdoor Pool   💪 Health Club   💳 Credit Cards

# Shopping

**Befitting a city of its size and sophistication, Rio is an alluring shopping destination. Despite the recent escalation of prices, there are still bargains to be had and treasures to be found. The most interesting purchases you can make in Rio include beachwear, musical recordings by classic and contemporary artists, jewelry wrought from Brazil's dazzling array of precious and semiprecious stones, and traditional art and crafts culled from around the country.**

Like all Brazilians, Cariocas are beholden to their "*shoppings*." Far from mere malls, these artically air-conditioned centers are where Cariocas of all ages and socioeconomic backgrounds go to eat, drink, stroll, hang out, watch movies, and even ice skate. In between, they also shop until they drop; the vast majority of Brazilian designers and labels have at least one outpost in a shopping. Regardless of how you feel about malls, they are great for multitasking, not to mention people-watching.

**Shopping Rio Sul** *(Rua Lauro Müller 116, Botafogo, tel 21/2122-8070, www.riosul.com.br)* is one of the oldest shoppings in town. Its strategic location next to the Túnel Novo, which leads to Copacabana, ensures that pretty much every Zona Sul–bound bus stops in front of its main entrance. The biggest and glitziest mall in the Zona Sul is **Shopping Leblon** *(Av. Afrânio Melo Franco 290, Leblon, tel 21/2430-5122, www.shoppingleblon.com.br)*, which has more than 200 stylish stores and a food court overlooking the Lagoa and Corcovado. More chic and rarefied is the sleek and skylit **São Conrado Fashion Mall** *(Estrada da Gávea 899, São Conrado, tel 21/2111-4444, www.fashionmall .com.br)*. Meanwhile, in a neighborhood notorious for its megashoppings, **BarraShopping** *(Av. das Américas 4666, Barra da Tijuca, tel 21/4003-4131, )* reigns supreme with more than 600 stores, not to mention an indoor amusement park known as the Hot Zone. It also has a brand new annex called Village Mall with the most exclusive

brands and labels.

Shoppings aside, there are fashionable boutiques galore along the tree-lined streets of Ipanema, particularly on the main street of Rua Visconde de Pirajá, and to a lesser extent, Leblon—as well as micro-malls known as *galerias*. Befitting its layered history, Lapa's Rua do Lavradio is lined with antique stores, while bohemian Santa Teresa has an intriguing smattering of ateliers where local artists display their creative wares. Traditional old *bairros* such as Centro and Copacabana have some interesting decades-old stores tucked away in unexpected corners.

## Antiques

During its centuries as Brazil's imperial and republican capital, Rio was also the center of the nation's lavish aristocratic life. When luck and fortunes ran dry, many goods—domestic and imported— were sold to pay off debts. There are still some interesting treasures tucked away for those with patience and a good eye.

**Ateliê e Movelaria Belmonte**
Rua do Lavradio 34, Lapa
Tel 21/2507-0934
www.ateliebelmonte.com.br
Owned by architect-decorator Luciano Cavalcanti do Albuquerque (whose great-great-grandmother, the Countess of Belmonte, tutored Pedro II), this atelier/boutique sells restored Brazilian furnishings and design objects.

**Mercado Moderno**
Rua do Lavradio 130, Lapa
Tel 21/2508-6083

One of the best places in Rio for mid-20th-century furniture and decorative objects, this emporium has a soft spot for Carioca designers such as Zanini de Zanine, Sérgio Rodrigues, Joaquim Tenreiro, and Ricardo Fasanello.

**Shopping dos Antiquários**
Rua Siqueira Campos 143, Copacabana
Tel 21/2255-3461
Built in the 1960s, Rio's first shopping offers three floors of antique stores where you can find everything from baroque sacred art and colonial furniture to art deco dishes and Bakelite jewelry. A great mixture of serious finds and kitschy fun.

## Arts & Crafts

Although Rio and the surrounding state don't possess much of a folk art tradition, the city has an innovative contemporary art scene and is also a good place to pick up authentic *artesanato* from other regions of Brazil.

**Brasil & Cia**
Rua Maria Quitéria 27, Ipanema
Tel 21/2267-4603
www.brasilecia.com.br
This boutique works with a selection of artists from around the country who draw on local traditions to create original decorative objects from such materials as sisal, clay, fabric, papier-mâché, and *capim dourado*, "golden grass" harvested from the stems of a rare flower in the Amazonian state of Tocantins.

**La Vereda**
Av. Almirante Alexandrino 428,
Santa Teresa
Tel 21/2507-0317
www.lavereda.com.br
This cozy boutique on Santa's winding main drag attracts its share of tourists without being a trap. The compact interior is artfully stuffed with carefully chosen artesanato from all four corners of Brazil as well as pieces by neighborhood artists.

**Novo Desenho**
Av. Infante Dom Henrique 85,
Glória
Tel 21/2524-2290
The Museu de Arte Moderno's airy design shop showcases some of the best of Brazilian modern and contemporary design, with decorative objects, housewares, furnishings, toys, and accessories by the acclaimed likes of the Campana brothers, Lina Bo Bardi, Rodrigues, Zanini de Zanine, and Fasanello.

**Pé de Boi**
Rua Ipiranga 55, Laranjeiras
Tel 21/2285-4395
www.pedeboi.com.br
This gallery-like boutique sells a carefully curated ensemble of sculptures, toys, and decorative objects that hail from the folk-art-rich regions of the Northeast, the Amazon, and Minas Gerais. The welcoming owner knows a great deal about Brazilian *arte popular*.

## Books & Music

Rio's *livrarias* (bookstores) aren't just for browsing and buying books. Many have charming cafés and host events such as readings and live musical performances. They're also great places to find CDs and DVDs of all types of Carioca and Brazilian music.

**Arlequim**
Praça XV de Novembro 48,
Loja 1, Centro

Tel 21/2533-4359
www.arlequim.com.br
Lodged inside the Paço Imperial, this inviting bookstore/music store/café has a particularly rich selection of Brazilian music—ranging from erudite to contemporary—sold in CD, DVD, and Blu ray versions. Often hosts great live pocket shows.

**Baratos da Ribeiro**
Rua Barata Ribeiro 354, Loja D,
Copacabana
Tel 21/2256-8634
www.baratosdaribeiro.com.br
Rio's biggest *sebo* (secondhand bookstore) beckons those who love to scavenge for lost literary treasures or comb through comics, CDs, vinyl (particularly independent labels and *raríssimo* samba and bossa nova recordings), and DVDs.

**Biscoito Fino**
Rua Lauro Müller 116, Shopping
Rio Sul, Botafogo
Tel 21/2279-3605
www.biscoitofino.com.br
This local indie label—*biscoito fino* (fine biscuit) is a slang expression for "high quality"—is devoted to promoting emerging young talents and resuscitating forgotten legends from Brazil's musical past. Its Biscoitinho label specializes in popular Brazilian music for kids.

**Bossa Nova & Cia**
Rua Duvivier 37, Copacabana
Tel 21/2295-8096
www.bossanovaecompanhia.com.br
Tucked away in the Beco das Garrafas, the legendary alleyway in which bossa nova sprouted into life, this music store is actually more of a treasure trove for samba aficionados in search of CDs and vinyl, books, and percussion instruments.

**Casa Oliveira**
Rua da Carioca 70, Centro
Tel 21/2508-8539
www.casaoliveirademusica.com.br

One of the few surviving music stores that once littered Rua da Carioca, this traditional address is highly recommended for those in search of Brazilian string and percussion instruments.

**Livraria Argumento**
Rua Dias Ferreira 417, Leblon
Tel 21/2239-5294
www.livrariaargumento.com.br
This cozy neighborhood bookstore feels like a second home for Leblon residents who drop in to browse, have a coffee, and take part in the many readings and recitals. During the military regime, it bravely stocked books by prohibited Brazilian writers.

**Livraria da Travessa**
Rua Visconde de Pirajá 572,
Ipanema
Tel 21/3205-9002
www.travessa.com.br
There are several branches of this mellow, well-stocked bookstore around town, but this Ipanema outpost has a particularly warm vibe (in addition to a great café). Aside from English books, art books, and scads of interesting Rio books, the CD and DVD selection is stellar.

**Maracatu Brasil**
Rua Ipiranga 49, Laranjeiras
Tel 21/2557-4754
www.maracatubrasil.com.br
This combination music school/recording studio sells a terrific array of used and new Brazilian string and percussion instruments. The staff is friendly and knowledgable.

## Fashion

In keeping with the climate and culture, Carioca fashion leans toward casual sportswear and beachwear. In fact, Rio sets the standard in terms of cutting-edge *biquini* and *sunga* (male trunks) technology and design. Renowned labels include **Blue Man** *(www.blueman.com.br)*,

**Lenny** *(www.lenny.com.br)*, **Rosa Chá**, and **Salinas** *(www.salinas-rio.com.br)*, all of which can be found at shoppings throughout the city. Rio is also home to a handful of interesting and innovative designers (it hosts a Fashion Week of its own), who capture the city's vibe with the use of vivid colors, artisanal details, and sensual shapes. Women, in particular, will succumb to the original (often chunky) jewelry and platform sandals.

**Aüslander**
Av. Afrânio de Melo Franco 290,
Shopping Leblon
Tel 21/2422-2405
www.auslander.com.br
Fashion-conscious, body-baring Cariocas love the strikingly graphic, form-fitting, limited-edition T-shirts whose faded softness is achieved by a special treatment.

**Farm**
Rua Visonde de Pirajá 365,
Lojas C–D, Ipanema
Tel 21/3813-3817
This funky flagship store is the place for young women to go if they want to be mistaken for a typical *garota da Ipanema*. A wide assortment of jeans, skirts, and colorful print dresses conjure up breezy Zona Sul beach living.

**Galeria River**
Rua Francisco Otaviano 67,
Arpoador
Tel 21/2247-8387
www.galeriariver.com.br
For decades, this micro-mall has been a pioneer for surfers in search of the perfect boards, shorts, and other wave-related paraphernalia. Today, the alternative offerings—both sartorial and lifestyle-related (you can get a tattoo, haircut, energy drink, vegan burger, and even a bong)—embrace skateboarding and extreme sports too.

**Isabela Capeto**
Rua Garcia D'Ávila 173, Ipanema
Tel 21/2523-0052
www.isabelacapeto.com.br
One of Brazil's top designers, Capeto produces handmade women's clothes that are romantic without slipping into over-the-top melodrama. Recurrent characteristics include delicate embroidery, visible stitching, and extravagant colors (and prices).

**Liga Retrô**
Rua Visconde de Pirajá 303,
Loja 201, Ipanema
Tel 21/3202-1057
www.ligaretro.com.br
Die-hard Carioca soccer fan Leonard Klarnet fashions replicas of original jerseys sported by world soccer legends of the past. A stonewashing technique is responsible for the well-worn look that makes shirts appear scavenged from players' closets.

**Osklen**
Rua Maria Quitéria 85, Ipanema
Tel 21/2227-2911
www.osklen.com
Designer Oskar Metsavaht has a knack for taking casual and beachwear items and turning them into high fashion, without stripping them of their just-stepped-off-the-sand quality.

**Reserva**
Rua Maria Quitéria 77, Loja F,
Ipanema
Tel 21/2247-5980
www.usereserva.com
Started by three Carioca pals (whose favorite beach, Reserva, is located between Barra and Recreio), this men's line runs the gamut from sporty beachwear that's often tattooed with Carioca references to more dressy attire.

**Sementeira**
Rua Visconde de Pirajá 414,
Loja 211, Ipanema

Tel 21/2521-8408
www.sementeira.com
This mint-scented boutique specializes in stylish and comfortable yoga and meditation gear for men and women, fashioned out of 100 percent organic fibers.

**Totem**
Rua Visconde de Pirajá 550,
Loja M, Ipanema
Tel 21/2540-9977
www.totempraia.com.br
Big, bright, psychedelic prints are not for the conservative dresser, but Totem's well-tailored, highly original beachwear for men, women, and kids screams tropical, not tacky.

## Jewelry & Accessories

Carioca designers are experts at using the country's wealth of precious minerals, stones, and other alternative materials and natural resources to create innovative yet exquisite products you won't find anywhere else.

**Antônio Bernardo**
Rua Garcia D'Ávila 121, Ipanema
Tel 21/2512-7204
www.antoniobernardo.com.br
Goldsmith, artist, and orchid expert (he maintains the Jardim Botânico's Orquidário), Bernardo designs fluid, contemporary jewelry, often making use of white, yellow, and red gold.

**Gilson Martins**
Rua Visconde de Pirajá 462,
Loja B, Ipanema
Tel 21/2227-6178
www.gilsonmartins.com.br
Martins's funky jewelry, bags, accessories, and design objects are quintessentially Carioca. Improvised using found, recycled materials such as rubber and plastic, many depict or take the form of such Rio icons as Sugarloaf and Christ the Redeemer, which makes them excellent souvenirs.

### Granado

Rua Primeiro de Março 16, Centro
Tel 21/3231-6746
www.granado.com.br

Brazil's oldest pharmacy has been selling natural remedies and cosmetics made from pure oils and extracts of Brazilian herbs, plants, and flowers since the 1880s. Today, it sells its vintage products as well as a host of newer but no less natural lines for men, babies, and even pets. Although there are several branches around town, the original *botico*, with its antique vials, exudes historic charm.

### H. Stern

Rua Visonde de Pirajá 490, Ipanema
Tel 21/2274-3447
www.hstern.com.br

Brazil's most famous jeweler, H. Stern, makes dazzling use of the country's abundance of precious and semiprecious stones. Known for classic designs, it also has a line of more unusual contemporary pieces, beautifully displayed at this flagship store.

### Maria Oiticica

Av. Afrânio de Melo Franco 290, Shopping Leblon
Tel 21/3875-8025
www.mariaoiticicabiojoias.com.br

Growing up in Manaus, Maria Oiticica thought nothing of the exotic Amazonian seeds she strung into necklaces. Today, her bio-bijoux sell at Macy's. Moreover, Oiticica's creations are as refined as they are sustainable—her designs incorporate materials like tree bark, plant fibers, and even fish scales.

### Sobral

Rua Visconde de Pirajá 351, Loja 105, Ipanema
Tel 21/2267-0009
www.rsobral.com.br

At first sight, the chunky, candy-hued jewelry and accessories designed by Roberto Sobral appear appetizing enough to sink your teeth into. The fact that they happen to be made out of polyester resin makes them ideal instead for eye-catching bangles, boxes, key chains, toilet seats, and other "poetic objects" that add color to any environment.

## Markets

Rio possesses many vibrant outdoor *feiras* (markets). While food and produce markets migrate from bairro to bairro during the week, others—featuring less perishable items—take place on weekends.

### Feira Babilônia Hype

Av. Borge de Medeiros 701, Leblon

Traditionally held at Gávea's Jockey Club every couple of months, and more recently at the Lagoa's Clube Monte Libano, this funky, fashion-forward market showcases clothing, accessories, and decorative objects from up-and-coming local designers.

### Feira de Antiguidades

Praça XV de Novembro, Centro (Sat.), and Praça Santos Dumont, Gávea (Sun.)

One of Rio's oldest and most picturesque markets, this antique fair will seduce trollers who have the inclination (and humor) to sift through mounds of interesting objects in search of the odd treasure.

### Feira de São Cristovão

Campo de São Cristovão, São Cristovão
Tel 21/2580-5335
www.feiradesaocristovao.org.br

From Tuesday through Sunday, this vast open-air feira is a gathering point for Rio's residents from the Brazilian Northeast, who satiate their longings for the food, culture, music, and sheer vibrancy of their home states among the bars and restaurants. Some 700 stalls hawk everything from bottles of herb-infused cachaça and bricks of *coalho* cheese to handwoven hammocks and CDs and DVDs of typical *brega* and *forró* music.

### Feira do Rio Antigo

Rua do Lavradio, Lapa

On the first Saturday of every month, the stores along Lapa's antique row take their wares out into the street alongside independent antique dealers. As if the open-air bazaar weren't vibrant enough to draw you in, there is also food, drink, and free live performances.

### Feira Hippie

Praça General Osório, Ipanema

On Sundays ever since the 1960s, this Ipanema square has hosted the Feira Hippie, where vendors (some of them aged hippies) hawk a colorful, somewhat ragtag collection of handicrafts, souvenirs, and flea-market finds that lures tourists (and pickpockets).

# Entertainment

Rio possesses a dynamic arts and cultural scene with a wide variety of events held at venues whose architectural or natural features often more than justify the price of admission. One of the city's major aces is its vast number of public and private cultural centers. Housed in historic buildings, the majority host trendy events and performances for prices that are extremely affordable or even free.

## Live Music

Rio is justly famed for its virtually limitless musical offerings, which mine rich homegrown traditions such as samba, *chorinho*, and bossa nova while nourishing a constantly evolving, extremely vital contemporary scene that yields hybrids such as samba-rock and bossa-lounge. Depending on the rhythm, live performances naturally segue into spontaneous *festas* in which audience members groove along with the upbeat rhythms.

### Bip Bip

Rua Alimirante Gonçalves 50, Copacabana
Tel 21/2267-9696
Just off Copacabana beach, this tiny, atmospheric hole-in-the-wall hosts live samba jams on Sundays and Mondays and chorinho on Tuesdays. It also has bossa nova on Wednesdays and samba on Fridays and Saturdays.

### Carioca da Gema

Av. Mem de Sá 79, Lapa
Tel 21/2221-0043
www.barcariocadagema.com.br
This pioneer of Lapa's revival movement is a great place to catch high-caliber samba and chorinho performances. To avoid crowds, come early in the week. Delicious pizza is served upstairs.

### Clube dos Democráticos

Rua do Riachuelo 91, Lapa
Tel 21/2252-4611
www.clubedosdemocraticos.com.br
This humongous ballroom originally opened in 1867 as a social club for the abolitionists and republicans who were members of the Democráticos Carnaval society. Rescued from oblivion in 2004, it lures all stripes of Cariocas; those too timid to cut loose on the dance floor can soak up the live music and eclectic ambience.

### The Maze

Rua Tavares Bastos 414, Casa 66, Catete
Tel 21/2558-5547
www.jazzrio.com
The bimonthly Friday-night jazz jam sessions held at Englishman Bob Nadkarni's pioneering favela inn have become an alternative institution—helped in no small part by the bewitching views of Guanabara Bay.

### Rio Scenarium

Rua do Lavradio 20, Lapa
Tel 21/3147-9005
www.rioscenarium.com.br
One of Rio's most stunningly beautiful venues, the three floors of this handsome building are stuffed with thousands of antiques and a lively mixture of locals and gringos who gather to listen to samba, chorinho, and *forró*.

### Studio RJ

Av. Vieira Souto 110, Arpoador
Tel 21/2523-1204
www.studiorj.org
This cutting-edge club programs a heady mix of compelling homegrown and imported bands and DJs. Tuesday's Jazzmania sessions are a ritual in themselves. Aside from great acoustics, a bar offers impressive views of Ipanema beach.

### Teatro Odisséia

Av. Mem de Sá 66, Lapa
Tel 21/2226-9691
One of Lapa's pioneering musical venues is also its most eclectic, where performers of regional styles such as forró and *maracatu* alternate with up-and-coming garage and alternative rock bands and Carnaval *blocos*. Featuring rough stone walls and exposed beams, this atmospheric old warehouse houses a stage, bar/restaurant, dance floor, and performance space. Theme parties with intriguing names—like the Festa do Bigode (Moustache Party)—lure legions of young blood.

### Trapiche Gamboa

Rua Sacadura Cabral 155, Saúde
Tel 21/2516-0868
Housed in a beautifully restored 19th-century warehouse, this is one of the city's top samba venues. Aside from the musical offerings, the mixed crowd can rely on delicious appetizers and cocktails such as caipirinhas made with *cupuaçu*.

### Vinícius Show Bar

Rua Vinícius de Moraes 39, Ipanema
Tel 21/2287-1497
www.viniciusbar.com.br
Those nostalgic for bossa will find it alive and well at this intimate piano bar where daily live performances of Vinicius's classic compositions are given by noted musical artists.

## Theater & Concert Venues

Although often eclipsed by the multitude and wealth of its popular music forms, Rio is an important stage for local and global performances of erudite music, dance, and opera. Increasingly, it's also a hothouse for daring contemporary dance and theater (although the latter will be challenging for non-Portuguese speakers).

### Centro Cultural Banco do Brasil (CCBB)

Rua Primeiro de Março 66, Centro
Tel 21/3808-2020
Banco do Brasil is a major sponsor of the arts, and its former headquarters—a magnificent turn-of-the-20th-century building—features an excellent selection of national and international theater, dance, and music. Performances that aren't free are very affordable.

### Centro Cultural Carioca

Rua do Teatro 37, Centro
Tel 21/2252-6468
www.centroculturalcarioca.com.br
From the 1930s to the '60s, this cultural center went by the name Dancing Eldorado and was the most legendary of Rio's many dance halls. Today, this charmingly retro venue is one of the best places to hear live samba and forró and to take in performances by the house dance troupe.

### Centro Cultural Estudantina Musical

Praça Tiradentes 79, Centro
Tel 21/2232-1149
www.estudantinamusical.com.br
Dating from 1928, the Estudantina is one of Rio's last remaining traditional gafieiras (dance halls). Its musical roster alternates samba, hip-hop, and funk with big-band classics played by live orchestras on Saturday nights.

### Cidade das Artes

Avenida das Américas 5300, Barra
Designed by French architect Christian de Portzamparc, this state-of-the-art complex—finally inaugurated in 2013—is meant

to add a heaping dose of culture to Barra's suburban sprawl. The second largest symphony concert hall and opera house in Latin America, this contemporary palace also houses performance spaces for chamber music, MPB, and jazz in addition to a trio of art-house cinemas.

### Circo Voador

Rua dos Arcos, Lapa
Tel 21/2533-0354
The "Flying Circus" is a historically important Lapa venue where international indie bands alternate with local underground artists and samba legends. After sweating up a storm on the sunken dance floor, cool off on the palmy outdoor terrace.

### Espaço SESC Copacabana

Rua Domingos Ferreira 160, Copacabana
Tel 21/2547-0766
www.sescrj.org.br
It's worth keeping an eye out for the free and inexpensive offerings at this cultural center, housed in a building designed by Oscar Niemeyer. Its small, state-of-the-art theater hosts underground theater performances, as well as festivals devoted to experimental music and dance.

### Fundição Progresso

Rua dos Arcos 24, Lapa
Tel 21/2220-5070
www.fundicaoprogresso.com.br
This historic iron fundição (foundry) is a multipurpose artistic space equipped with a stage, dance floor, and bleacher-style seating. Its eclectic roster of performers runs the gamut from international indie rock stars to homegrown sambistas and the Petrobras Symphony Orchestra. It's also home to the Intrépida Troupe, an innovative performance group whose works incorporate theater, dance, and circus.

### Miranda

Av. Borges de Medeiros 1424, Lagoa
Tel 21/2239-0305
www.mirandabrasil.com.br
Part of the swank Lagoon entertainment complex overlooking the Lagoa Rodrigo de Freitas, this new supper-clubby bar/concert space plays host to an eclectic but top-notch roster of major Brazilian musical and performing artists.

### Oi Futuro

Rua Dois de Dezembro 63, Flamengo
Tel 21/3131-3060
www.oifuturo.org.br
Operated by Oi, a major Brazilian telecommunications company, this avant-garde cultural center—housed in a cleverly renovated, early 20th-century phone company building—hosts pocket shows, film screenings, and dance performances.

### Teatro João Caetano

Praça Tiradentes, Centro
Tel 21/2332-9166
www.cultura.rj.gov.br/espaco/teatro-joao-caetano
The shabby facade of Rio's oldest theater—dating back to 1813—belies the fact that it plays host to some of the city's most interesting theatrical, dance, and musical performances, in addition to plain old musicals.

### Theatro Municipal

Praça Floriano, Centro
Tel 21/2332-9134
www.theatromunicipal.rj.gov.br
A dead ringer for Paris' Opera Garnier, Rio's premier—and most opulent—theater attracts the biggest national and international names in music, opera, dance, and theater and is also home to its own acclaimed symphony orchestra, opera company, and ballet troupe.

### Teatro Rival Petrobras

Rua Álvaro Alvim 33, Centro

Tel 21/2240-4469
www.rivalpetrobras.com.br
Hidden away on a little alley behind Cinelândia, the Rival is a faded but beloved art deco gem of a supper club theater that's been around since 1934. Unpretentious and affordable, it's a great place to catch both leading and up-and-coming performers of MPB in an intimate setting.

**Vivo Rio**
Av. Infante Dom Henrique 85, Parque do Flamengo
Tel 21/2272-2900
www.vivorio.com.br
An annex of the Museu de Arte Moderno, this stark contemporary space shelters a vast concert hall for 4,000 and two small lounges. Big dance music events as well as an eclectic roster of national and global performers can be enjoyed against the spectacular backdrop of Guanabara Bay.

## Movie Theaters

One of Latin America's biggest film markets, Rio's cinemas screen everything from Hollywood blockbusters to commercial, indie, art, and documentary films from Brazil and around the world. Aside from multiplexes at the malls, there is a thriving art-house cinema scene. Shown in their original version, foreign films are usually subtitled in Portuguese.

**Cine Odeon Petrobras**
Praça Floriano 7, Centro
Tel 21/2240-1093
Cinelândia's sole surviving cinema is a restored art deco gem dating back to 1926. In addition to screening films (often national and independent) on an immense screen, this theater plays host to numerous cinematic events ranging from premiers and festivals to all-night film-centric *festas* that include dance-a-thons in the lobby.

**Cinépolis Lagoon**
Av. Borges de Medeiros 1424, Lagoa
Tel 21/3029-2544
www.cinepolis.com.br
Part of the high-end Lagoon entertainment complex, few other multiplexes boast a pre- or post-film terrace bar overlooking Lagoa Rodrigo de Freitas, with in-your-face views of Corcovado.

**Espaço Itaú de Cinema**
Praia de Botafogo 316, Botafogo
Tel 21/2559-8750
Hard-core cinephiles appreciate the Italian projectors, German lenses, and Lucas THX sound systems here, in addition to the versatile mix of commercial and arts films. A cool bar and bookstore devoted to the seventh art round out the offerings.

**Estação Rio**
Rua Voluntários da Pátria 35, Botafogo
Tel 21/2266-9952
Frequented by devoted cinephiles and artsy young Cariocas, this glossy, three-screen cinema is always one of the first to premier important Brazilian and international art films. Aside from its bookstore, the modern lobby's café is a major draw. Across the street, its sister cinema, Estação Botafogo *(Rua Voluntários da Pátria 88, tel 21/2226-1988)* has been a major supporter of art-house cinema since 1985.

**Instituto Moreira Salles (IMS)**
Rua Marquês de São Vicente 476, Gávea
Tel 21/3284-7400
http://ims.uol.com.br
One of Rio's most enticing private cultural centers, the former residence of the Salles family (which includes Walter Salles, Jr., acclaimed film director of *Central Station*) is a modernist masterpiece set amid lush gardens landscaped by Roberto Burle Marx. While the streamlined, airy spaces shelter art exhibits and live music performances, a small cinema screens documentaries and independent films and hosts retrospectives and film festivals.

**Roxy**
Av. Nossa Senhora de Copacabana 945-A, Copacabana
Tel 21/2461-2461
www.kinoplex.com.br
A happy remnant of Copa's days of glamour, this art deco cinema dating back to 1938 has retained its sweeping grand staircase and tradition of screening Hollywood blockbusters.

# Activities

With so many natural attractions to choose from, it's not surprising that Cariocas are fond of sports and other outdoor recreational pastimes. Beach activities—from power walking and yoga to soccer, volleyball, and surfing—are particularly popular. So are extreme sports that pit climbers, hikers, and rappellers against Rio's splendid mountain peaks. In addition to the city's many parks, the lush Tijuca Forest offers trails and hikes for those in need of a nature fix.

## Climbing

Rio is a climber's paradise, not just because it boasts around 1,000 climbing routes but also because the scalable topography is breathtaking. The following oufits offer outings and courses for beginners.
**Climb in Rio**
Tel 21/2557-7299
www.climbinrio.com
**Companhia da Escalada**
Tel 21/2567-7105
www.companhiadaescalada.com.br

## Cycling

Rio has more than 80 miles (130 km) of bike paths. Easy, scenic routes circle the Lagoa Rodrigo de Freitas and stretch along the coastline from Flamengo to Recreio. More arduous, but no less captivating, are the mountain trails leading through the Tijuca Forest. There are many places to rent bikes along the Zona Sul beaches and around the Lagoa.
**Bike & Lazer**
Rua Visconde de Pirajá 135 B, Ipanema
Tel 21/2267-7778
www.bikelazer.com.br
Aside from selling all types of fitness gear, this store rents bikes for all ages. There's a branch in Laranjeiras, as well.

## Diving

One of Rio's best diving points is the region surrounding the Ilhas Cagarras, facing Ipanema beach. Recreio and Urca's Praia Vermelha are two other hot spots.
**Dive Point**
Av. Ataulfo de Paiva 1174, Loja 4, Leblon
Tel 21/7852-2546
www.divepoint.com.br
Aside from lessons for all levels, Dive Point organizes underwater diving, fishing, and photography excursions to aquatic paradises in Rio and destinations in the surrounding state, such as Cabo Frio, Búzios, and Angra dos Reis.

## Hang Gliding

Hang gliding is popular given the jaw-dropping scenery. The most popular trip is from Pedra Bonita down to Praia do Pepino in São Conrado. Major registered outfits are all based on Praia do Pepino.
**Fly Tour**
Tel 24/9984-5643
www.flytourbrazil.com
**Just Fly**
Tel 21/2268-0565
www.justflyinrio.blogspot.com

## Hiking

Rio shelters the world's largest urban rain forest, the Tijuca Forest, which means you can take a nature hike in the middle of the city.
**Jungle Me**
Tel 21/4105-7533
www.jungleme.com.br
This ecotourism outfit specializes in small hiking and trekking tours for all levels that offer exposure to some of Rio's most spectacular natural landmarks.
**Rio Hiking**
Tel 21/2552-9204
www.riohiking.com.br
Friendly, English-speaking Denise Werneck and her son, Gabriel, organize multilevel hiking excursions around the city. Trekking, cycling, and kayaking adventures are also available.

## Rappelling and Ziplining

**Lagoa Aventuras**
Av. Epitácio Pessoa 3000, Lagoa
Tel 21/4105-0079
www.lagoaaventuras.com.br
Based in the Parque da Catacumba, overlooking the Lagoa Rodrigo de Freitas, Lagoa Aventuras offers tree canopy tours and rappelling.

## Surfing

Since the 1970s, Rio has been a serious surfer mecca. The beaches of Arpoador, Barra, Recreio, Prainha, and Grumari are particularly popular. Those seeking gear or rental boards should head to **Galeria River** (www.galeriariver.com.br), in Arpoador.
**Rico Surf School**
Av. Lúcio Costa 3300
Tel 21/8777-7775
www.escoladesurfrico.blogspot.com
Barra's beach is sprinkled with surfing academies, but one of the oldest and most popular is Rico's, which offers affordable 2-hour courses twice daily for all levels (1-hour private lessons are also available).

## Wakeboarding/ Waterskiing

**Rio Wake Center**
Lagoa Rodrigo de Freitas in front of Rua Garcia D'Ávila
Tel 21/2239-6976,
The Lagoa is a major lure for practitioners of alternative water sports. Rio Wake Center offers lessons for all levels and outings for those interested in wakeboarding, wakeskating, or waterskiing.

# INDEX

Boldface indicates illustrations.
CAPS indicates thematic categories.

## A

A Gentil Carioca 87, **87**
Abraão, Ilha Grande 223–224
Activities 173, **174**, 174–175, **175**, 263
Addresses 238
Afonso de Sousa, Martim 23
Airports & airlines 236
Almeida, Júlia Lopes de 112
Andrade, Oswald de 43
Antiques, shopping for 256
Aqueducts 108, **110**, 223
Architecture
  art deco 45, **45**, 158–159
  history & culture 38–43, **39**, **42**, 45
  Oscar Niemeyer 208–210
  Palácio Gustavo Capanema 63–64
Arco do Teles 77–78
Arcos da Lapa 108, **110**
Armação dos Búzios 219
Art deco 45, **45**, 158–159
Art museums see MUSEUMS
Arts 38–49, 53–54, 56–57
  artistic cannibalism 43
  background reading 243
  fine arts 38–43, **41**
  folk art 135, **201**, 201–202
  literature 44, 46, **46**
  pop iconography 187
  shopping for 135, 256–257
  see also Architecture; Cinema; Music
Ateliê Pedro Grapiuna 114
Atlantic Forest (Mata Atlântica) 17, 23–24
ATMs 240
Avenida Koeler, Petrópolis 214–215
Avenida Niemeyer 165

## B

Bailes do funk 47, 54
Banks 240
Bar do David 155, 251
Bar do Mineiro 37, 115, 247
Barbosa, Rui 140–141
Bardot, Brigitte 221
Barra da Tijuca **188**, 190–191, **197**, 197–198, 253, 256, 261
Bars and clubs 117, **132**, 132–133, 241, 242
Bastos, Carlos 187
Beaches
  beach behavior 153
  beach culture **18**, 18–19, **152**, 152–153, **153**
  beach food 161
  Búzios **218**, 219–221, **220**
  Copacabana Beach **146**, **150**, 154, 155–156, **158**, 158–159
  Ilha Grande 224–225
  Leblon Beach **164**, 164–165
  Niterói 210–211, **211**
  Paraty **232**, 232–233
  Praia da Urca 145
  Praia Vermelha 145, **145**

Recreio & around **199**, 199–201
Zona Oeste Beaches 188–203
Zona Sul beaches 146–167
Beco das Garrafas 156
Beer 75, 214
Biblioteca Nacional **2–3**, **67**, 68, 82
Bicycling **234**, 238, 263
Birding 183
Bishop, Elizabeth 127
Boat trips
  Guanabara Bay 129–130
  Ilha de Paquetá 77
  to Rio 236
  swan boats 174, **175**
  taxi-boats 223
Body language 10
Bohemians & malandros **106**, 106–107, **107**
Bondes (trams) 111, 114–115
Books
  about Rio 243
  festivals 227
  history & culture 44, 46, **46**
  shopping for 257
Bossa nova 49, 163
Bossa Nova e Companhia 156, 257
Botafogo 125, 140–143
  entertainment 262
  hotels 247
  Museu do Índio 142–143
  restaurants 248
  Santa Marta 141–142
  shopping 256, 257
Botanical gardens see GARDENS
Botequins **132**, 132–133
Buarque, Chico 32, 107, **107**
Burle Marx, Roberto 43, 202–203
Bus travel 8, 236, 237
Búzios 206–207, 218–221
  Armação dos Búzios 219
  beaches **218**, 219–221, **220**
  hotels 253–254
  Manguinhos 219
  Ossos 219, **220**
  restaurants 254

## C

Cachaça **230**, 230–231, **231**
Cachoeira da Feiticeira, Ilha Grande 223–224
Caixa Cultural 69
Camboinhas beach, Niterói 211
Came e Café (bed-and-breakfast network) 113
Caminho do Ouro 233
Caminho Niemeyer, Niterói 209–210
Canopy tours 173, 263
Capela Mayrink 182
Capoeira 185
Car rentals & driving 68, 237–238
Carioca, definition of 24
Carioca da Gema **106**, 107, 260
Carnaval **4**, 50–52, **51**, **52**
  Ipanema **18**
  out of season 55
  shopping for 88, **89**
Casa Alto Vidigal 167
Casa Cláudio de Souza, Petrópolis 215
Casa da Cultura, Paraty 228

Casa da Ipiranga, Petrópolis 217
Casa da Princesa Isabel, Petrópolis 214–215
Casa de Santos Dumont, Petrópolis 217
Casa do Caminho 19
Casa do Pontal **201**, 201–202
Casa França-Brasil 80–81, 83
Cascatinha do Taunay **170**, 182
Cassino da Urca 143, 144
Castelo 61, 62–64
  Igreja de Nossa Senhora do Bonsucesso 63
  Museu Histórico Nacional **62**, 62–63
  Palácio Gustavo Capanema 63–64
Castro Maya, Raymundo Ottoni de 181, 183
Catedral de São Pedro de Alcântara, Petrópolis 214, 216, **217**
Catedral Metropolitana **70**, 71–72
Catete 103, 116–121
  entertainment 260
  getting there 117–118
  hotels 247–248
  The Maze 120, 260
  Museu da República 103, **119**, 119–121
  Museu do Folclore 121, **121**
  Palácio do Catete 30, **30**, 118–121, **119**
  Parque do Catete **116**, 121
Cell phones 239
Centro 58–99
  art deco architecture 45, **45**
  Castelo & Cinelândia **58**, 61, 62–73
  entertainment 261–262
  history 29, 73
  hotels 244–245
  maps 60–61, 83
  markets 97, 99, 259
  Port Zone 61, **90**, 90–93, **93**
  Praça Tiradentes & around 61, **84**, 84–87, **87**
  Praça XV & around 61, 74–81, **82**, 83
  restaurants 73, 78, 89, 245–246
  Saara **88**, 88–89, **89**
  São Cristóvão 61, **94**, 94–97, **97**, 99, **99**
  shopping 257, 259
  suggested itinerary 9–10
  walk in João VI's footsteps **82**, 82–83
Centro Cultural Banco do Brasil (CCBB) 80, **82**, 83, 261
Centro Cultural Carioca 86, 261
Centro Cultural da Justiça Federal 68
Centro Cultural dos Correios 80
Centro Cultural Estudantina Musical 86, 261
Centro de Arte Hélio Oiticica 86–87
Centro Histórico, Paraty 227, 228–229, **229**
Cervejaria Bohemia, Petrópolis 214, 215
Chorando (bargaining) 89
Choro (music) 48, **49**, 136

## ILLUSTRATIONS CREDITS

All photographs by Peter M. Wilson unless otherwise indicated below:

11, Celso Pupo/Shutterstock.com; 14-5, Johan Sjolander/iStockphoto; 22-3, Gianni Dagli Orti/The Art Archive at Art Resource, NY; 24, ricardoazoury/iStockphoto; 26-7, "Declaration of the Brazilian Independence by Emperor Pedro I on 7 September 1822." Oil on Canvas painting by Pedro Américo (1888)/Wikimedia Commons; 30, Bettmann/Corbis; 33, Bettmann/Corbis; 35, Pedro Ladeira/AFP/Getty Images; 36, Luiz Rocha Rocha/iStockphoto; 41, DeAgostini/Getty Images; 42, Elder Vieira Salles/Shutterstock.com; 46, STR/AFP/Getty Images; 49, Bettmann/Corbis; 54, Neftali/Shutterstock.com; 57, Theo Wargo/WireImage/Getty Images; 87, Photo by Paulo Innocêncio/A GENTIL CARIOCA; 89, Vanderlei Almeida/AFP/Getty Images; 97, Eric Gevaert/iStockphoto; 98, Celso Pupo/Shutterstock.com; 99, Erica Ramalho/AFP/Getty Images; 107, EDUARDO NICOLAU/dpa/Corbis; 146, Luiz Rocha/Shutterstock; 152, Jenny Leonard/Shutterstock; 157, Catarina Belova/Shutterstock.com; 158, GYI NSEA/iStockphoto.com; 162, Ekaterinabelova/Dreamstime.com; 167, luoman/iStockphoto; 184, Alexander Auler/LatinContent/Getty Images; 211, Elder Vieira Salles/Shutterstock; 230, tunart/iStockphoto.com; 231, wsfurlan/iStockphoto; 234, Cesar Okada/iStockphoto.com.

National Geographic
# TRAVELER
# Rio de Janeiro

**125**
**YEARS**

**Published by the National Geographic Society**
John M. Fahey, *Chairman of the Board and Chief Executive Officer*
Declan Moore, *Executive Vice President; President, Publishing and Travel*
Melina Gerosa Bellows, *Executive Vice President; Chief Creative Officer, Books, Kids, and Family*
Lynn Cutter, *Executive Vice President, Travel*
Keith Bellows, *Senior Vice President and Editor in Chief, National Geographic Travel Media*

**Prepared by the Book Division**
Hector Sierra, *Senior Vice President and General Manager*
Janet Goldstein, *Senior Vice President and Editorial Director*
Jonathan Halling, *Design Director, Books and Children's Publishing*
Marianne R. Koszorus, *Design Director, Books*
Barbara A. Noe, *Senior Editor, National Geographic Travel Books*
R. Gary Colbert, *Production Director*
Jennifer A. Thornton, *Director of Managing Editorial*
Susan S. Blair, *Director of Photography*
Meredith C. Wilcox, *Director, Administration and Rights Clearance*

**Staff for This Book**
Caroline Hickey, *Managing Editor*
Kay Kobor Hankins, *Art Director and Photo Editor*
Jane Sunderland, *Text Editor*
Doug Gray, *Researcher*
Carl Mehler, *Director of Maps*
Michael McNey and Mapping Specialists, *Map Production*
Marshall Kiker, *Associate Managing Editor*
Galen Young, *Rights Clearance Specialist*
Katie Olsen, *Production Design Assistant*
Jack Brostrom, Olivia Garnett, Abigail Cloft, Rose Davidson, Marlena Serviss, and Mary Stephanos *Contributors*

**Manufacturing and Quality Management**
Phillip L. Schlosser, *Senior Vice President*
Chris Brown, *Vice President, NG Book Manufacturing*
George Bounelis, *Vice President, Production Services*
Nicole Elliott, *Manager*
Rachel Faulise, *Manager*
Robert L. Barr, *Manager*

The National Geographic Society is one of the world's largest nonprofit scientific and educational organizations. Founded in 1888 to "increase and diffuse geographic knowledge," the member-supported Society works to inspire people to care about the planet. Through its online community, members can get closer to explorers and photographers, connect with other members around the world, and help make a difference. National Geographic reflects the world through its magazines, television programs, films, music and radio, books, DVDs, maps, exhibitions, live events, school publishing programs, interactive media, and merchandise. *National Geographic* magazine, the Society's official journal, published in English and 38 local-language editions, is read by more than 60 million people each month. The National Geographic Channel reaches 440 million households in 171 countries in 38 languages. National Geographic Digital Media receives more than 25 million visitors a month. National Geographic has funded more than 10,000 scientific research, conservation, and exploration projects and supports an education program promoting geography literacy. For more information, visit www.nationalgeographic.com.

For more information, please call 1-800-NGS LINE (647-5463) or write to the following address:

National Geographic Society
1145 17th Street N.W.
Washington, D.C. 20036-4688 U.S.A.

For information about special discounts for bulk purchases, please contact National Geographic Books Special Sales: ngspecsales@ngs.org

For rights or permissions inquiries, please contact National Geographic Books Subsidiary Rights: ngbookrights@ngs.org

ISBN: 978-1-4262-1165-2
Printed in Hong Kong
13/IHK/1

The information in this book has been carefully checked and to the best of our knowledge is accurate. However, details are subject to change, and the National Geographic Society cannot be responsible for such changes, or for errors or omissions.